# TODD JAMES

Other books by Todd James
ATTITUDE DANCER
STREET MARKET
REAS

The Henry Moore
Foundation

Contemporary Projects

Produced with the assistance of Henry Moore Foundation Contemporary Projects on the occassion of a new commission for 'The International 2002', Liverpool Biennial.

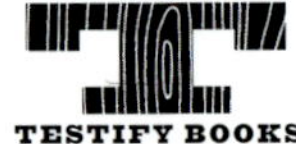
TESTIFY BOOKS



Designed by Todd James and Peter Girardi

ISBN: 0-9725920-0-8

Distributed by powerHouse Cultural Entertainment, Inc.

10 9 8 7 6 5 4 3 2

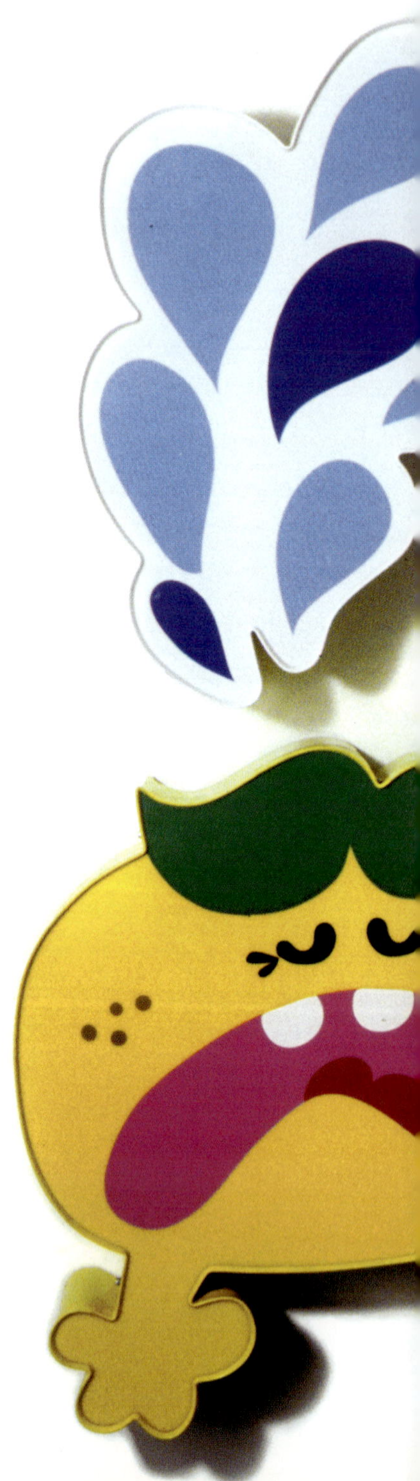

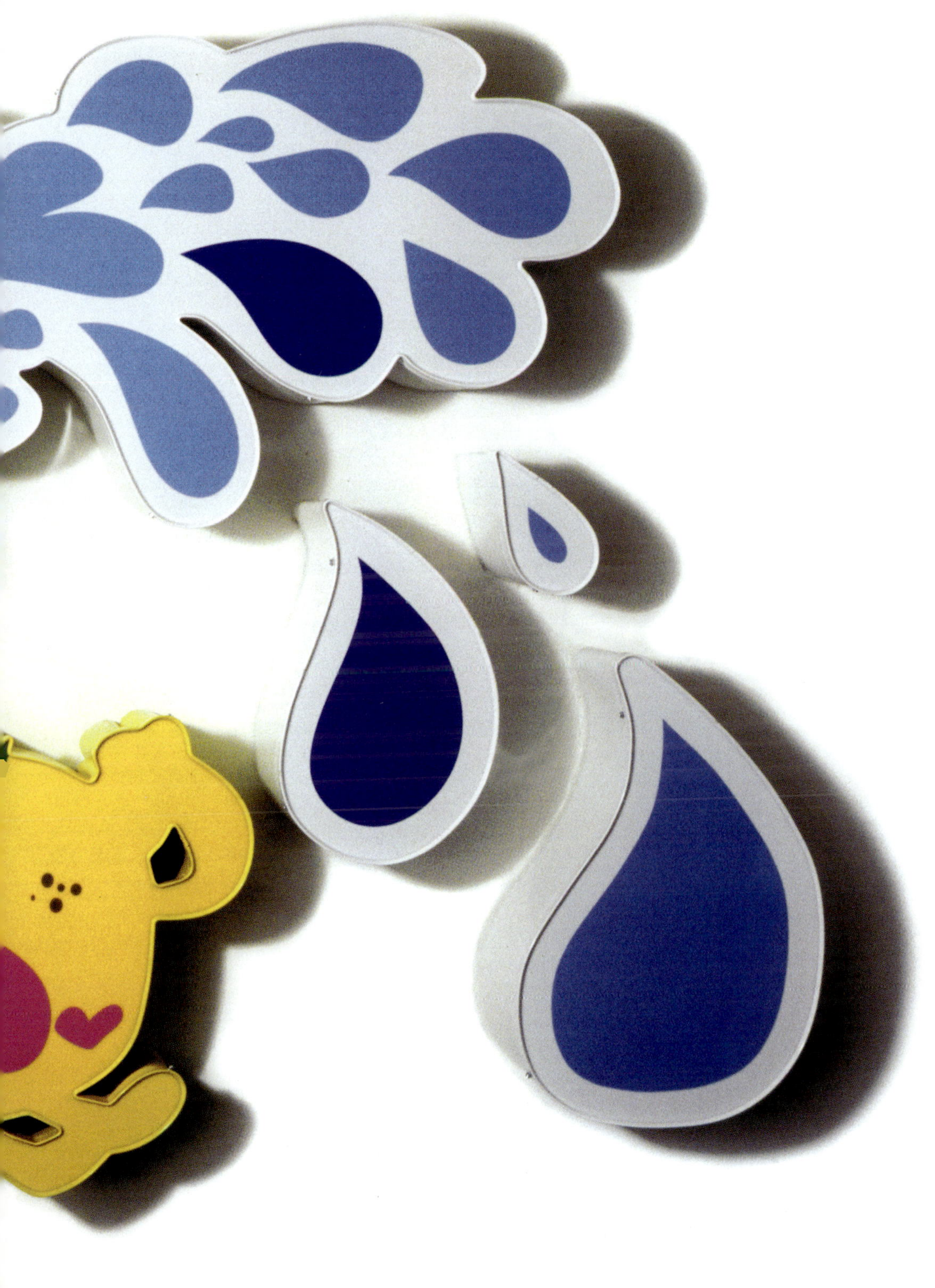

# BELOVED

Todd James belongs to a small, influential group of artists who acquired the earliest elements of their visual languages painting subway cars, and who have come to alter my generation's perception of urban aesthetics. In a New York market dominated by Conceptual artists, Todd's wide-ranging work (signs, paintings, animation, production designs, and drawings, etc.) display his prodigious skills, and poses challenges to those who can't work successfully across formats, who have repressed relationships to their locale, and over-determine their subjects and objects. With work similar in spirit to James' now appearing in various galleries and shows, like the Whitney Biennial 2002, we may be more accustomed to this kind of instinct and technique-based artistic practice, but James' outstanding talent and his advanced work in the commercial sector show endless ideas and astounding range and ability, like a young Hockney.

I first heard of James' work via the cool quotient that preceded him. Friends who grew up in downtown New York told me about this "Todd James" who had grown up making extraordinary subway graffiti, and was somewhat of a folk hero in that world. We met while working on animation projects for the design firm Funny Garbage, while James was in the process of developing his 2001 installation for Deitch Projects, *Street Market*. For Funny Garbage, we worked together on a cartoon that he largely designed, *Raptoons*, an urban variety show set somewhere like the Apollo Theater. Between *Street Market*, *Raptoons*, and Funny Garbage, where I was surrounded by a collection that included Peter Saul, Gary Panter, and Sue Coe, I began to think about the ways James' illustrations held their own compared to the aforementioned: his plush, brash line had the mark of raw talent, and a refined transgressive quality, but went into subject areas others did not venture: all five of New York's boroughs, jail, bodegas, train yards, old buses, unsupervised bedrooms.

For James, a sort of realignment took place after *Street Market*. That installation, which would later travel to Japan and then on to the Venice Biennale, featured the kinds of work he was known for as a hip young thing: signs, drawings, products, and sculptures were based on graffiti-related experiences and practices, and aspects of his New York life. REAS (James' tag) proliferated in a number of formats – paint, sequins, illustration, print, metal. Other paintings and illustrations in restricted palates focused on young women looking street and sexy. The catalog features pictures of James as a youth doing subway graffiti, juxtaposed with products he made

# FIEND

for the show's bodegas, cans of 'street cred,' 'shame' or 'REAS.' Unlike any other artist I can think of, many of James' figures were almost interchangeable with letterforms, type treatments and signs: both are colorful, brash, and architecturally lavish. I also recall some of the darker pieces from the show, such as a painting of the Pink Panther holding his huge penis, or the beautiful sculpture of brass knuckles. Many of these, showing bravura and a taste for the fucked up, were over the top, yet the purity of their forms transformed these gestural works into a elements of a larger, operatic, or melodramatic scene – *Street Market*.

In the last two years at Funny Garbage, I've watched James fluidly phase and move quickly through a number of art, design and illustration projects. Witnessing his work on television properties such as *Raptoons* and *Crank Yankers*, I saw that James has the ability to invent worlds almost effortlessly. Moreover, I saw his line, with its particular brand of emotional control, create defiant, modern universes that look both backwards to Saturday morning cartoons of the late 70s, and forwards into the zeitgeist subtleties of Little Italy and the Lower East Side. His backgrounds and landscapes quietly expel an urban power, and the terms of his characters are always clear and slightly slapstick, with a high level of descriptive detail that distinguishes them fully from other contemporary cartoon powerhouses.

I visited James' studio recently to view his new works for the Tate Liverpool, and was interested to see how REAS tags and cans had given way to new stylistic forms that include more sculptural signs, animations that play with spatial and temporal dimensions (yet are still grounded by weighty, stunning drawings), and two exciting painting projects that engage ambivalently with narrative.

One experiment with painting is a series done on wallpaper called 'Pro Thunder,' which is installed in comic book-like panels. Soft green wallpaper, punctuated with delicate, gold flowers, underwrites a dense, edgy composition of playful figures verging on accident or chaos. A woman is barely in her high-heeled shoes; a recurring James character called "Cepe" steals a cheap Huffy; kids wave naively; phrases suggest child's play turning rough ("It's a good thing not to be over there," "I think it's time for Troy to go home."). Cartoon shapes, kids flipping the bird, and letter forms all co-exist amidst the narrative structure, and one can extract from the mixed-up composition the importance of the color black in James' vocabulary, his love of early decorative graffiti, and his ability to isolate moments of transition and pending danger.

A group of paintings done mostly in black on black reveal another kind of fragility, and provide an almost cinematic backdrop for James' distinctive cartoon shapes, figures, and phrases. These compositions are more cluttered: figures are surrounded by tears; they overlap each other and are of varying gloss and emotion. Spatially ambiguous, these works use paint to extend pathos. Hovering between abstracted compositions and fucked up, cluttered comics, these paintings, with big bootied bodies, asses, and disenfranchised figures, have a jokey veneer, but are still much more emotionally amorphous works than the necessarily ego'd, bravura-laden tags and products of the Street Market show.

Although elements of James' work are reclusive within the world of his own ideas, experiences, and observations, his trajectory within the art world has introduced him to the complexes of academized art, institutional politics, and trend-based curating. His animation short featuring a group of graffiti writers from the seventies who are invited to install at a downtown gallery satirizes some of these dynamics. In the first degree, the cartoon is yet another example of James' format mastery: there is the refined, transgressive yet classical line again, and his usage of color and detail create visuals and spatial continuums as compelling and entertaining as television. But secondly, the piece is also helpful in recognizing the demands placed on the artist to be a "noble savage," a graffiti boy, a naïf. A genius at work, operating at such advanced levels in both the commercial and artistic worlds, James' "thing" can't be stopped, so he doesn't have to give a fuck. But don't think he doesn't notice.

Rachel Greene
Author of the forthcoming *Internet Art* (Thames & Hudson)
New York, 2002

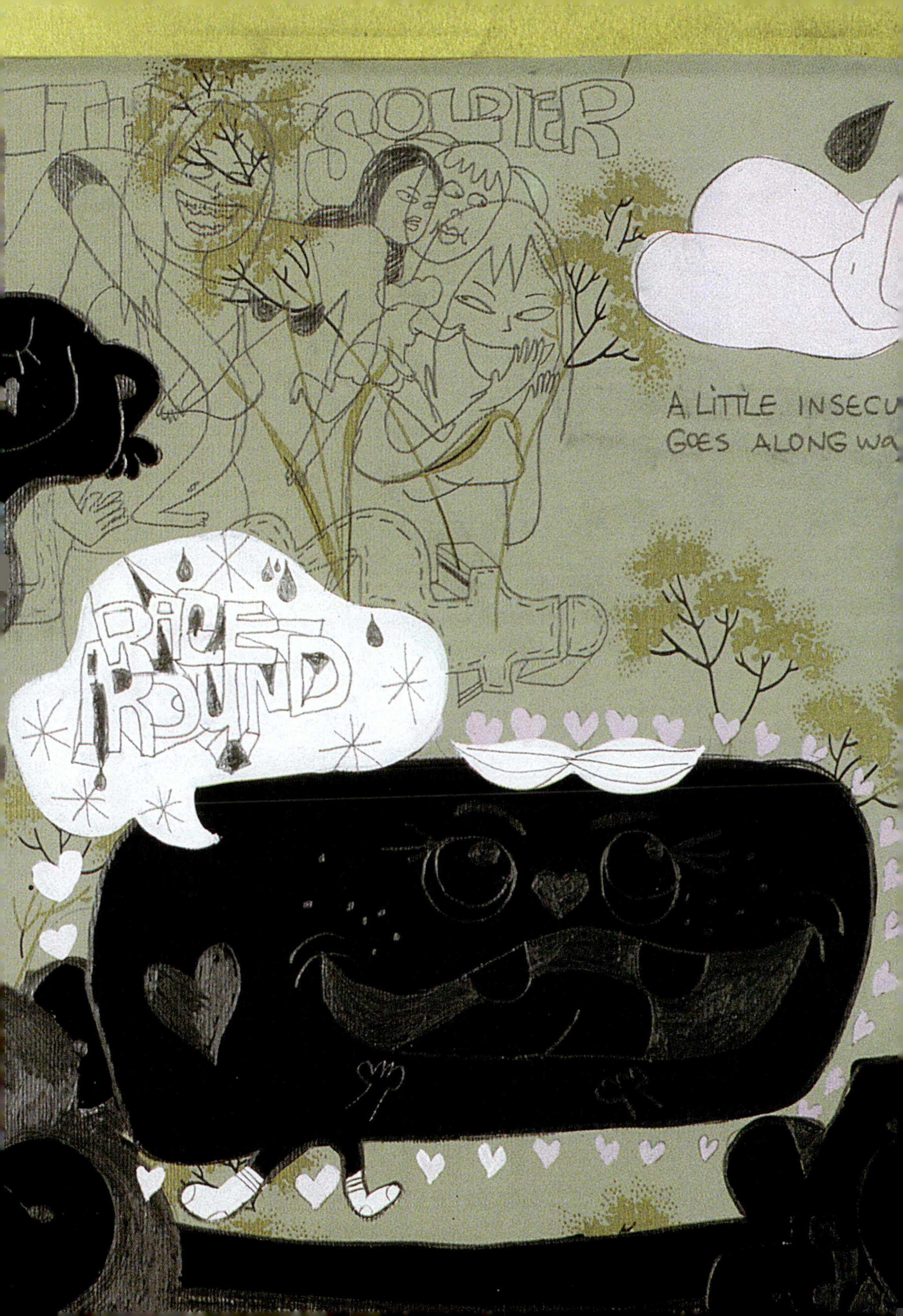
SOLDIER
A LITTLE INSECU
GOES ALONG wa

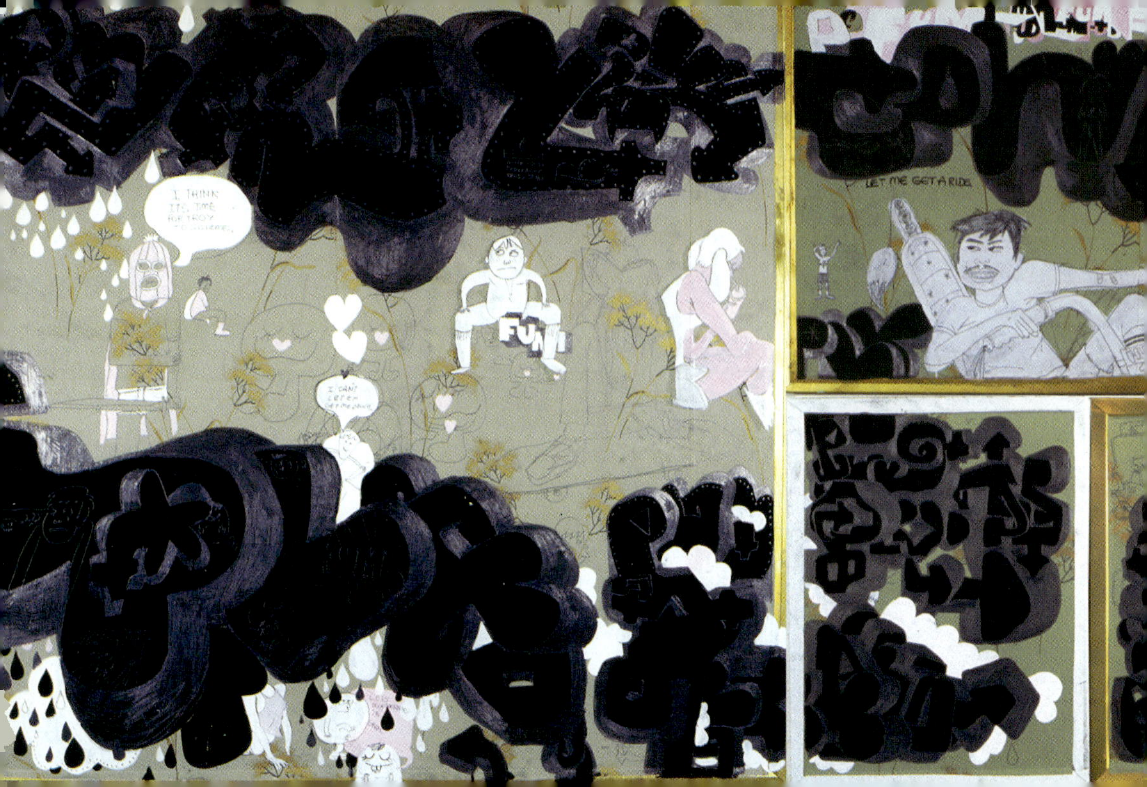
I THINK
ITS TIME
FOR TROY
FUN
LET ME GET A RIDE

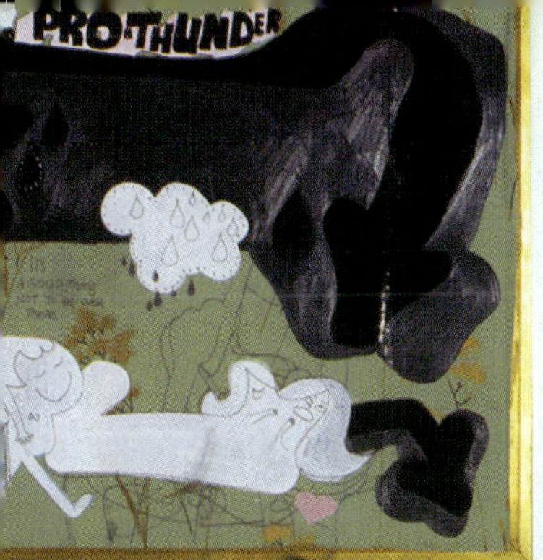
PRO-THUNDER

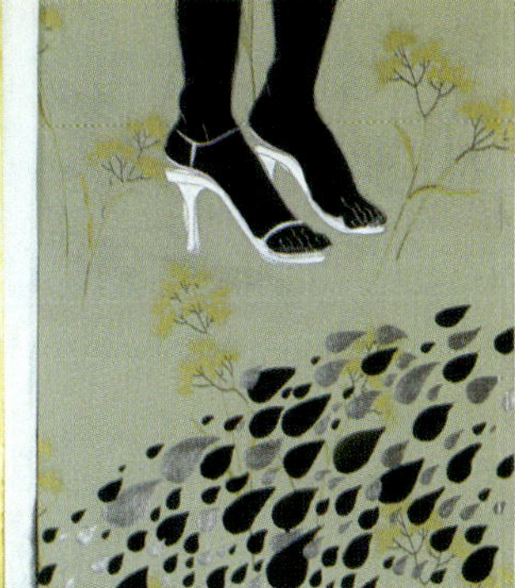

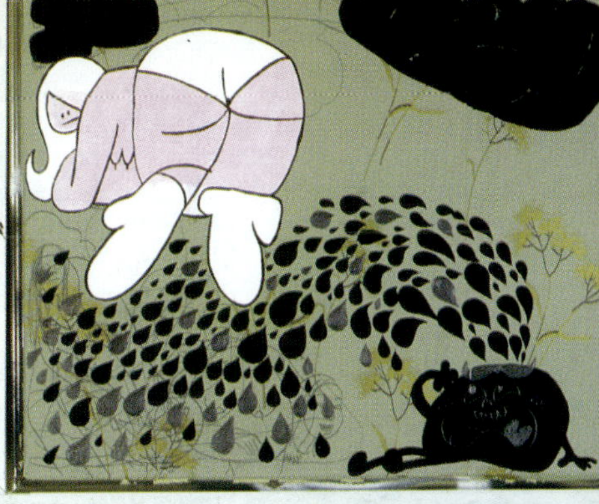

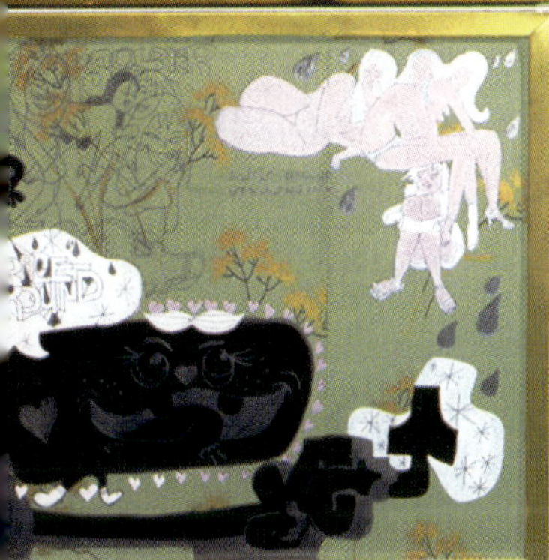

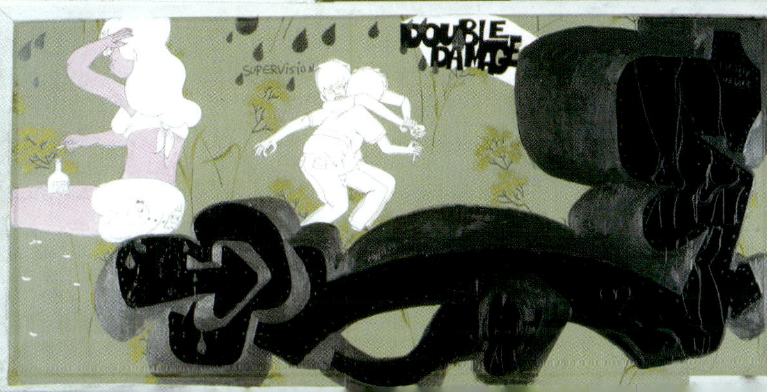
SUPERVISION
DOUBLE DAMAGE

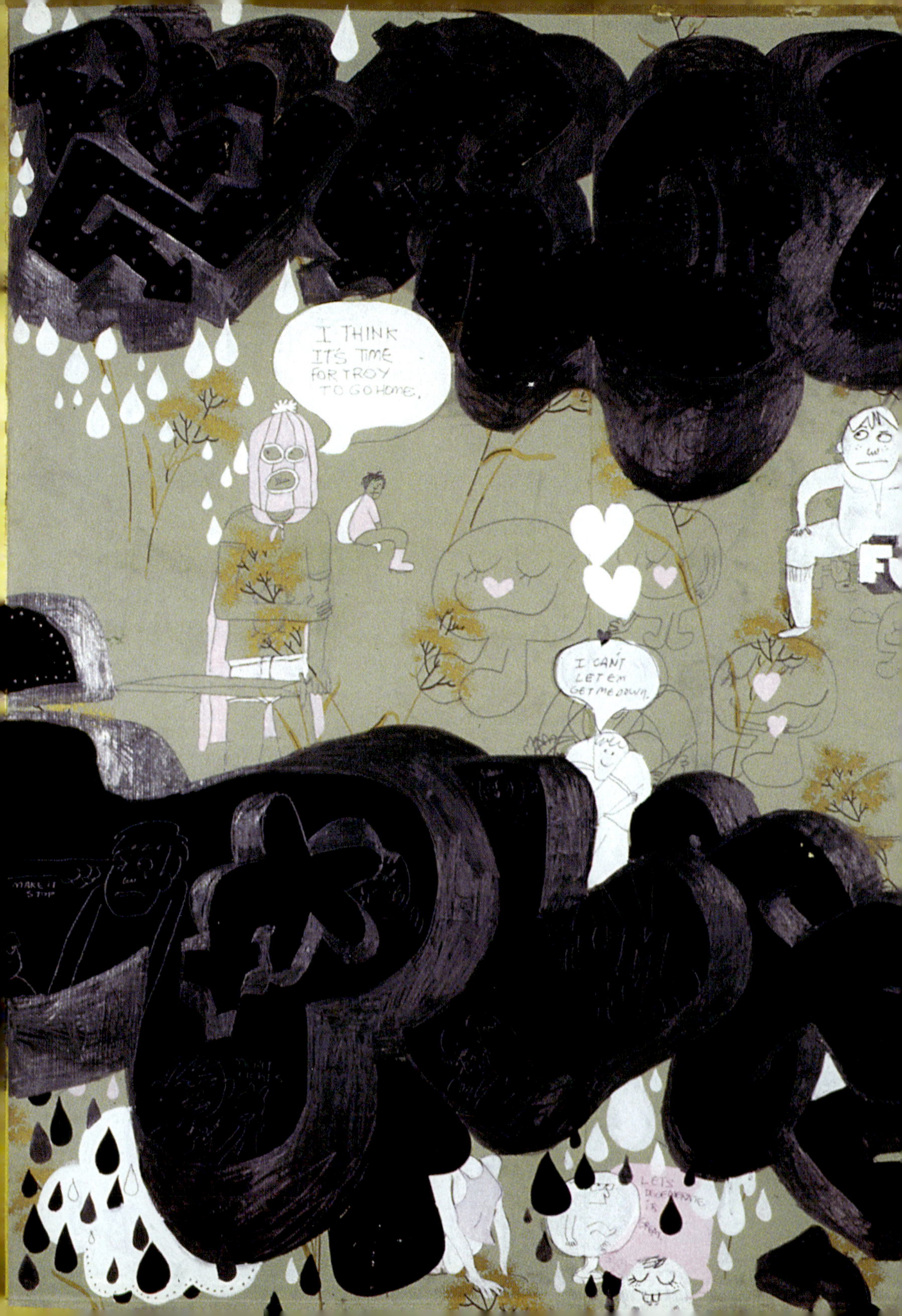
I THINK IT'S TIME FOR TROY TO GO HOME.
I CAN'T LET EM GET ME DOWN.
MAKE IT STOP

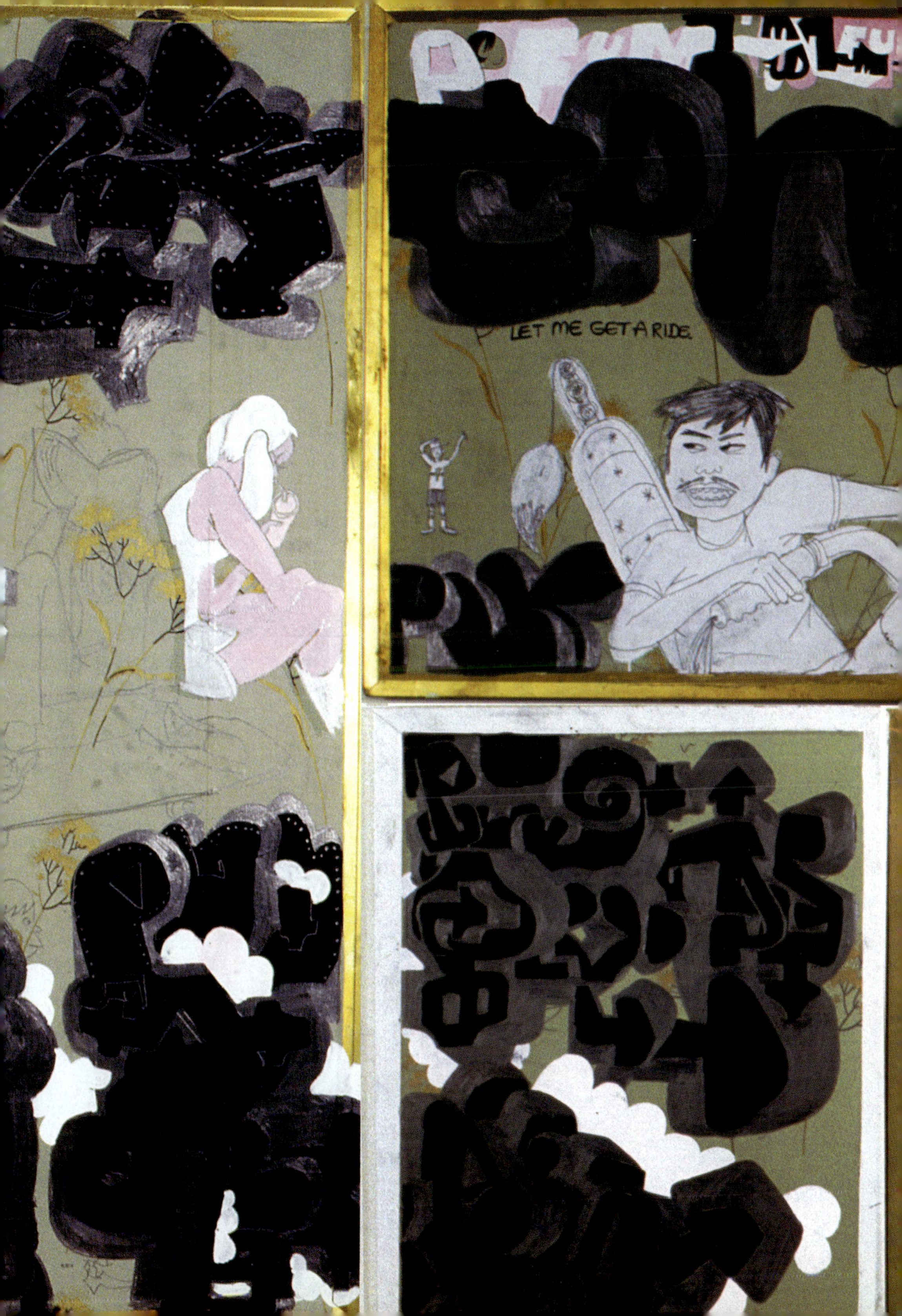

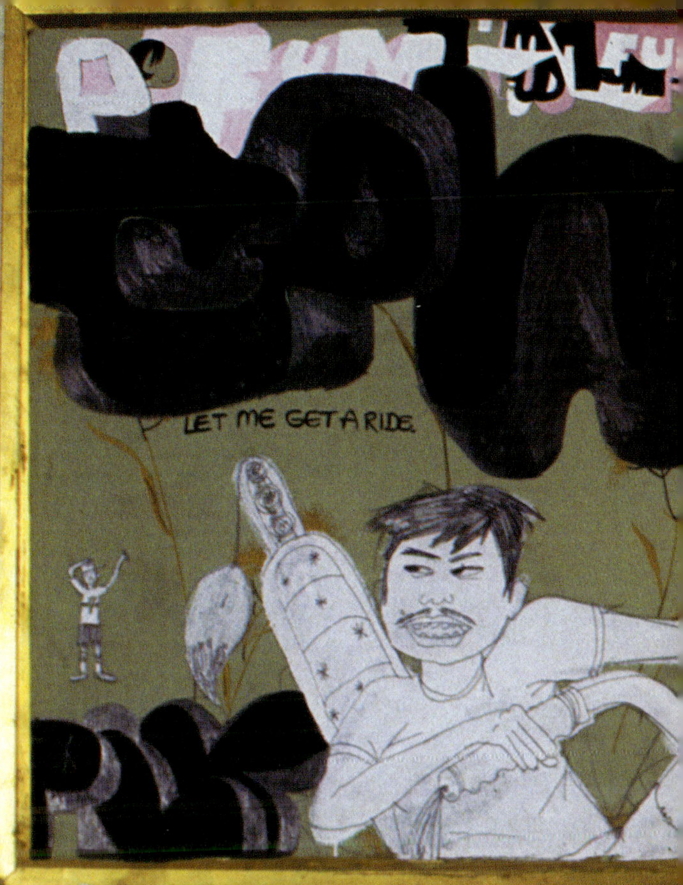
LET ME GET A RIDE

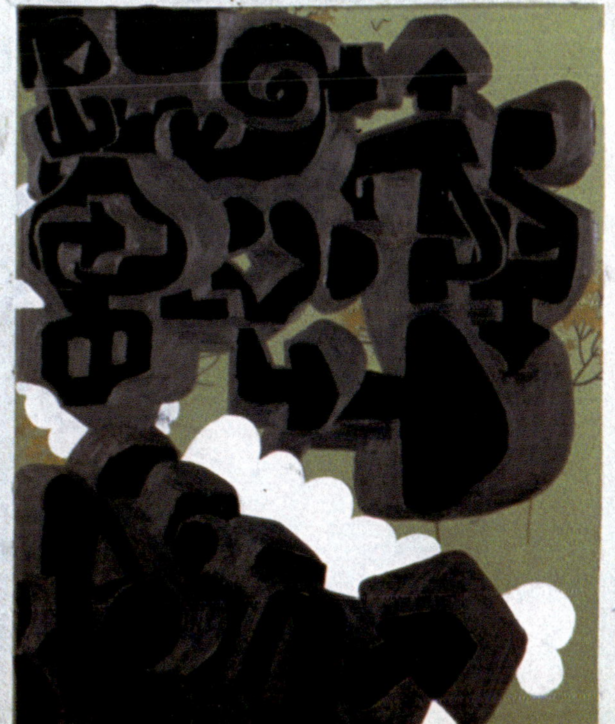

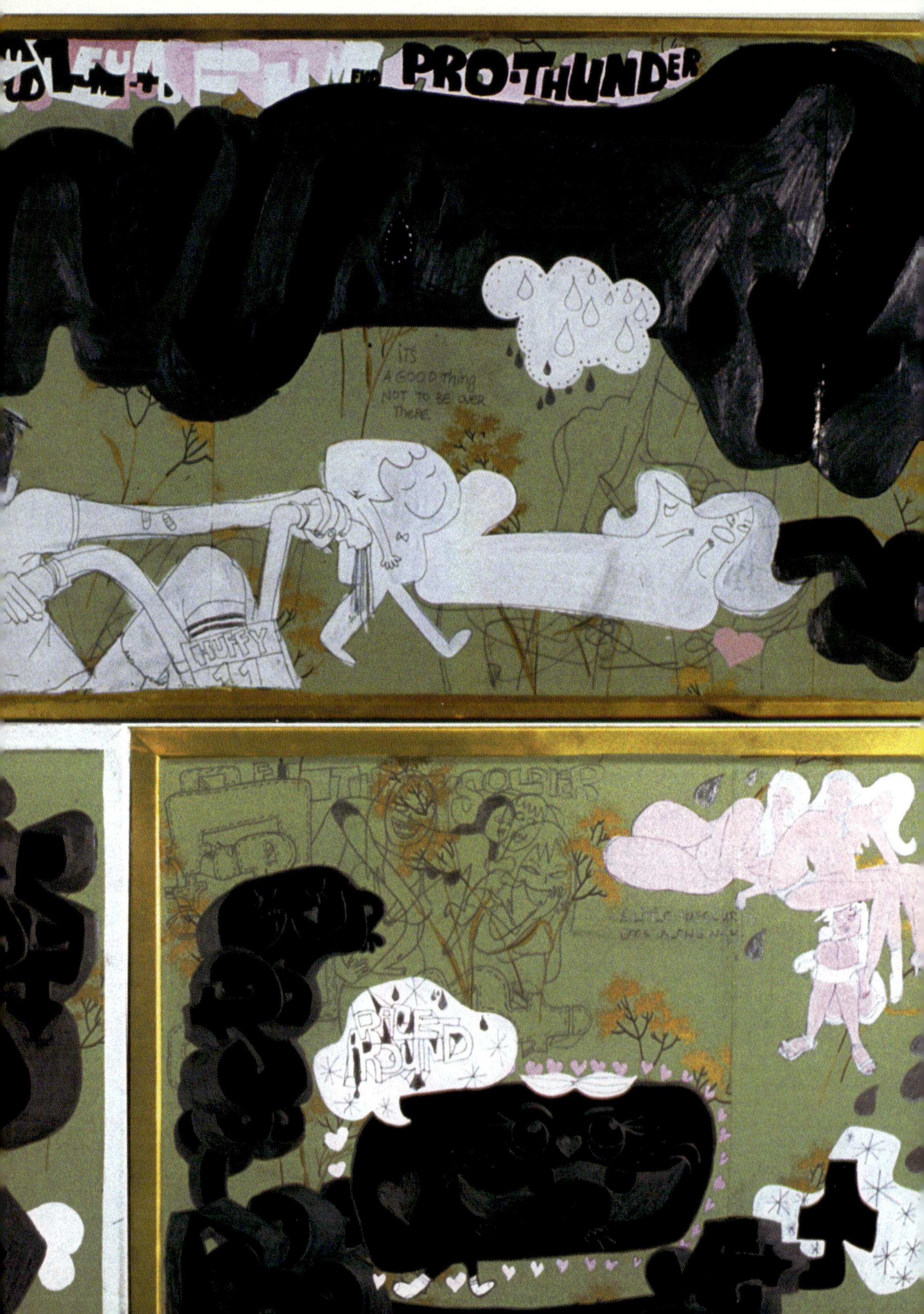
PRO·THUNDER
ITS A GOOD Thing NOT TO BE OVER THERE
HUFFY

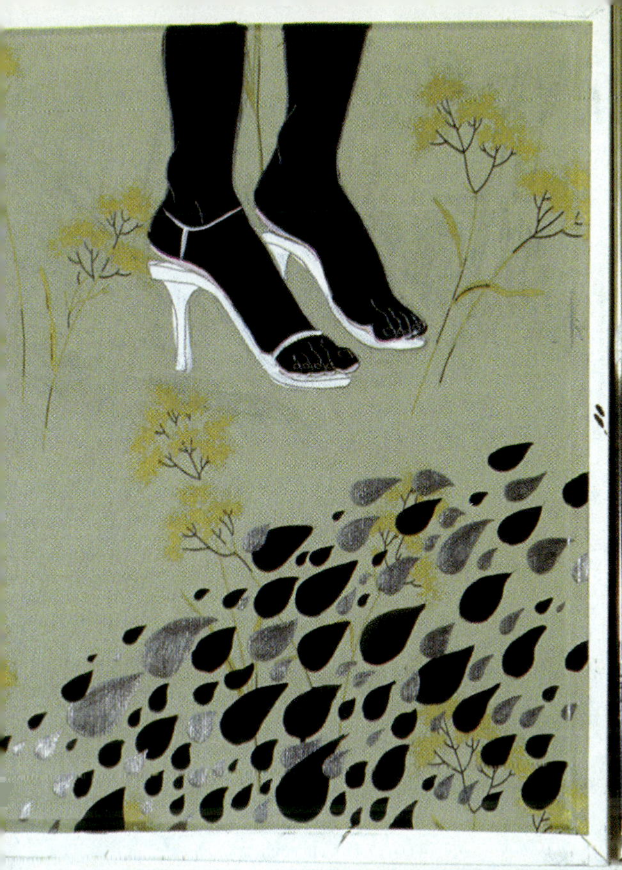

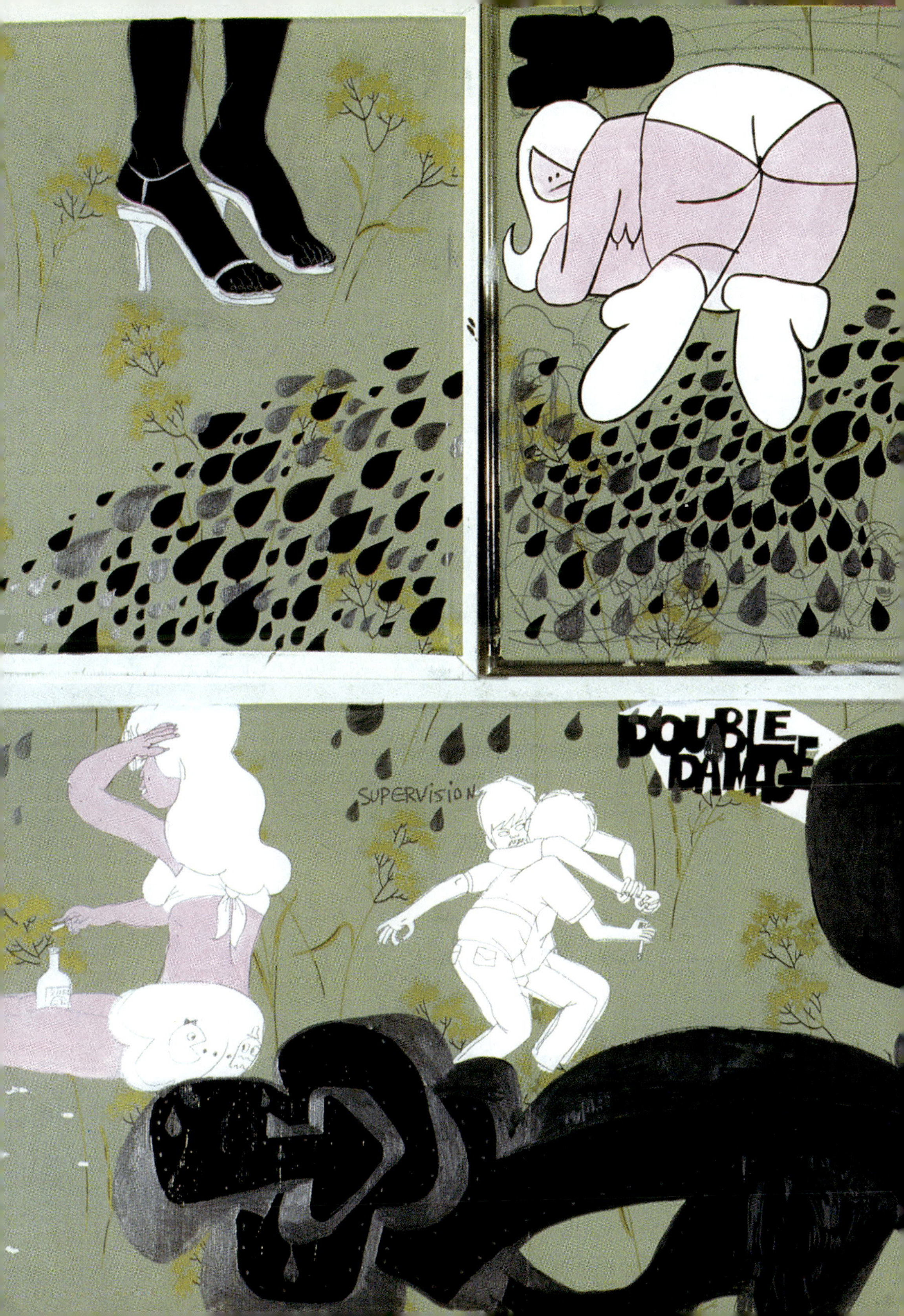

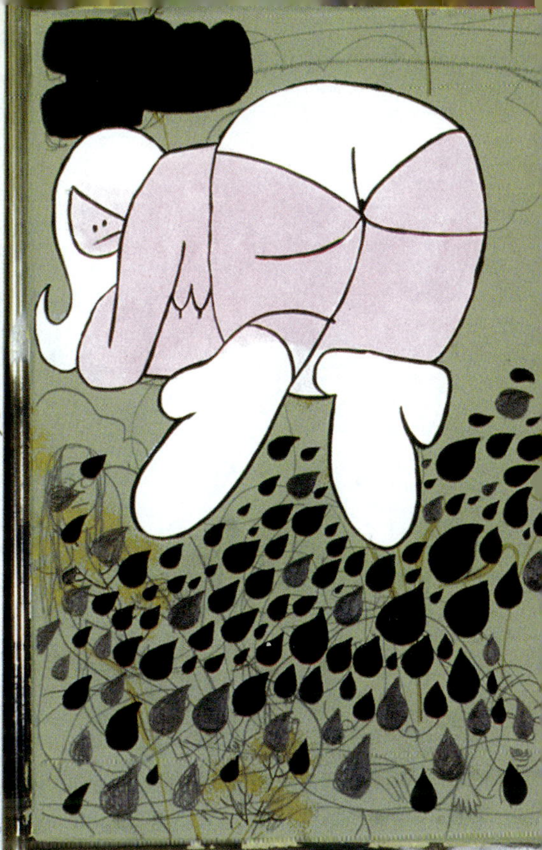

SUPERVISION

DOUBLE DAMAGE

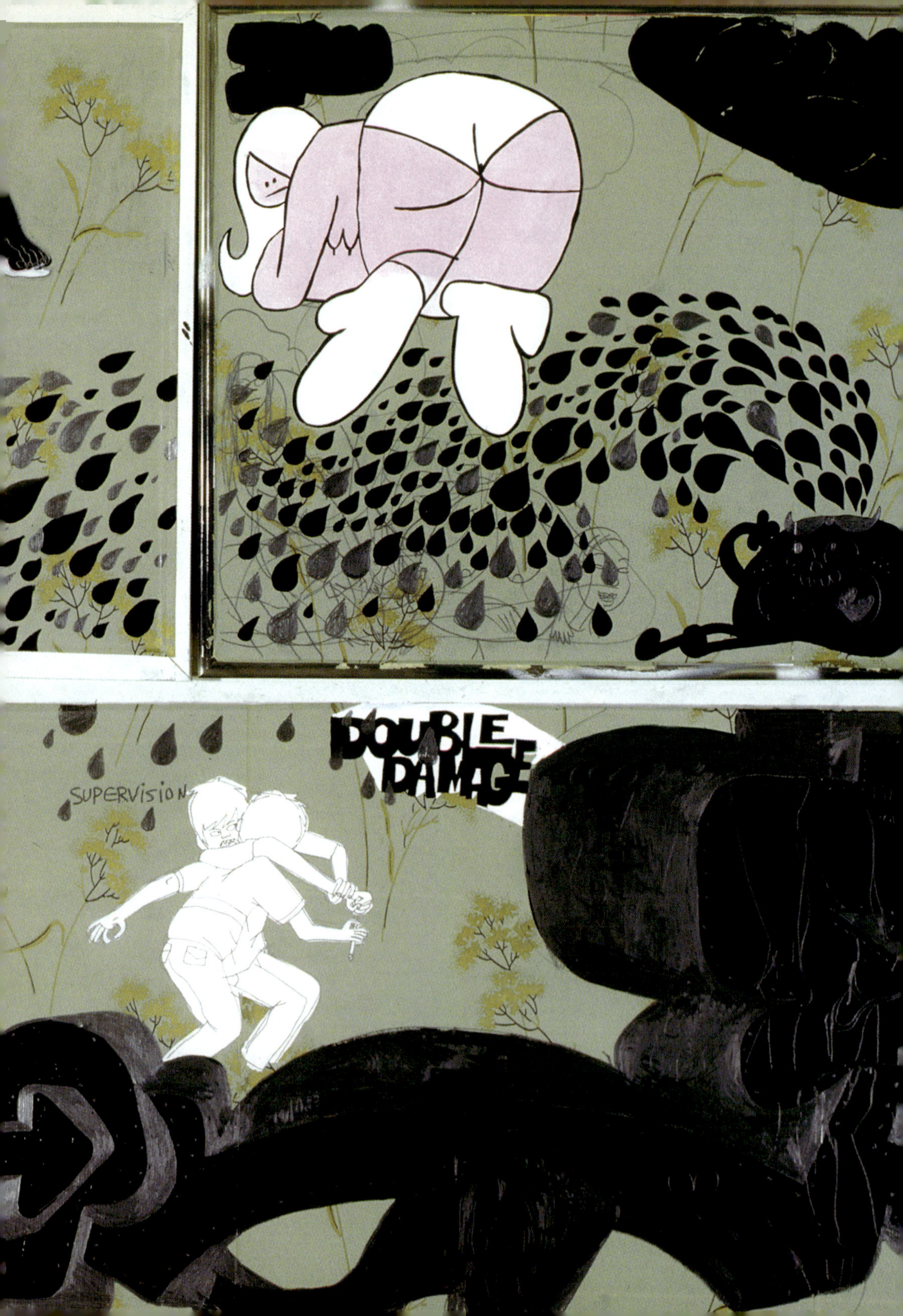

SUPERVISION

DOUBLE DAMAGE

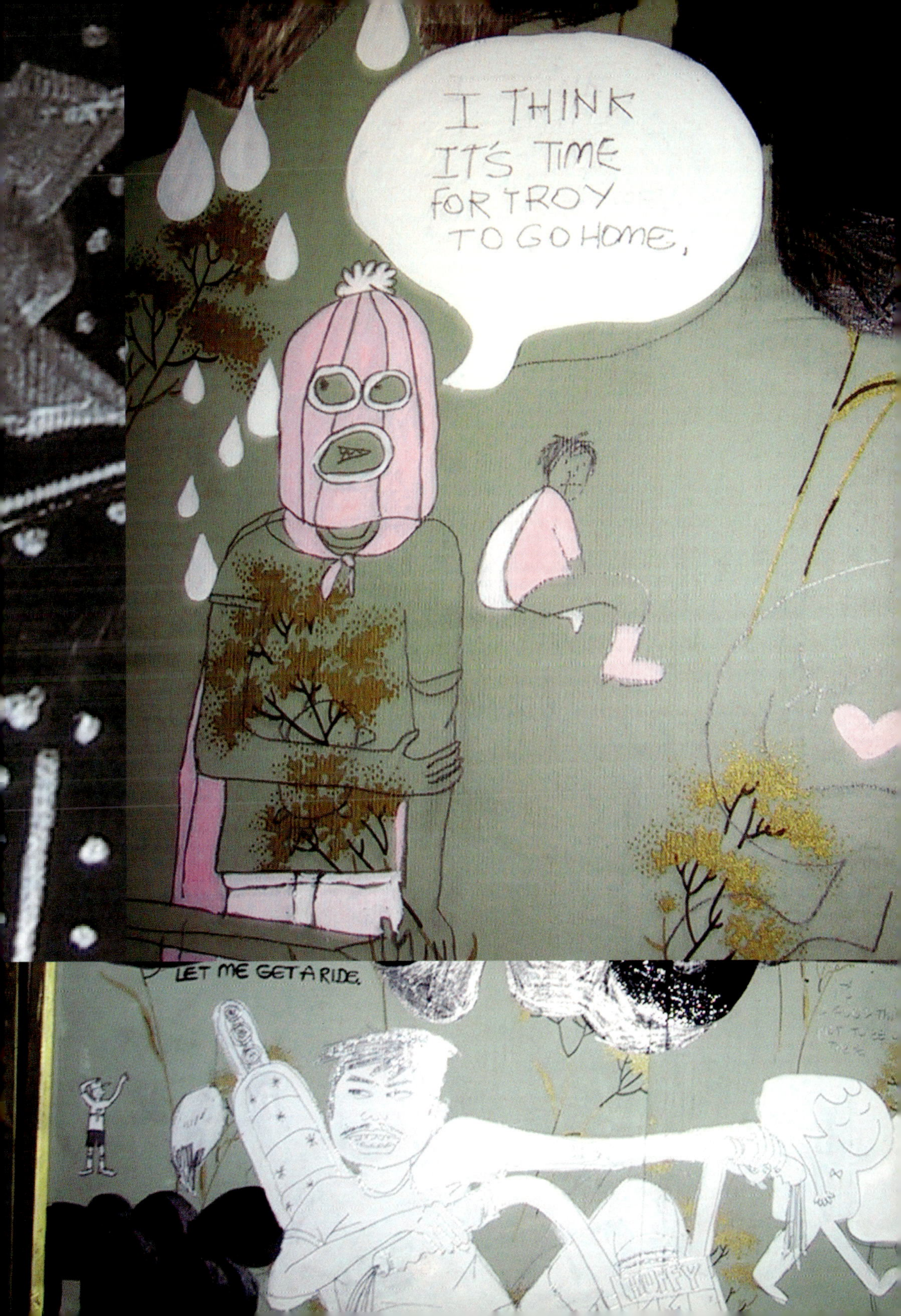
I THINK IT'S TIME FOR TROY TO GO HOME,
LET ME GET A RIDE.

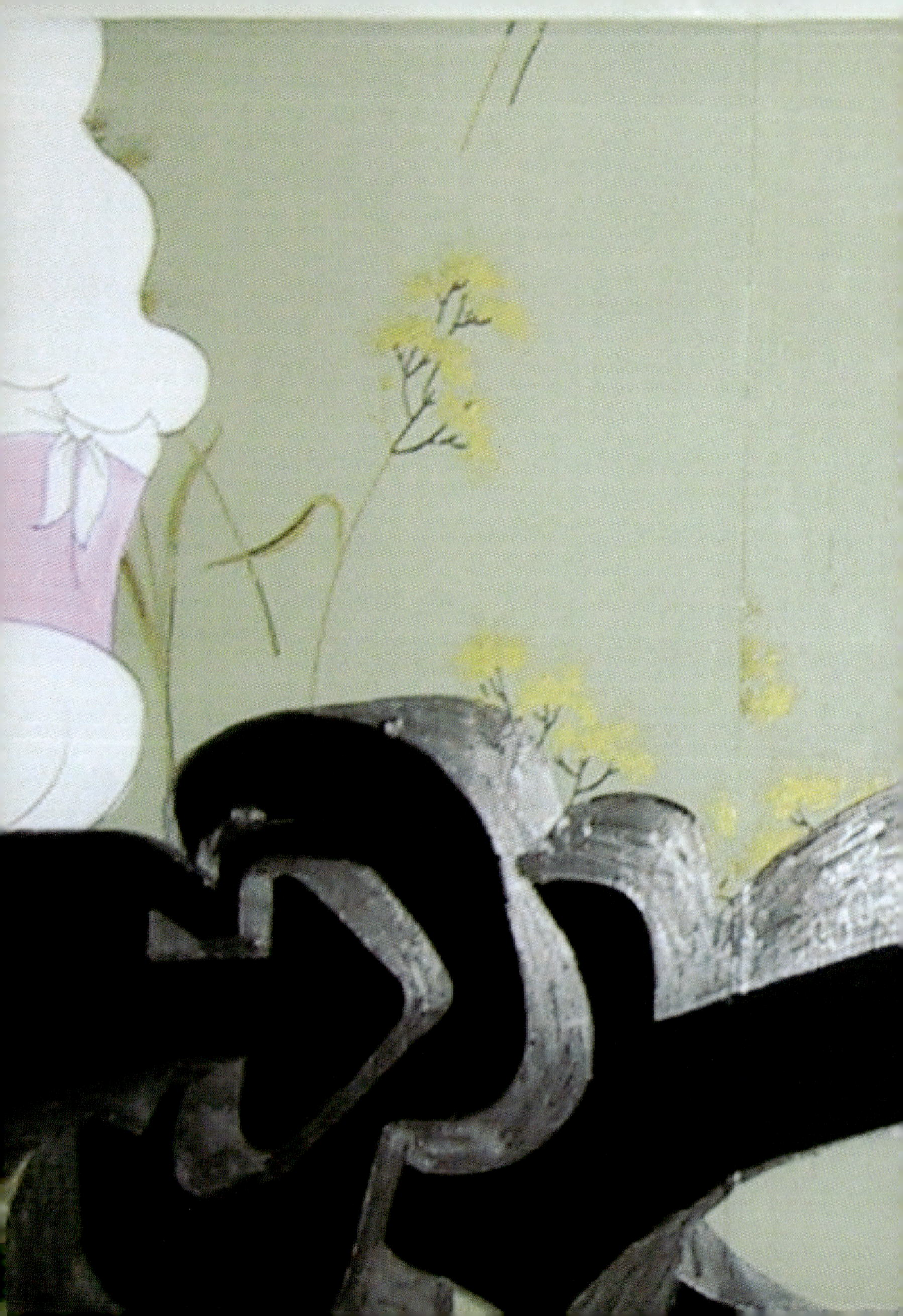

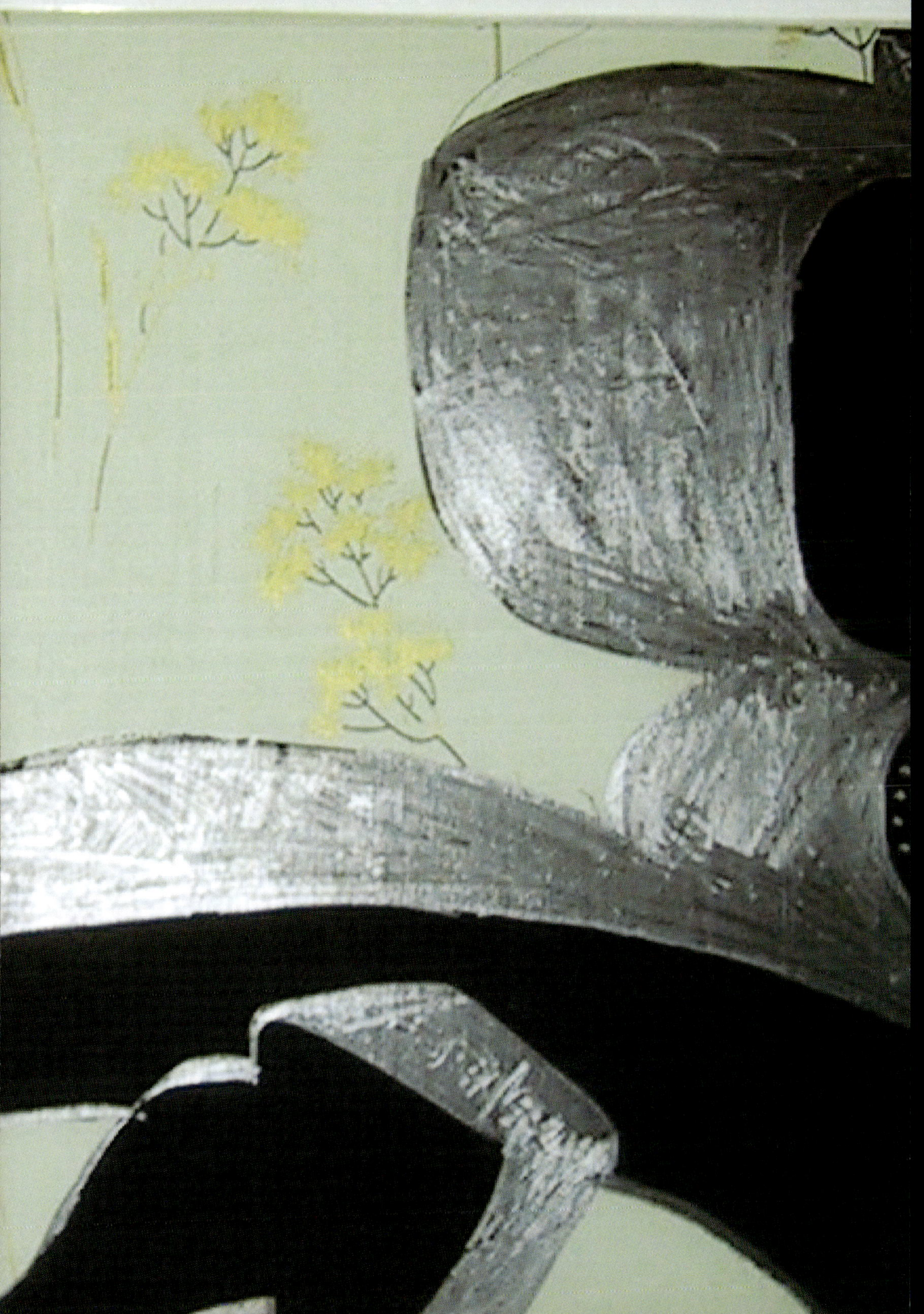

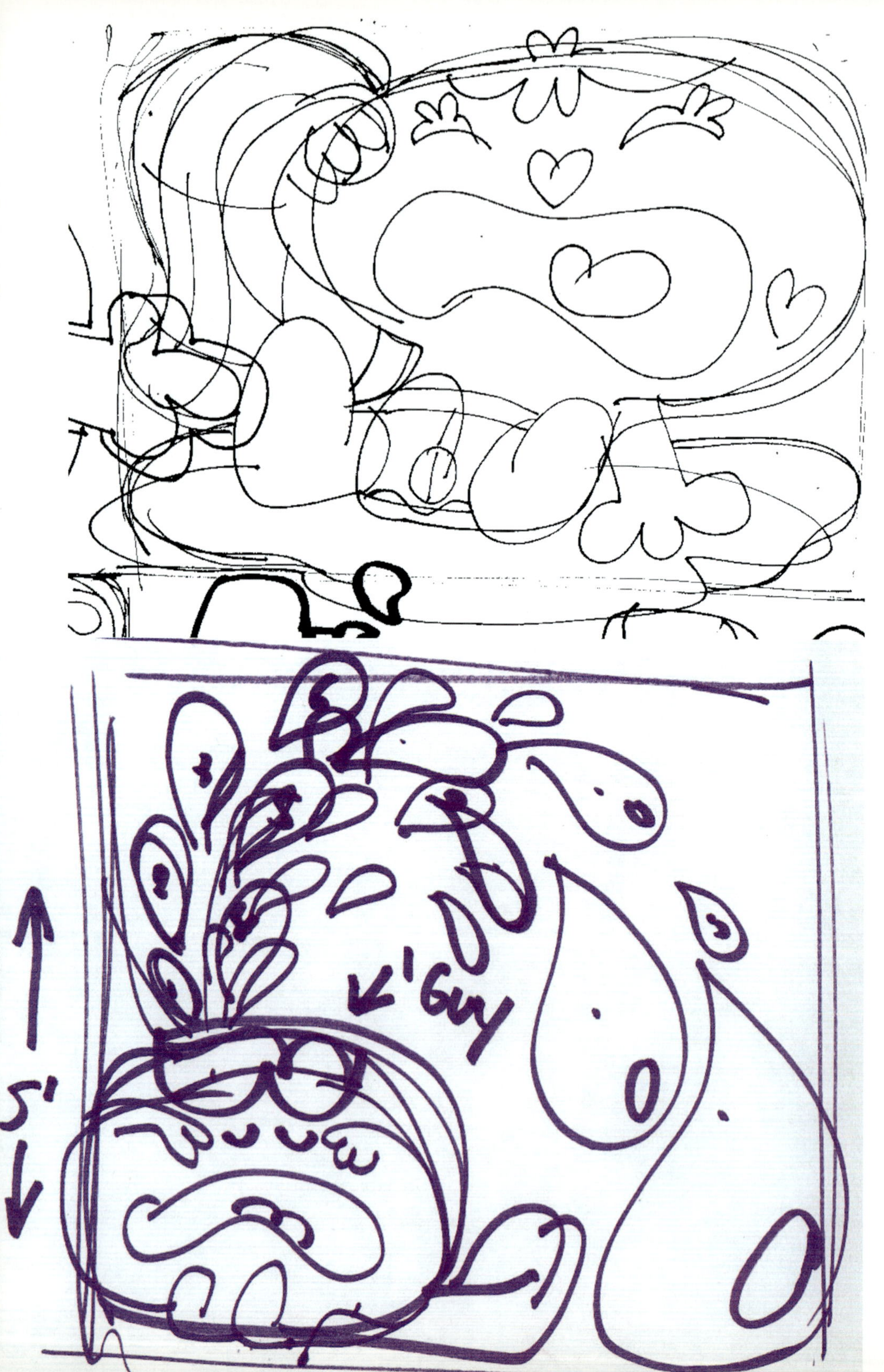

'GUY
5'

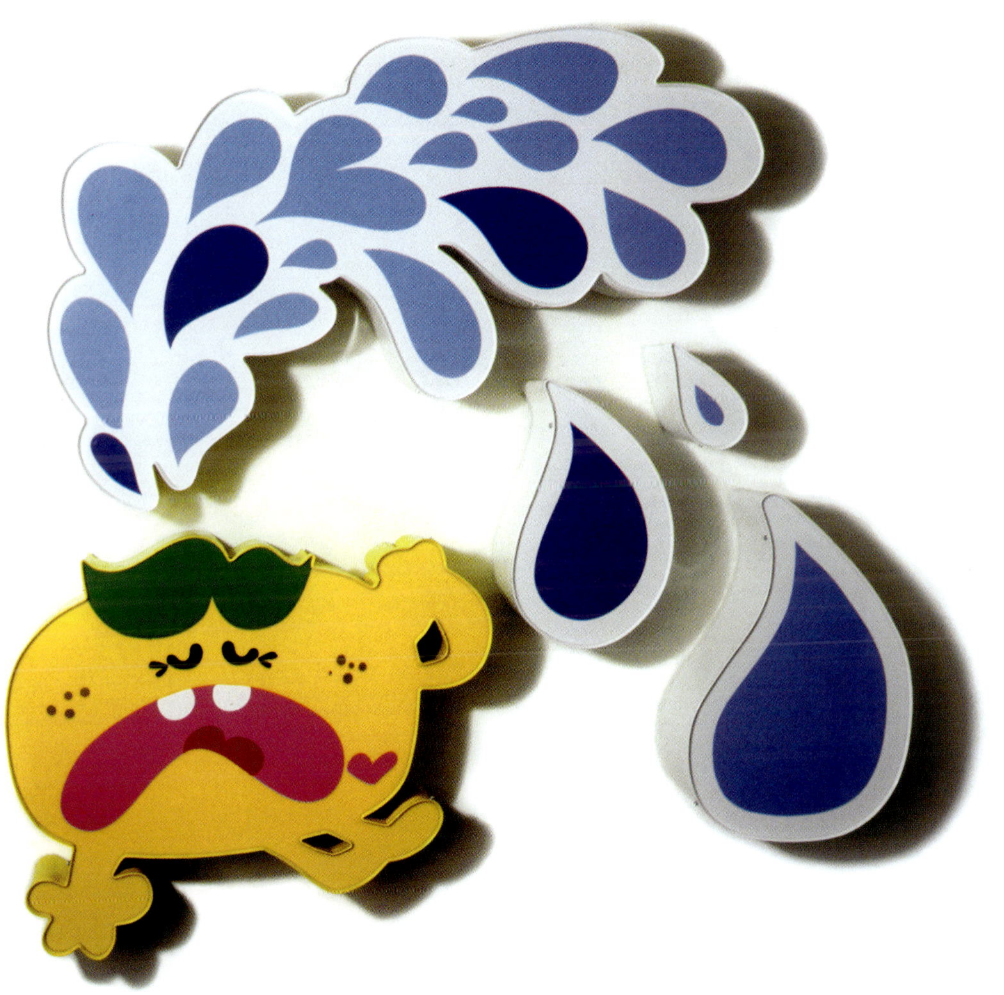

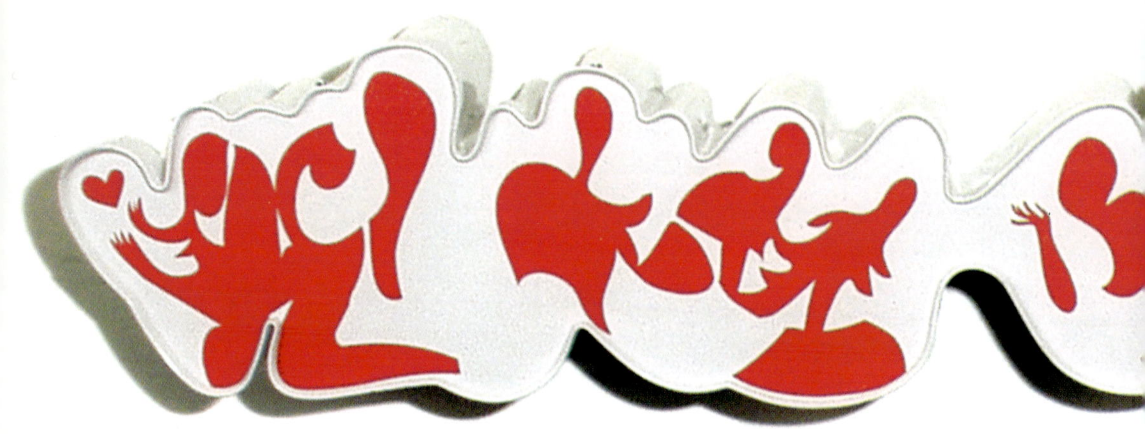

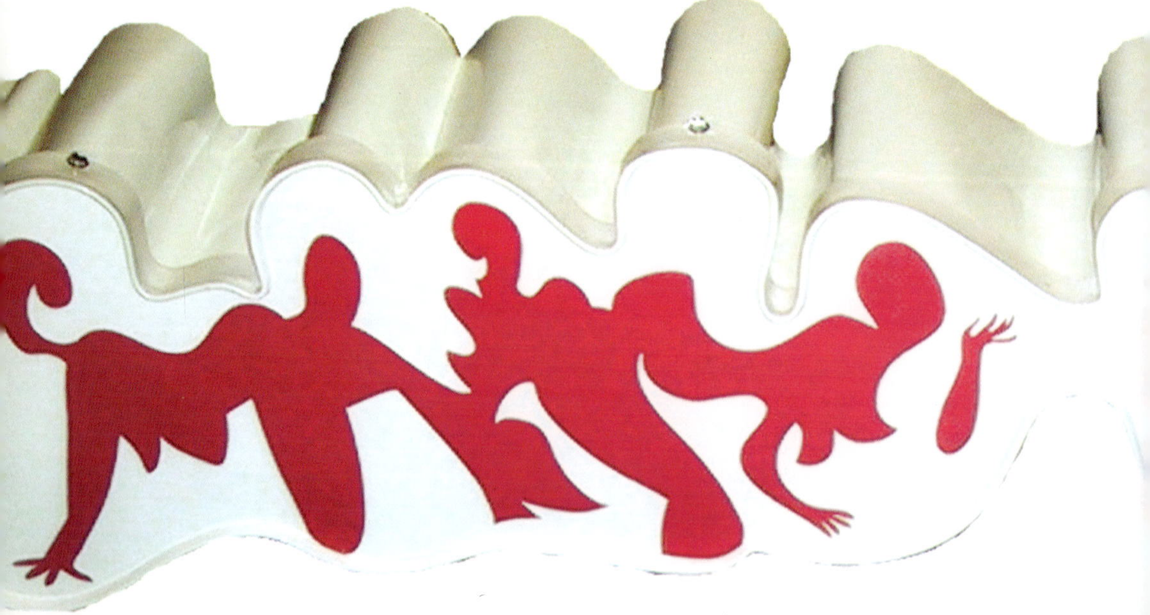

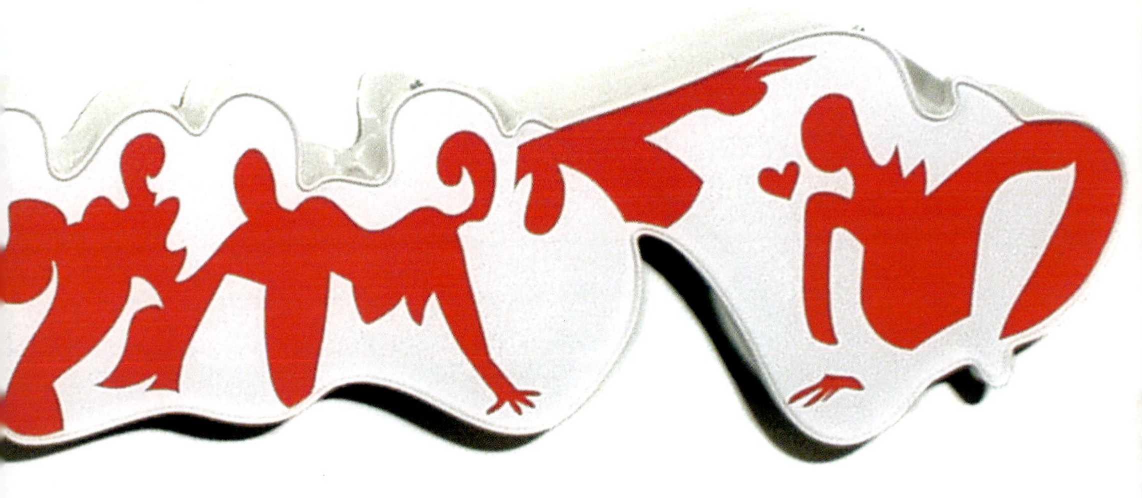

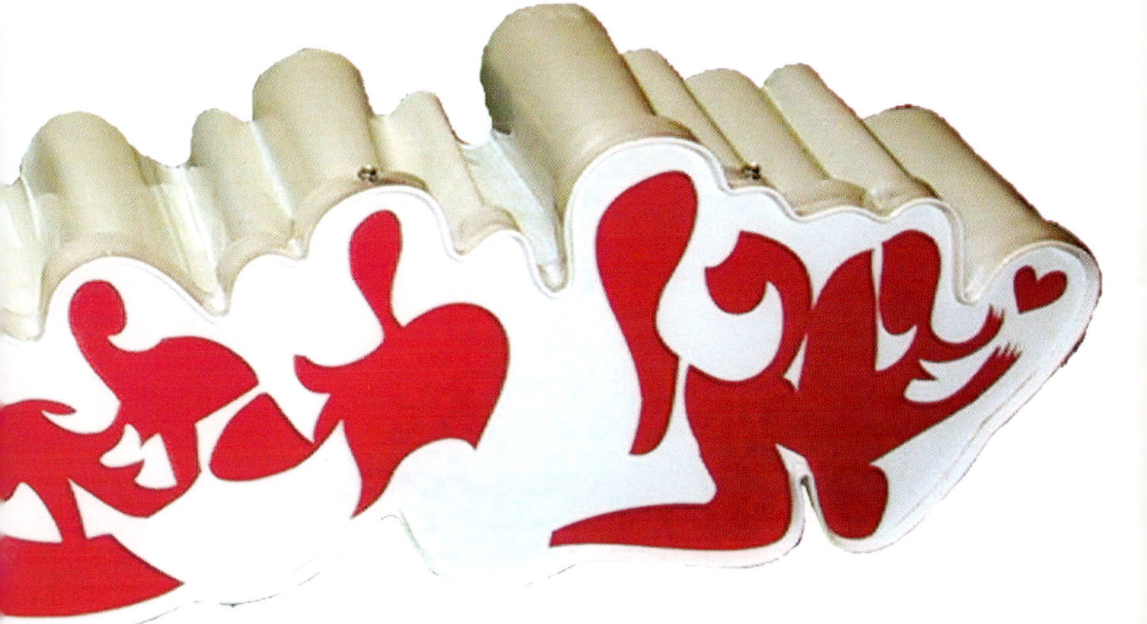

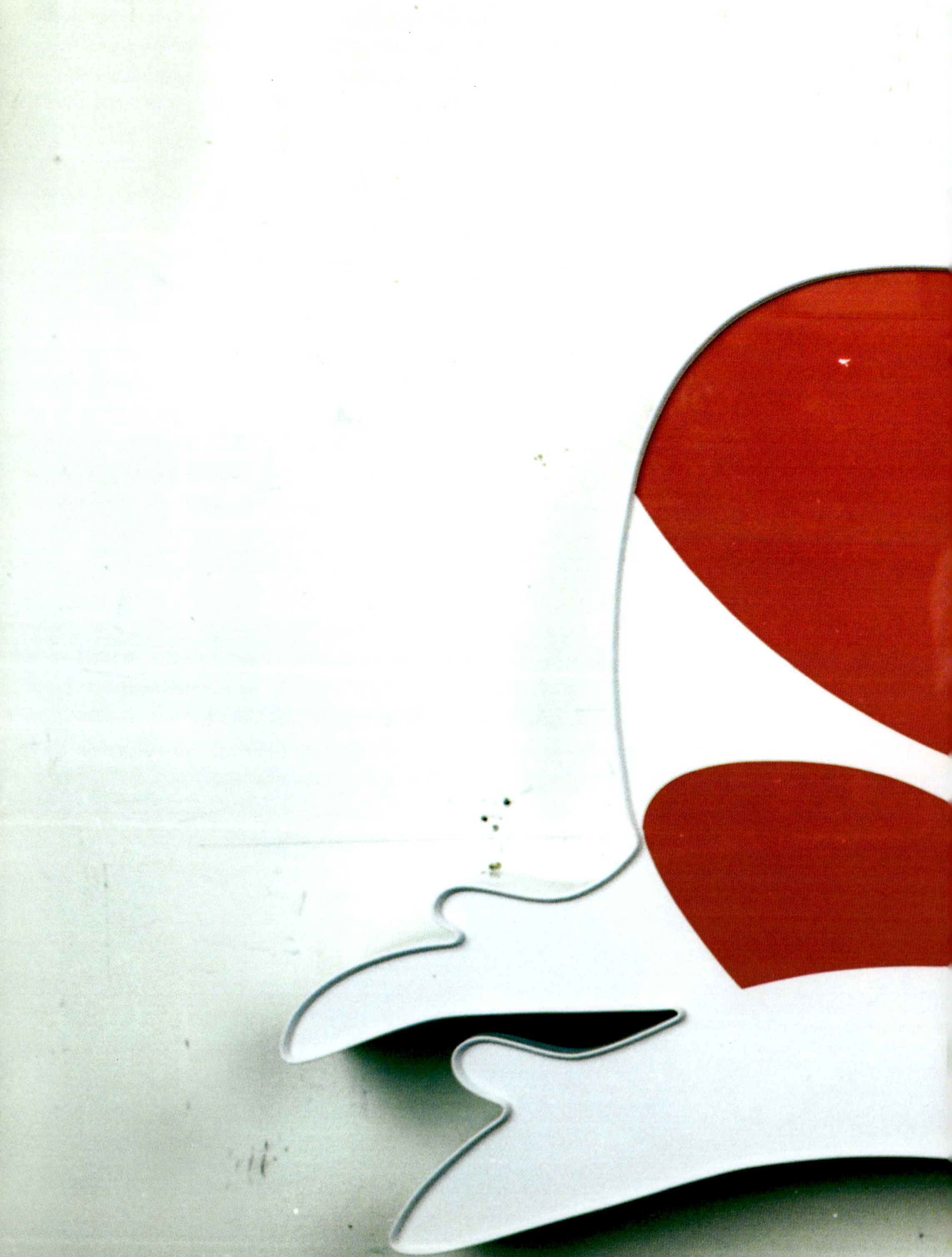

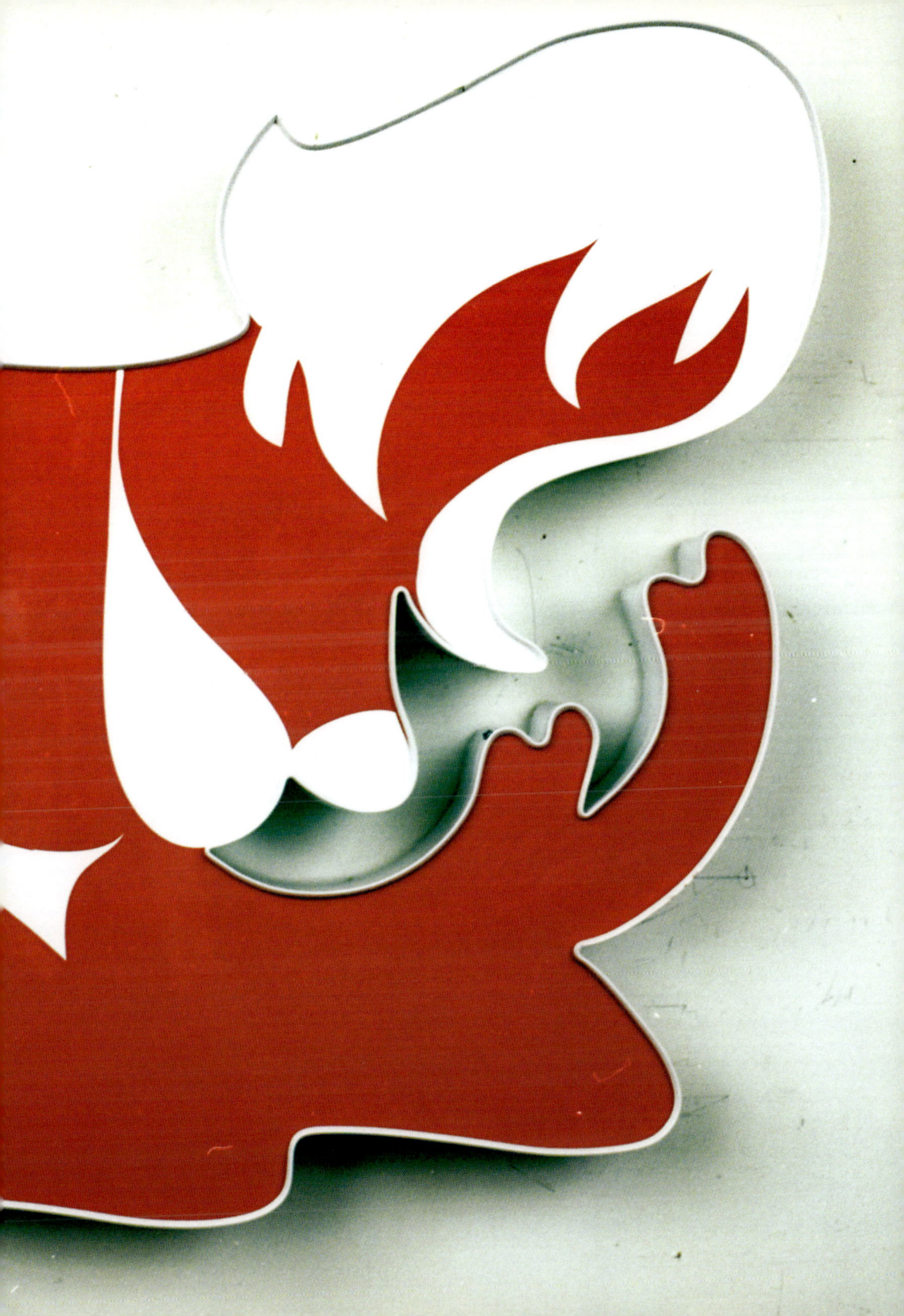

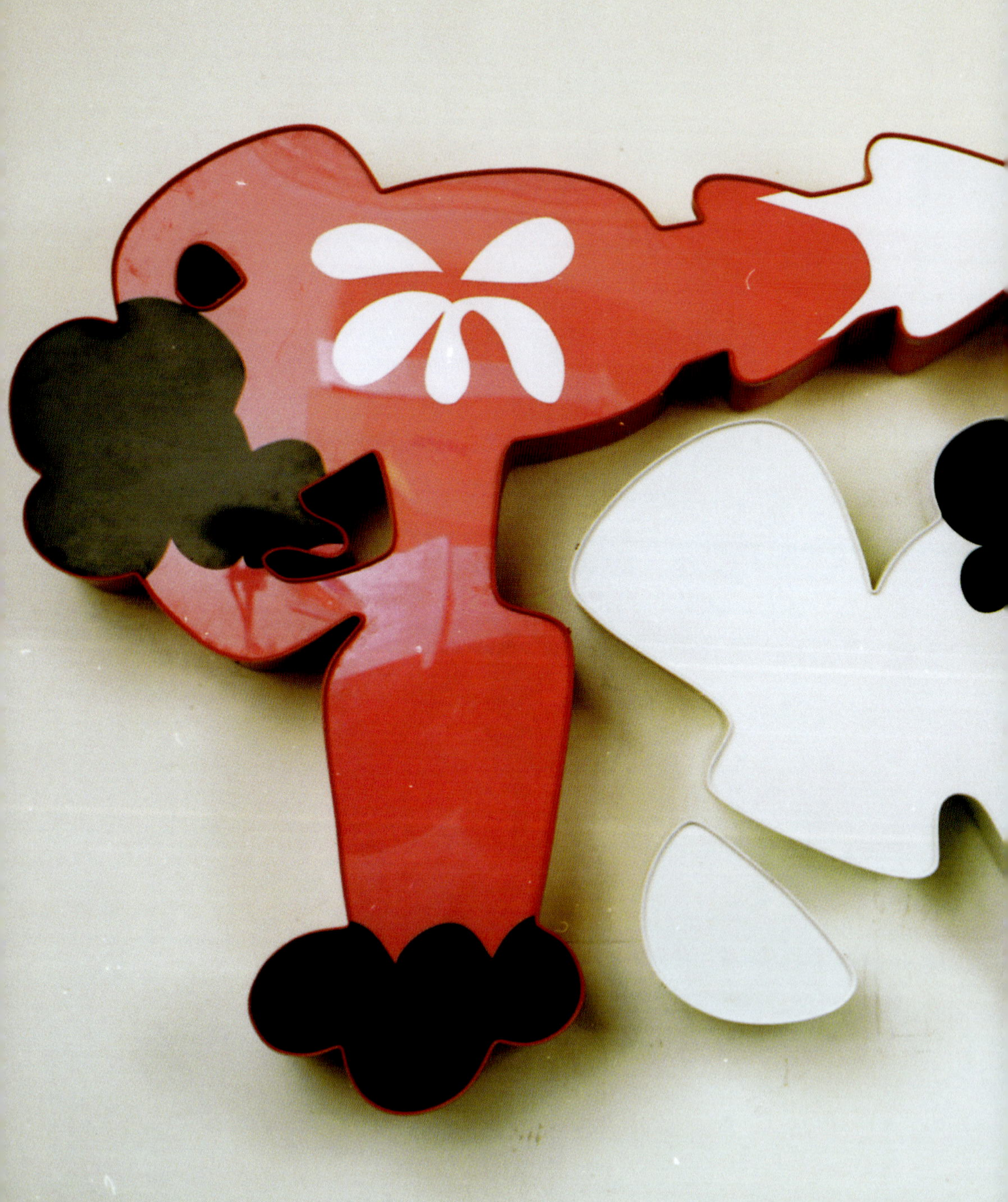

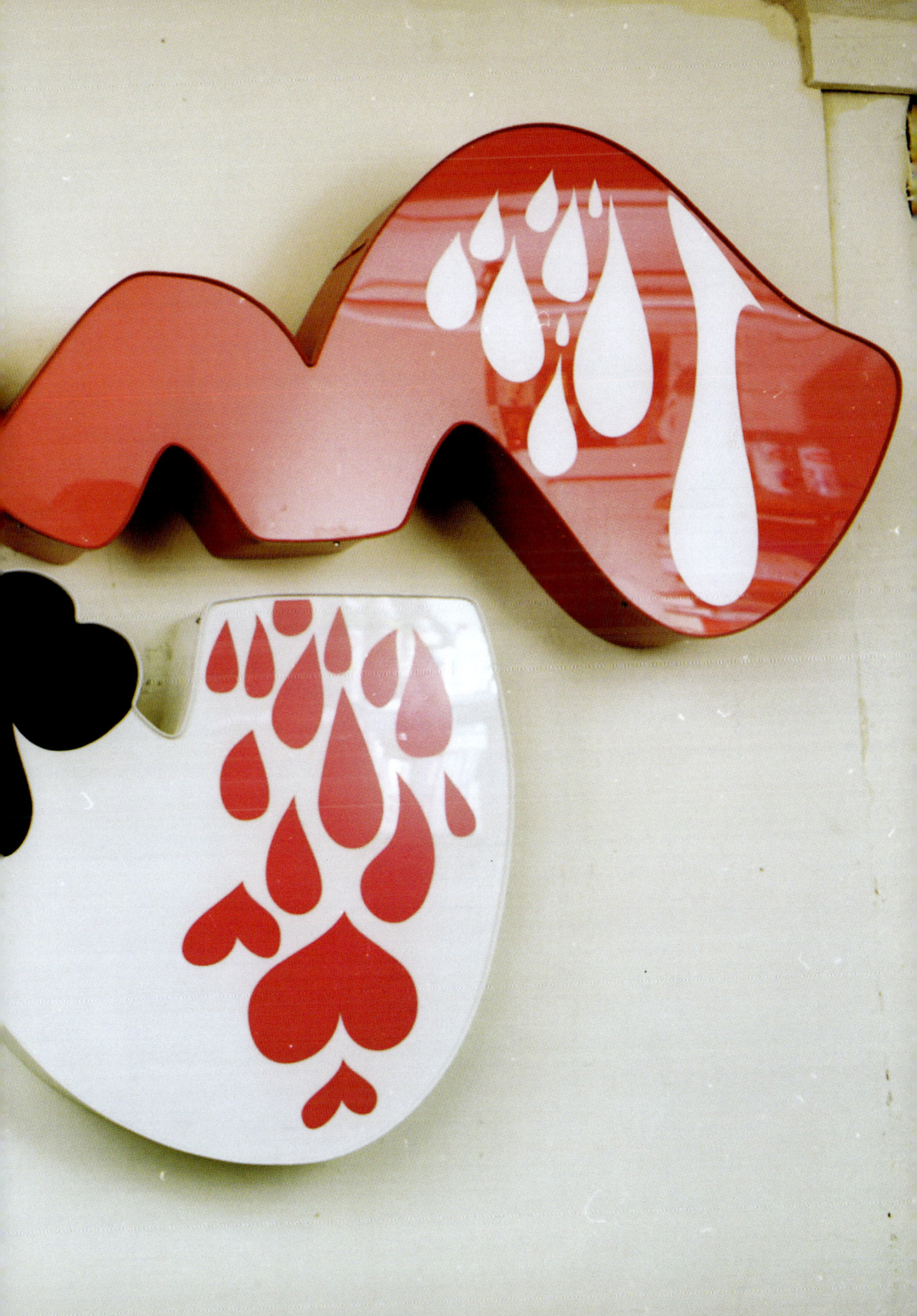

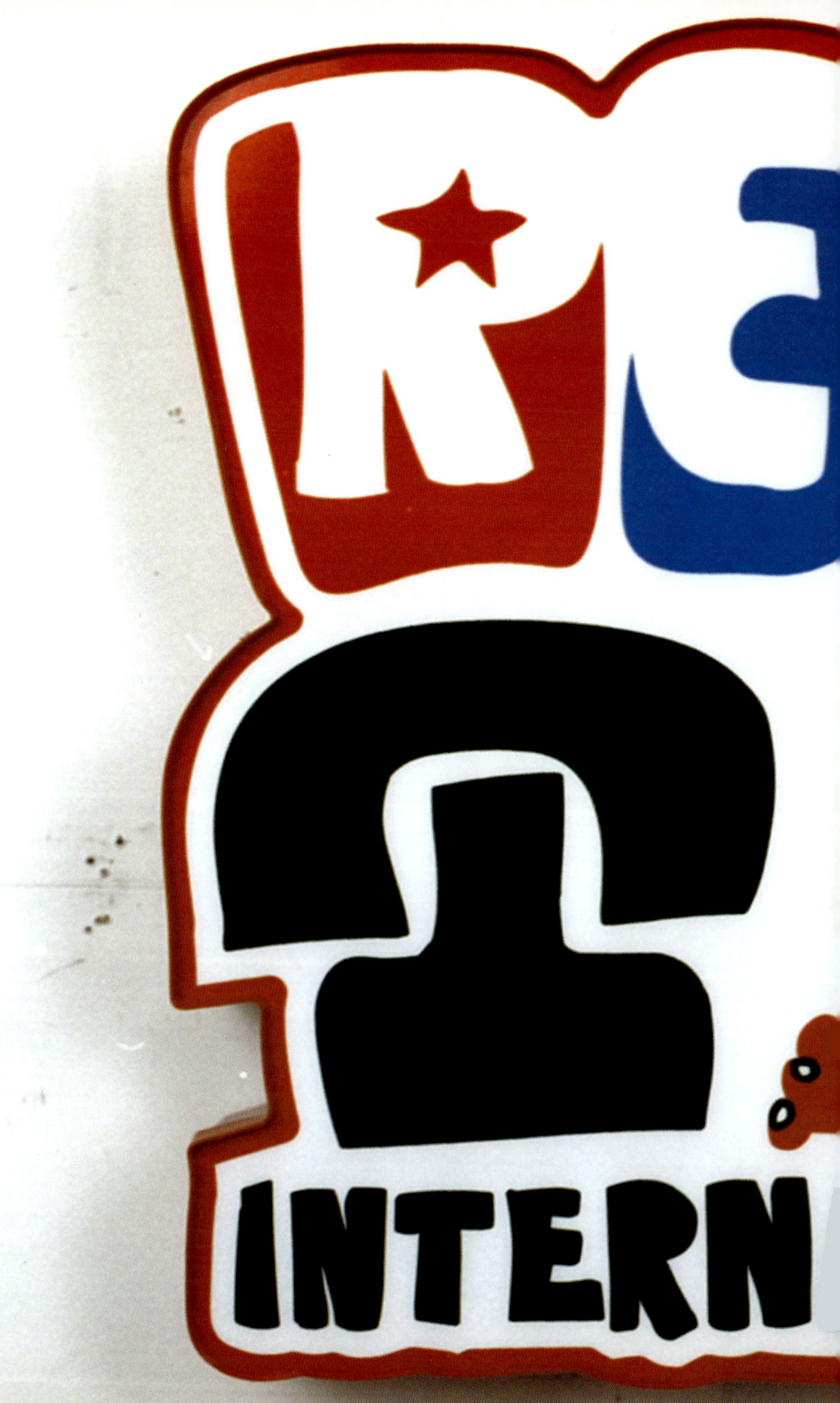
INTERN

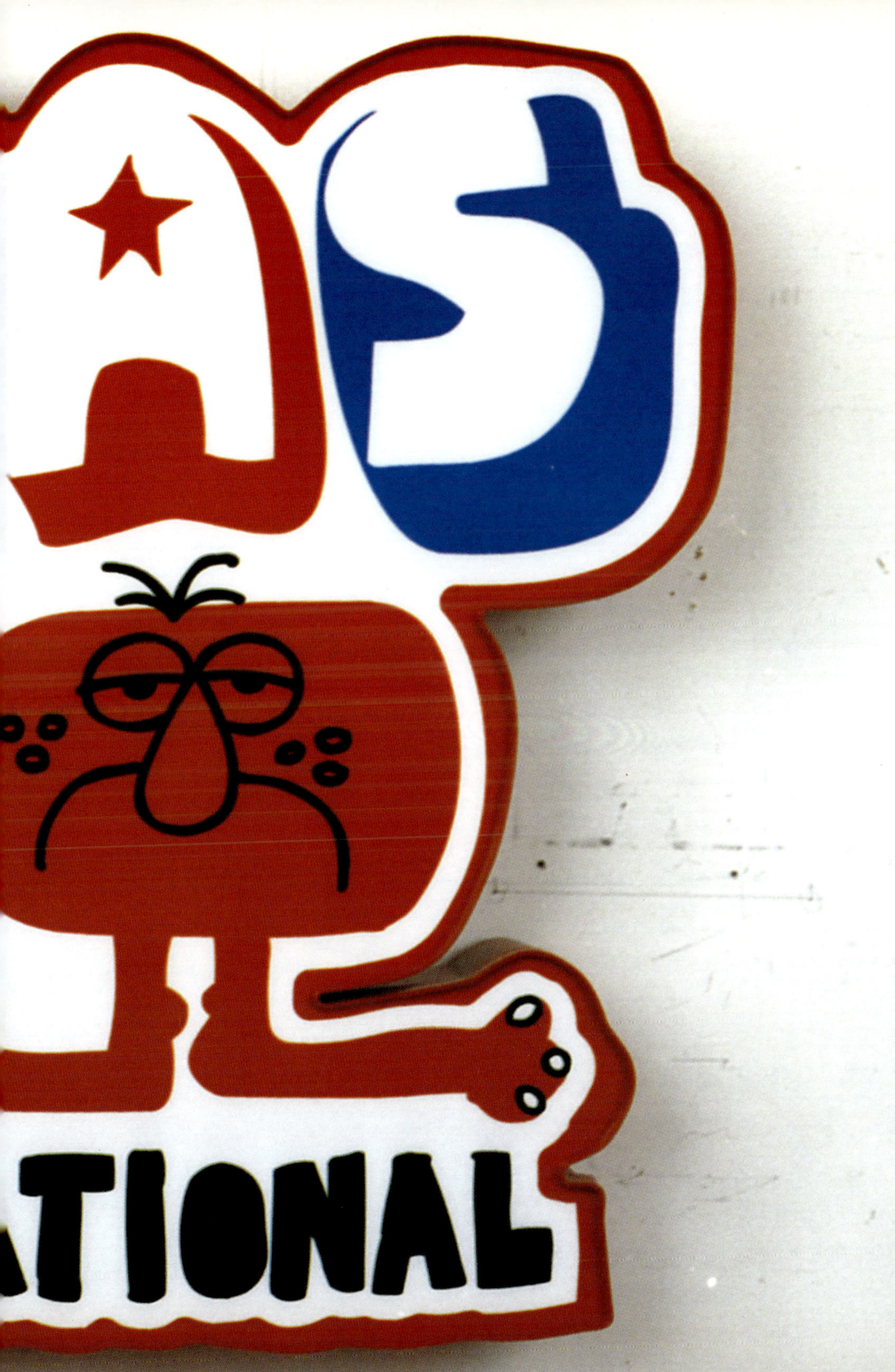
ATIONAL

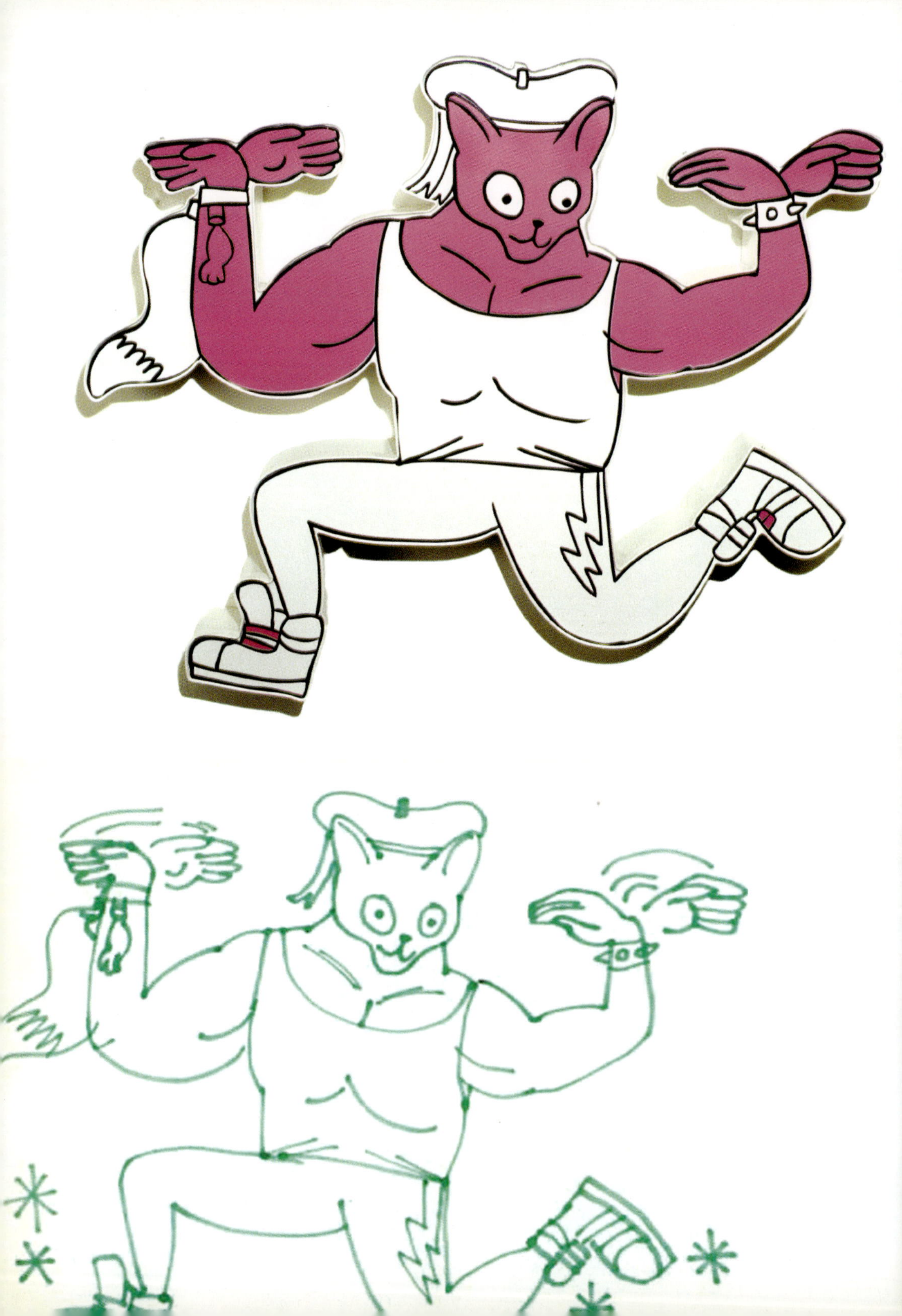

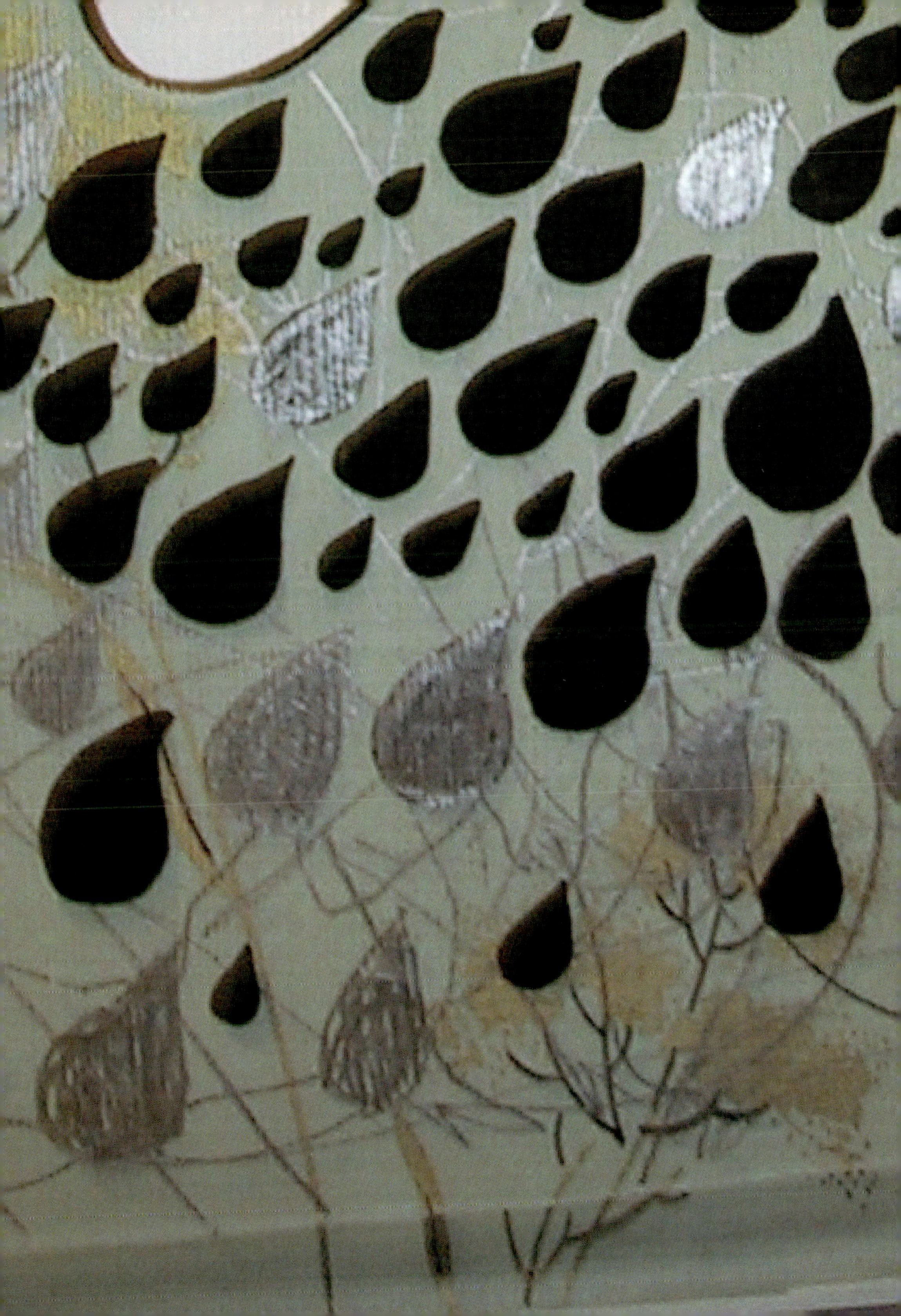

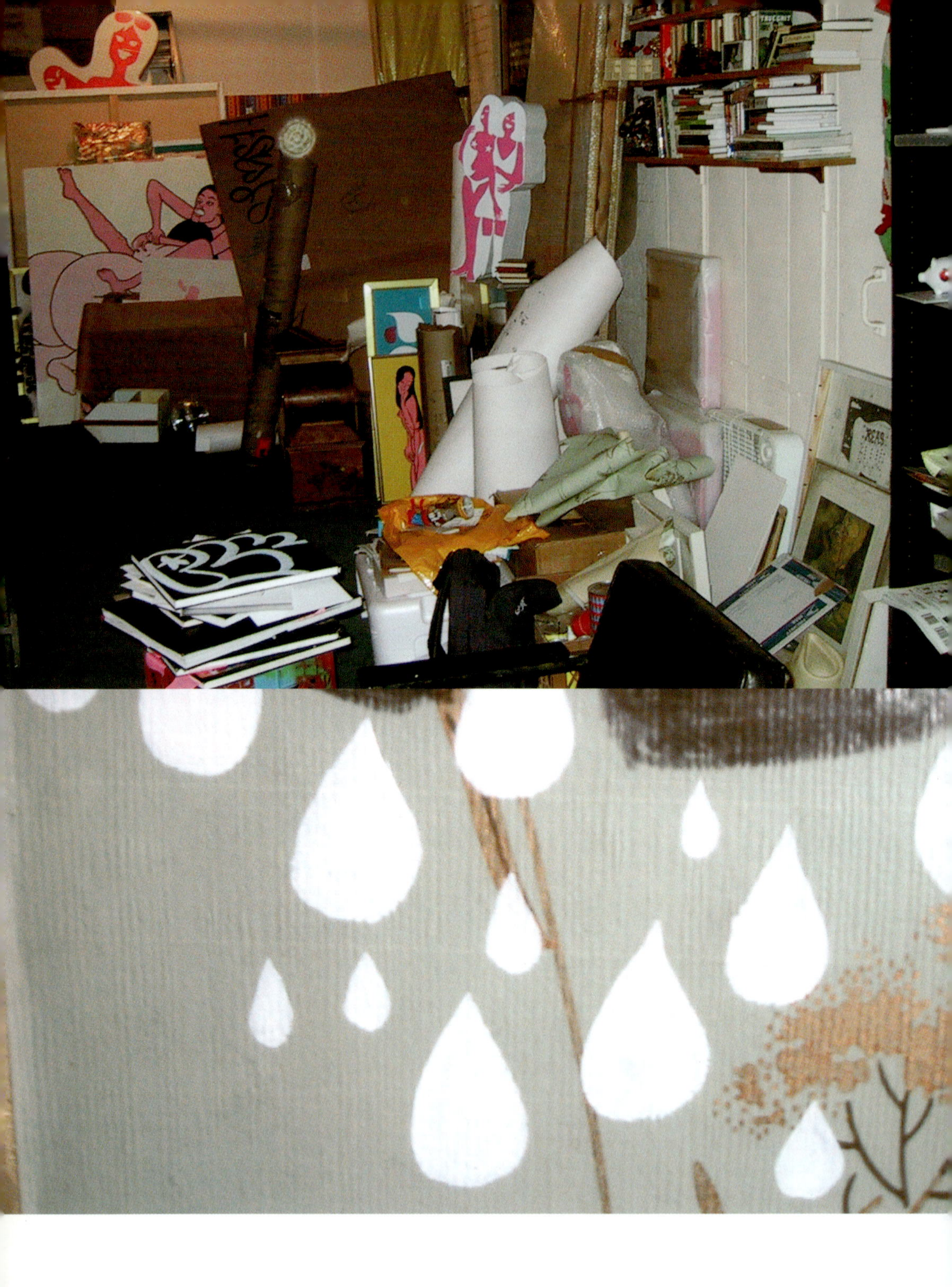

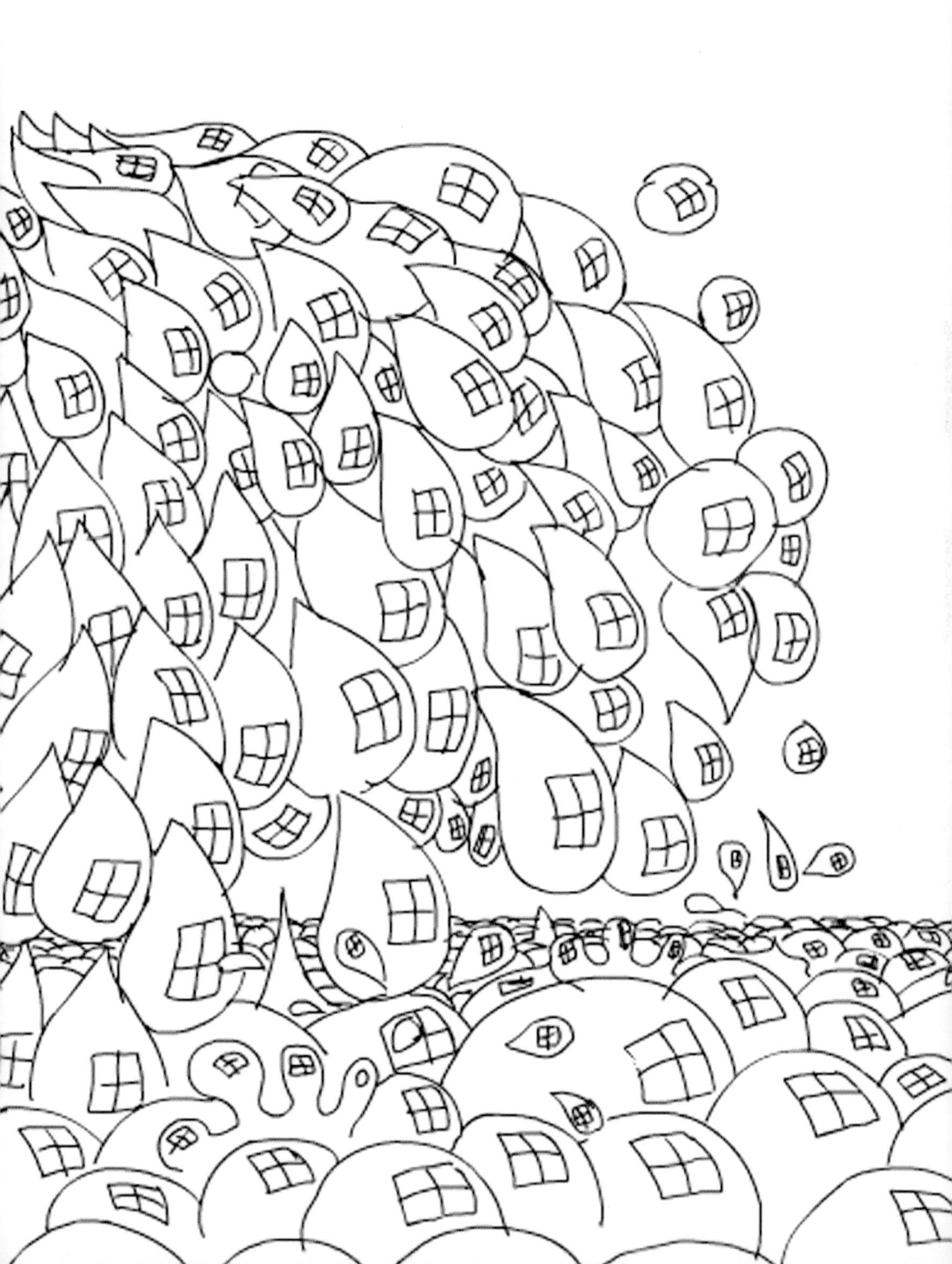

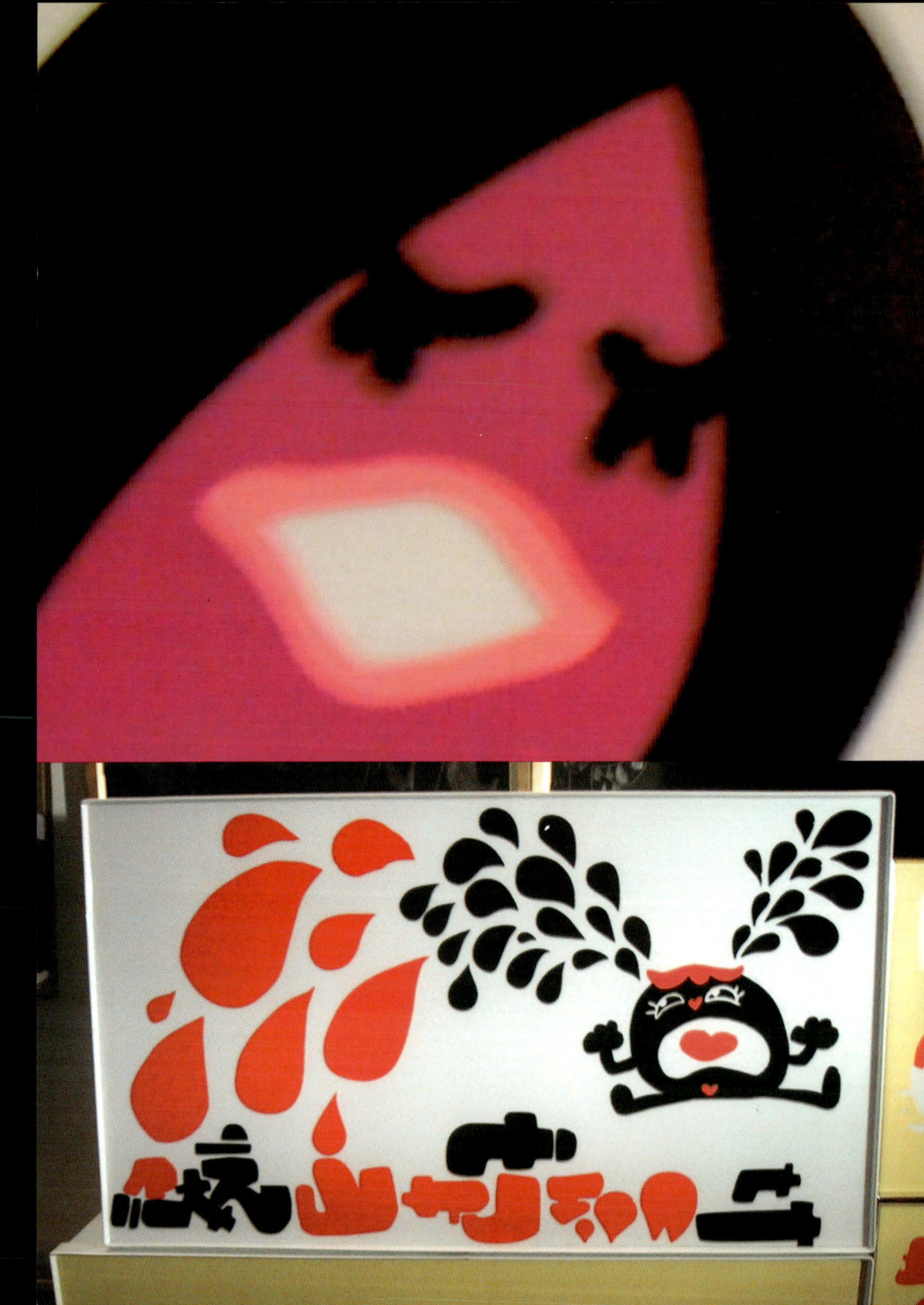

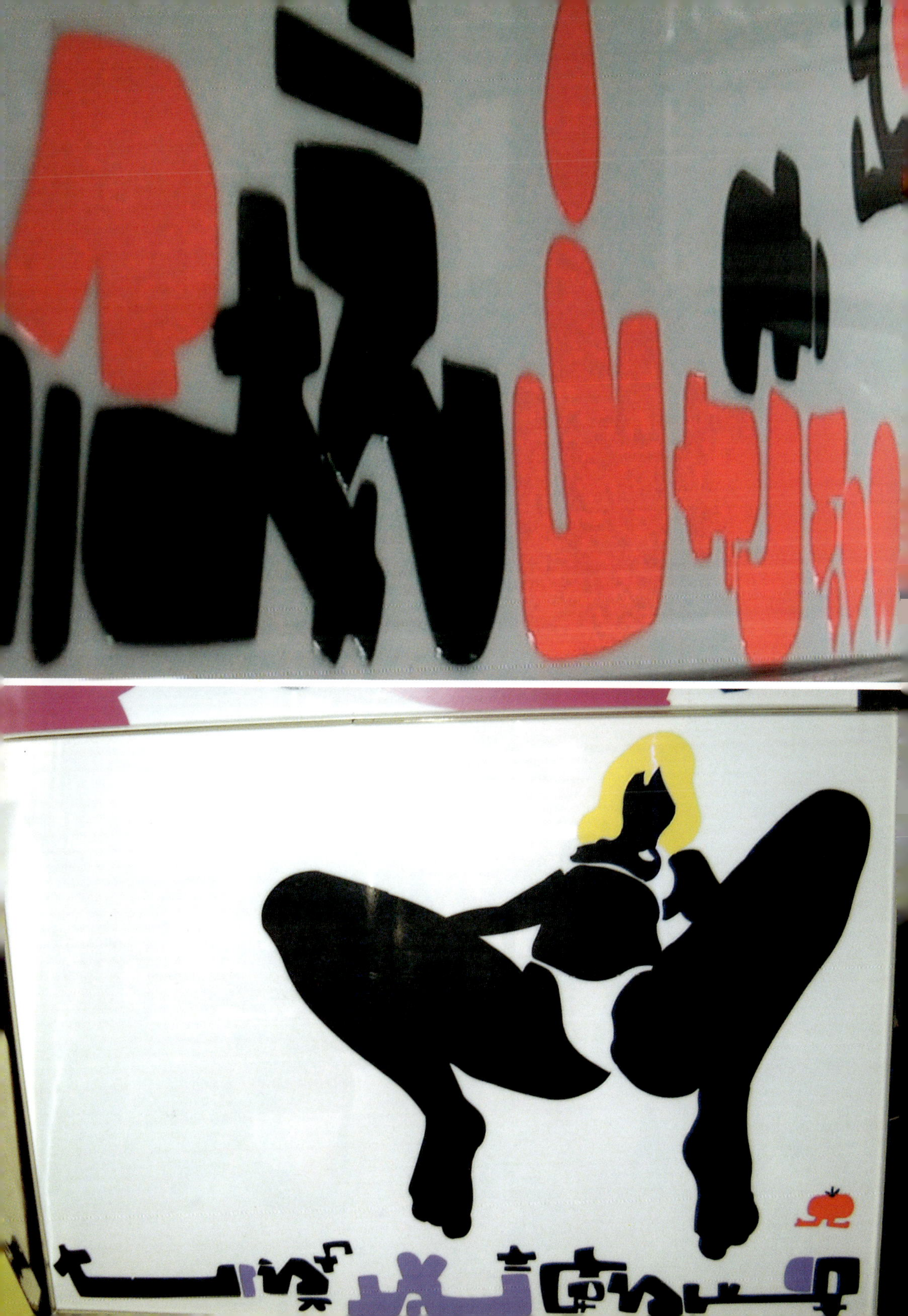

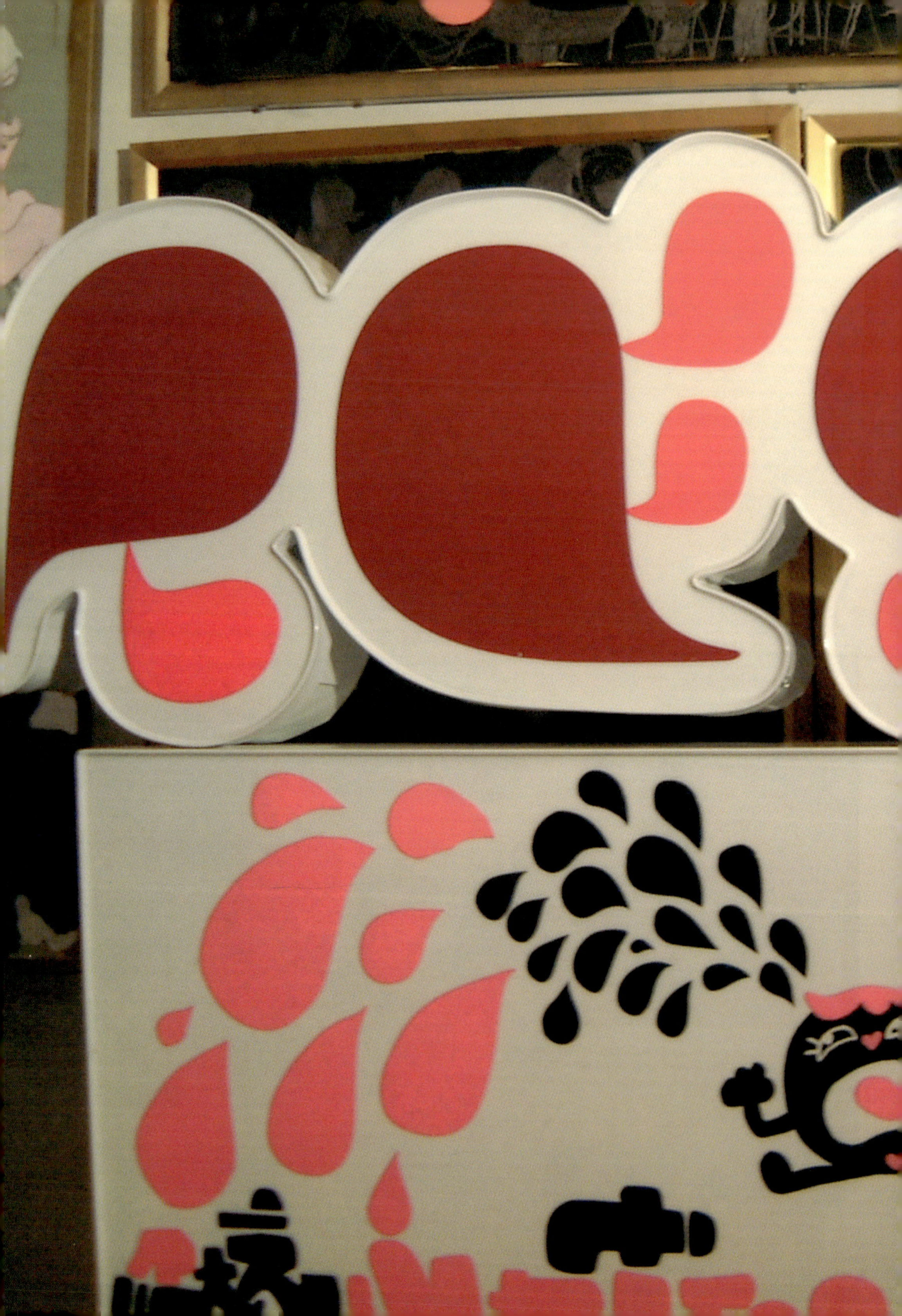

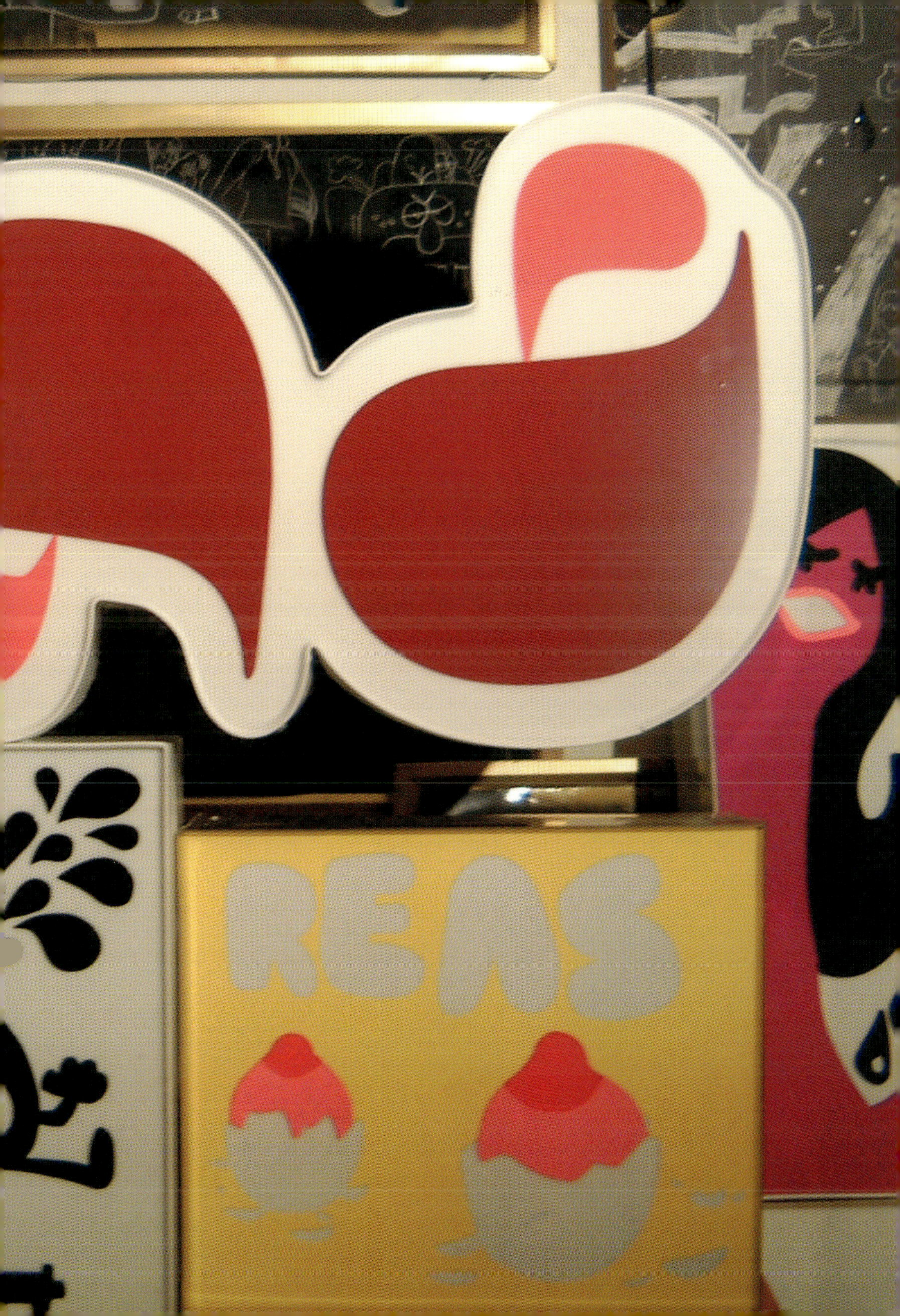
REAS

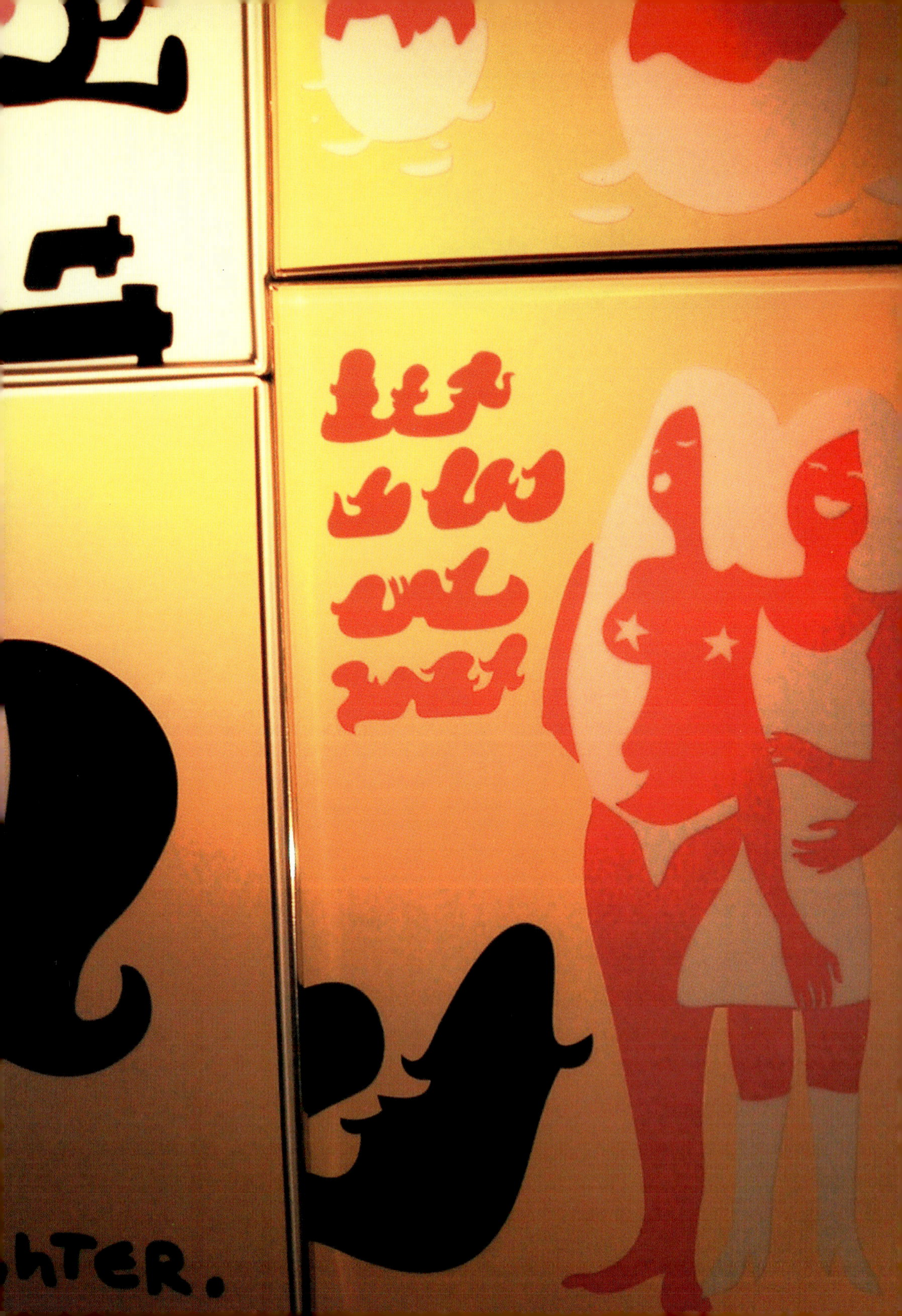
hTER.

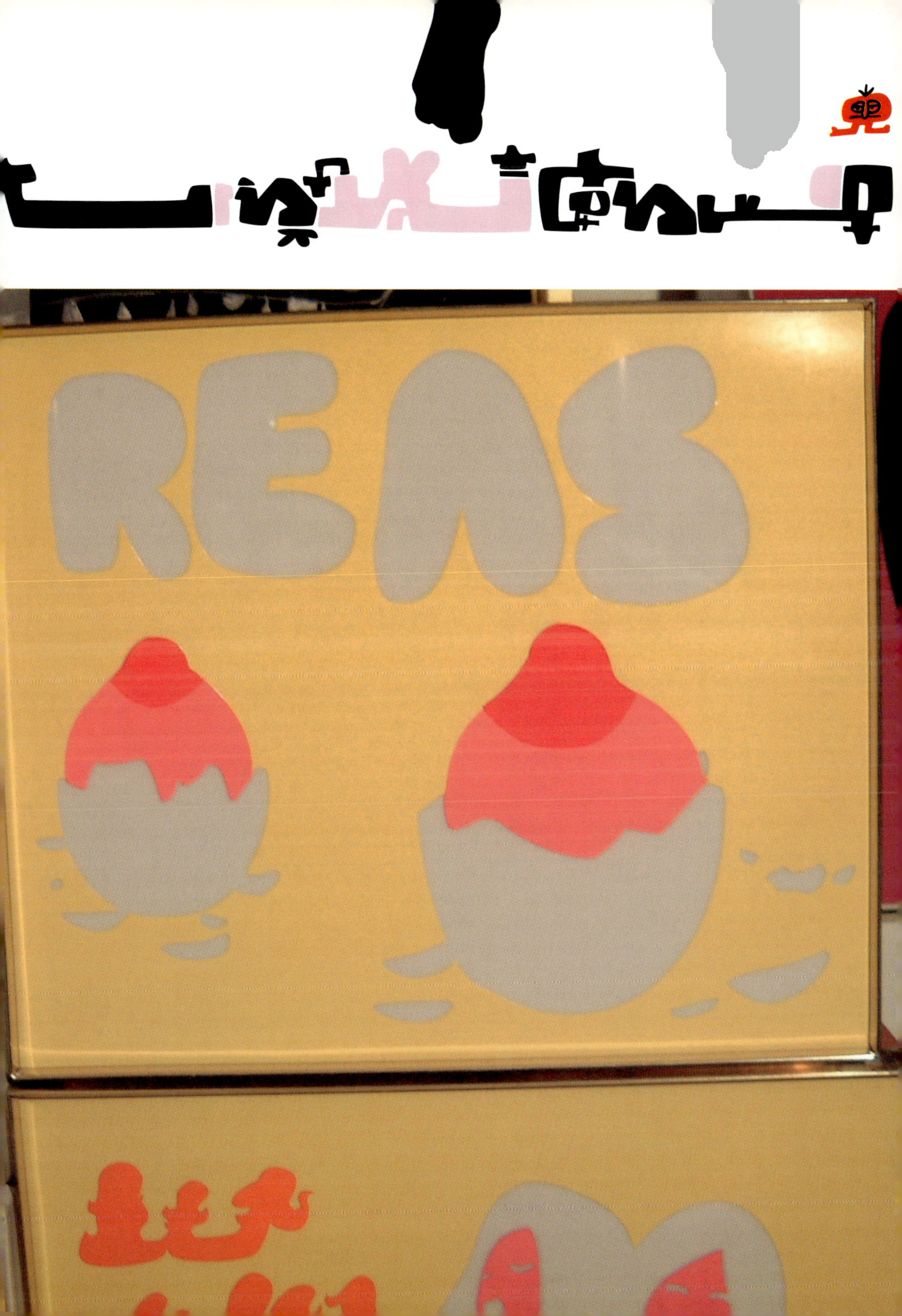
REAS

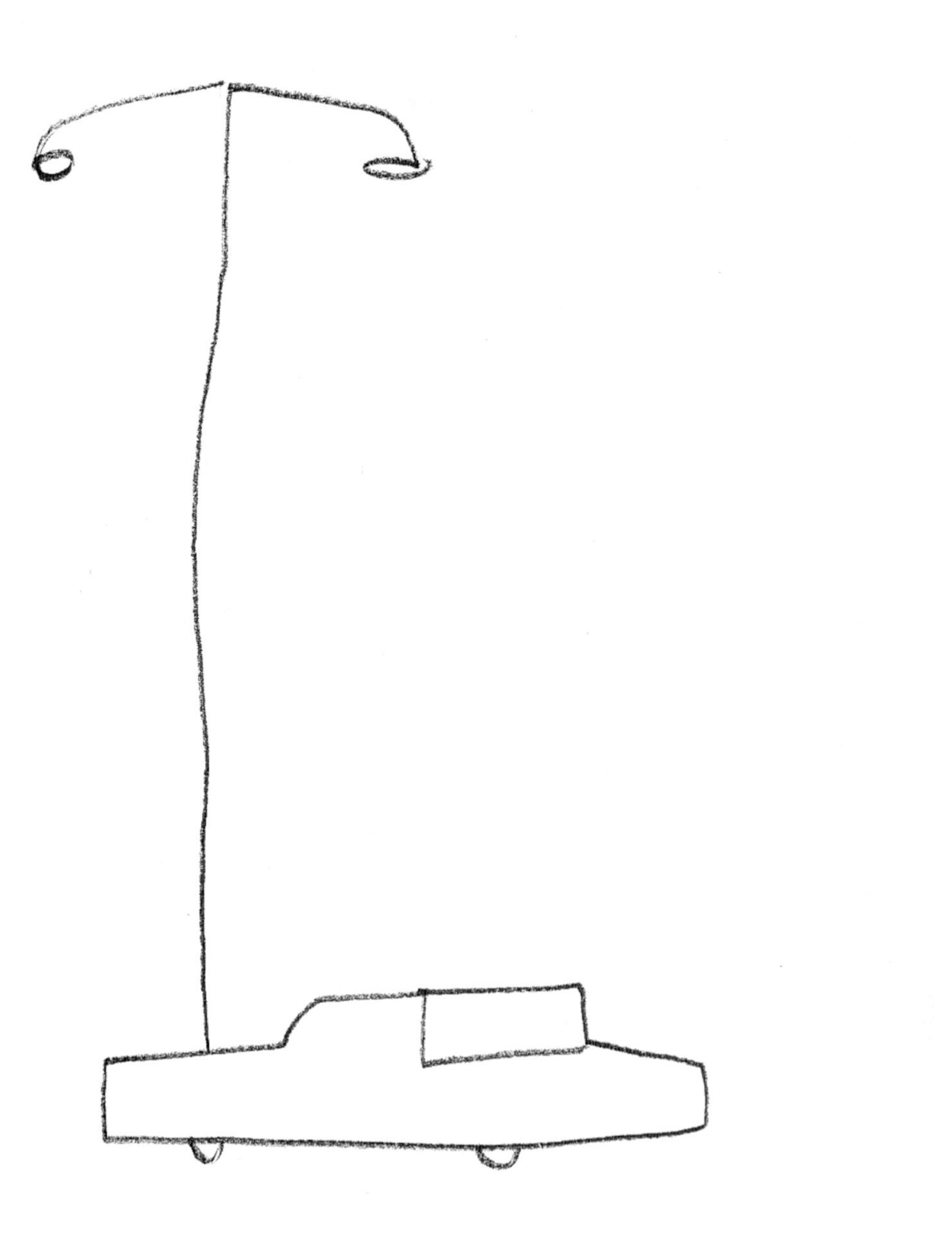

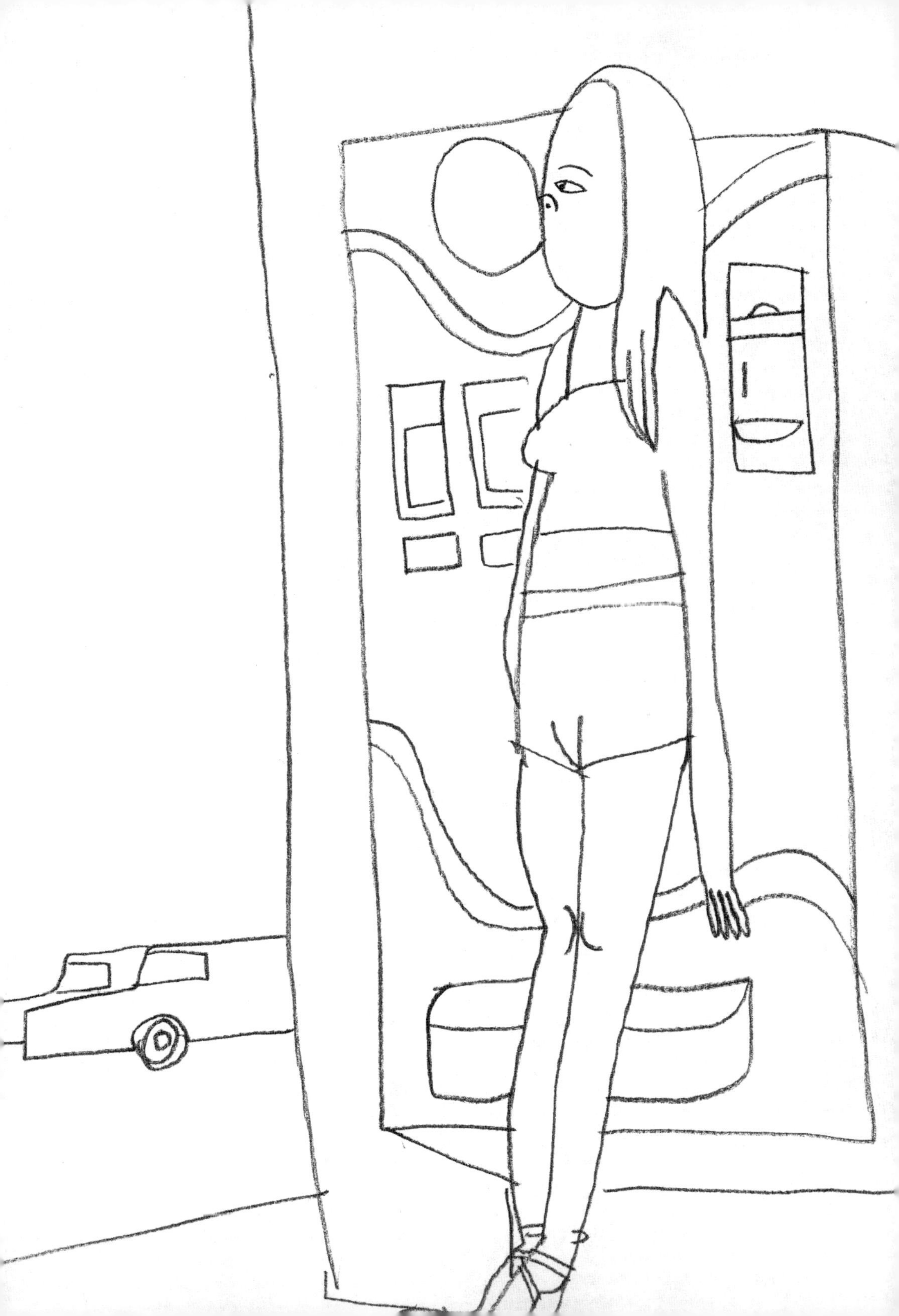

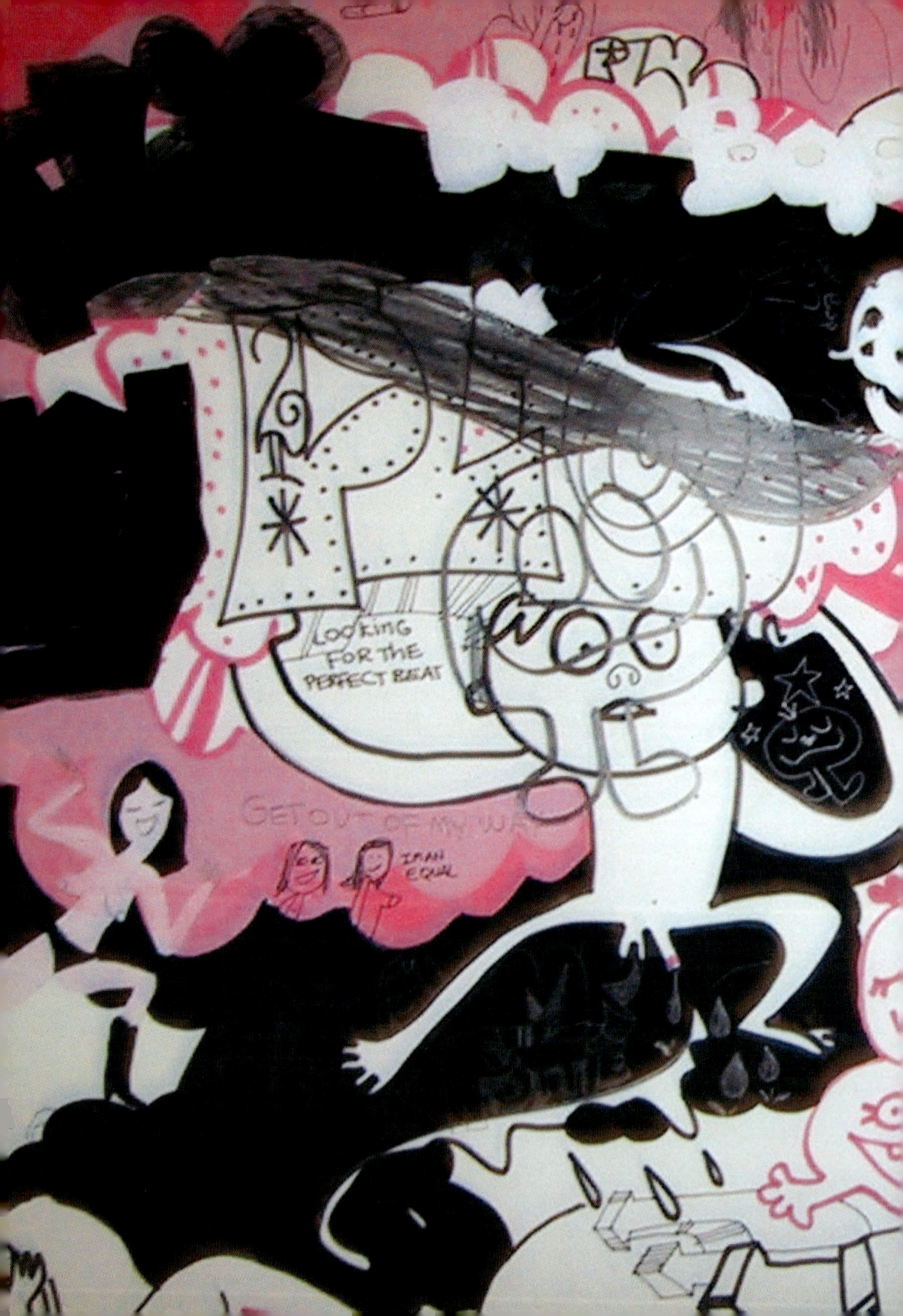
LOOKING FOR THE PERFECT BEAT

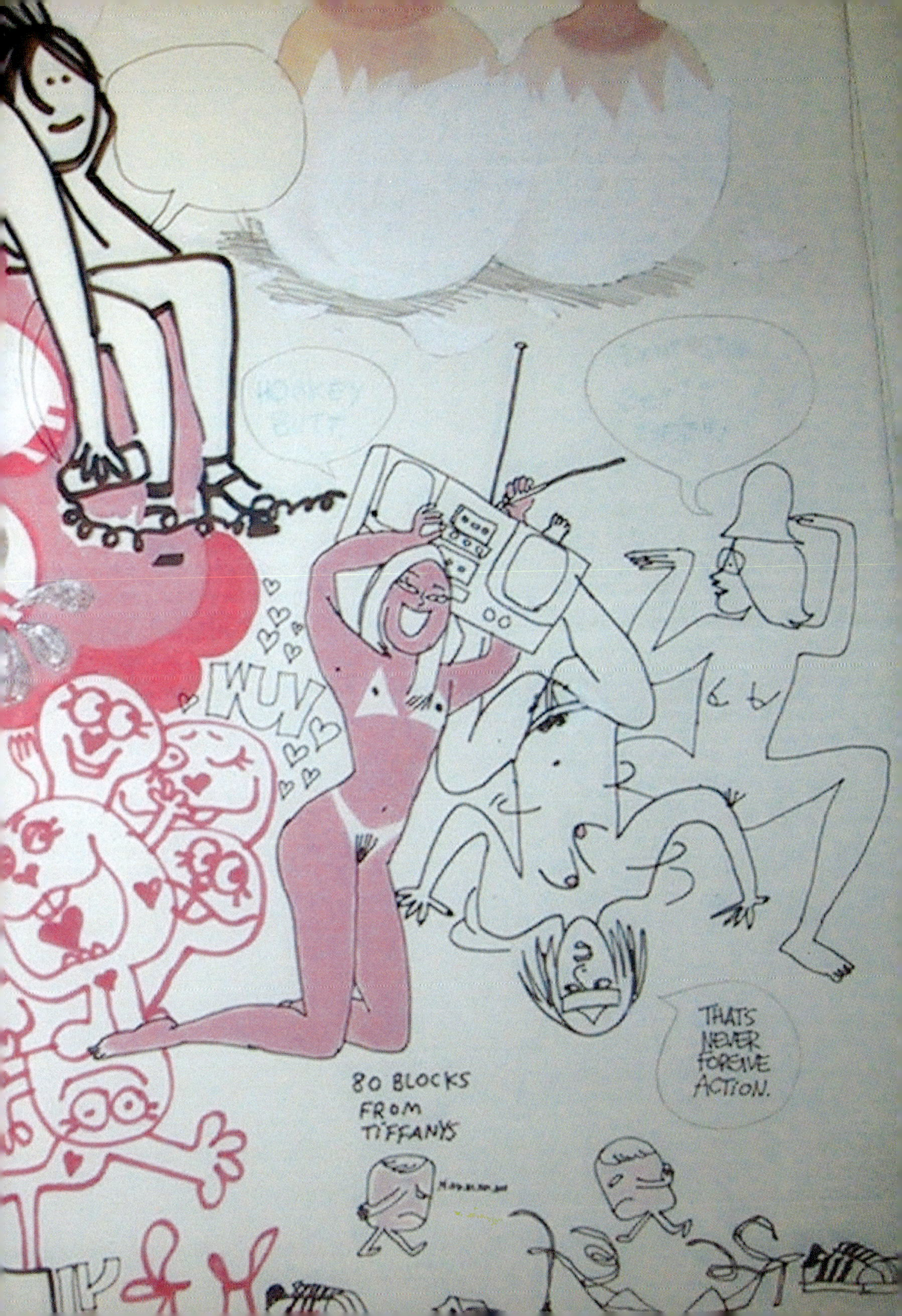
HOCKEY BUTT
WUV
THATS NEVER FORGIVE ACTION.
80 BLOCKS FROM TIFFANYS

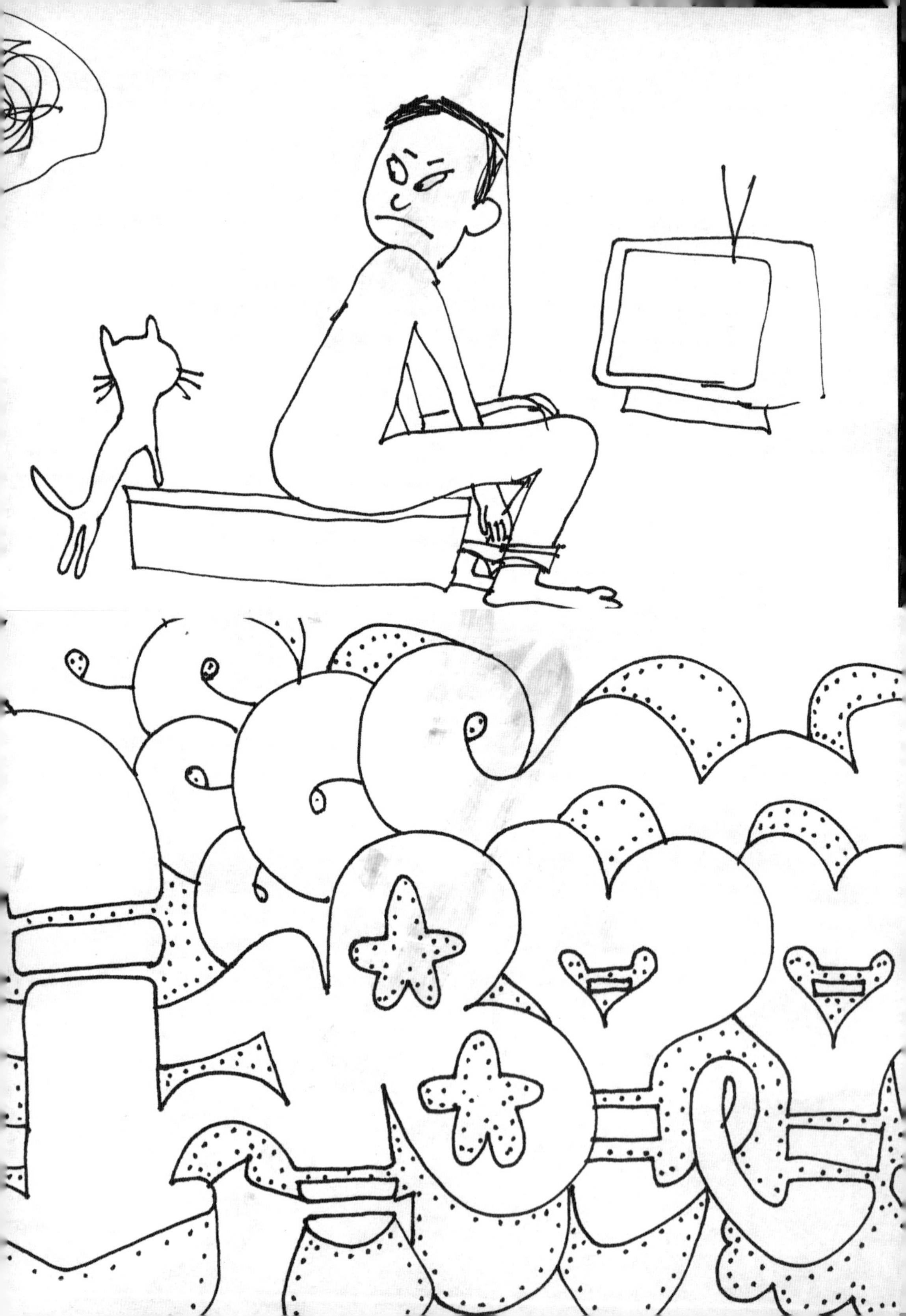

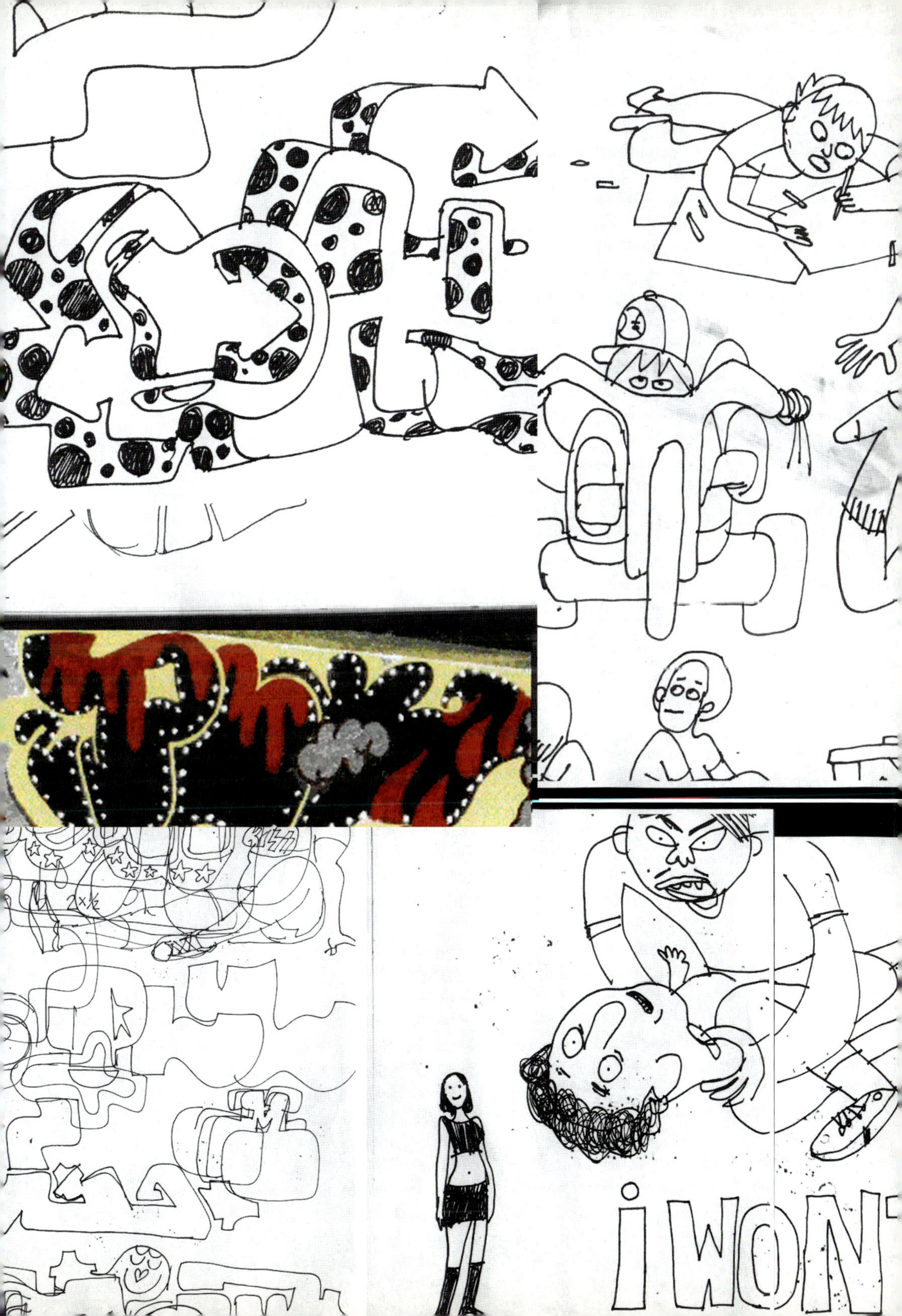
i WON

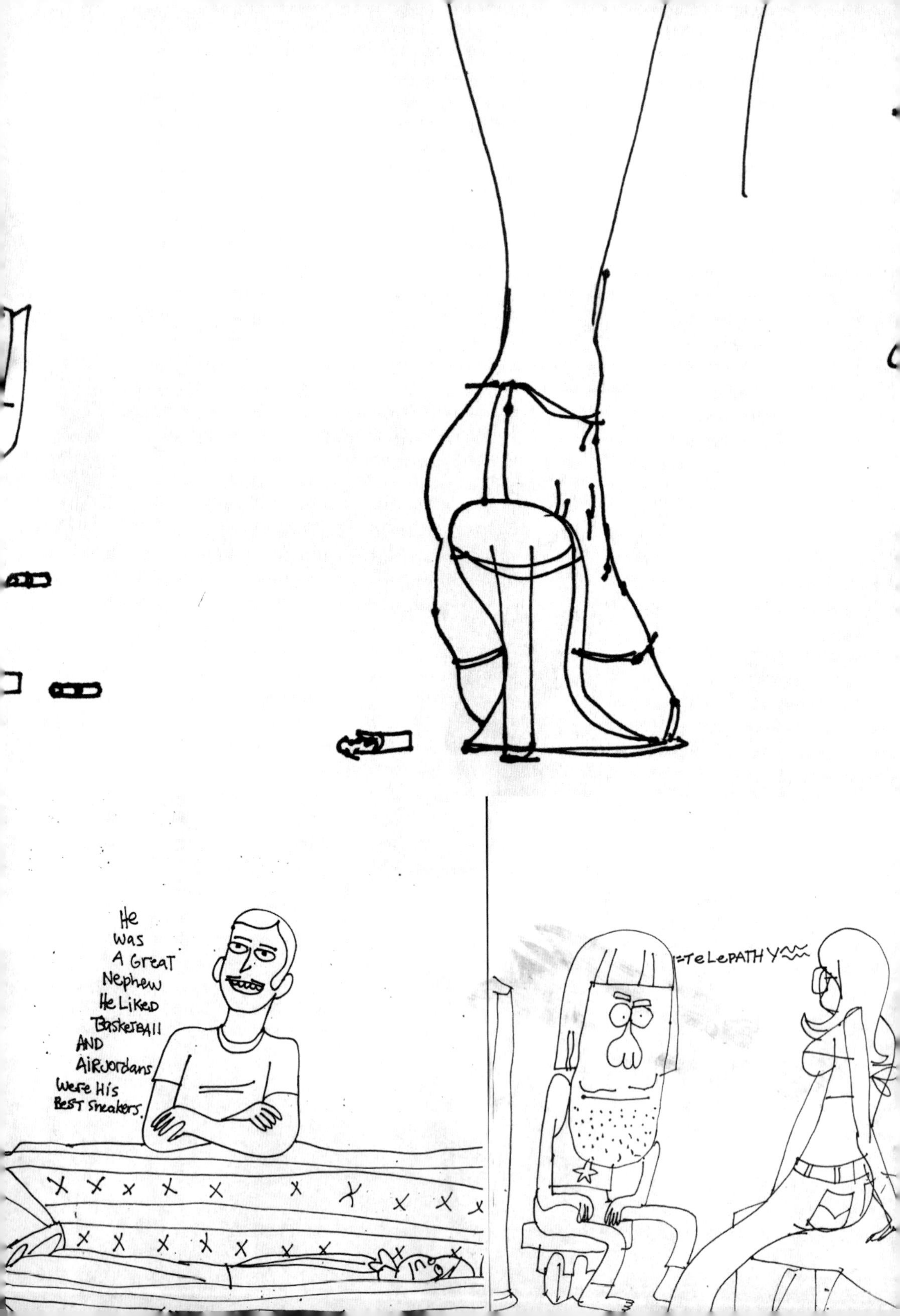
He
was
A GreaT
Nephew
He LikeD
BasketBAll
AND
AiRJordans
Were His
BesT Sneakers.
=TeLePATHY

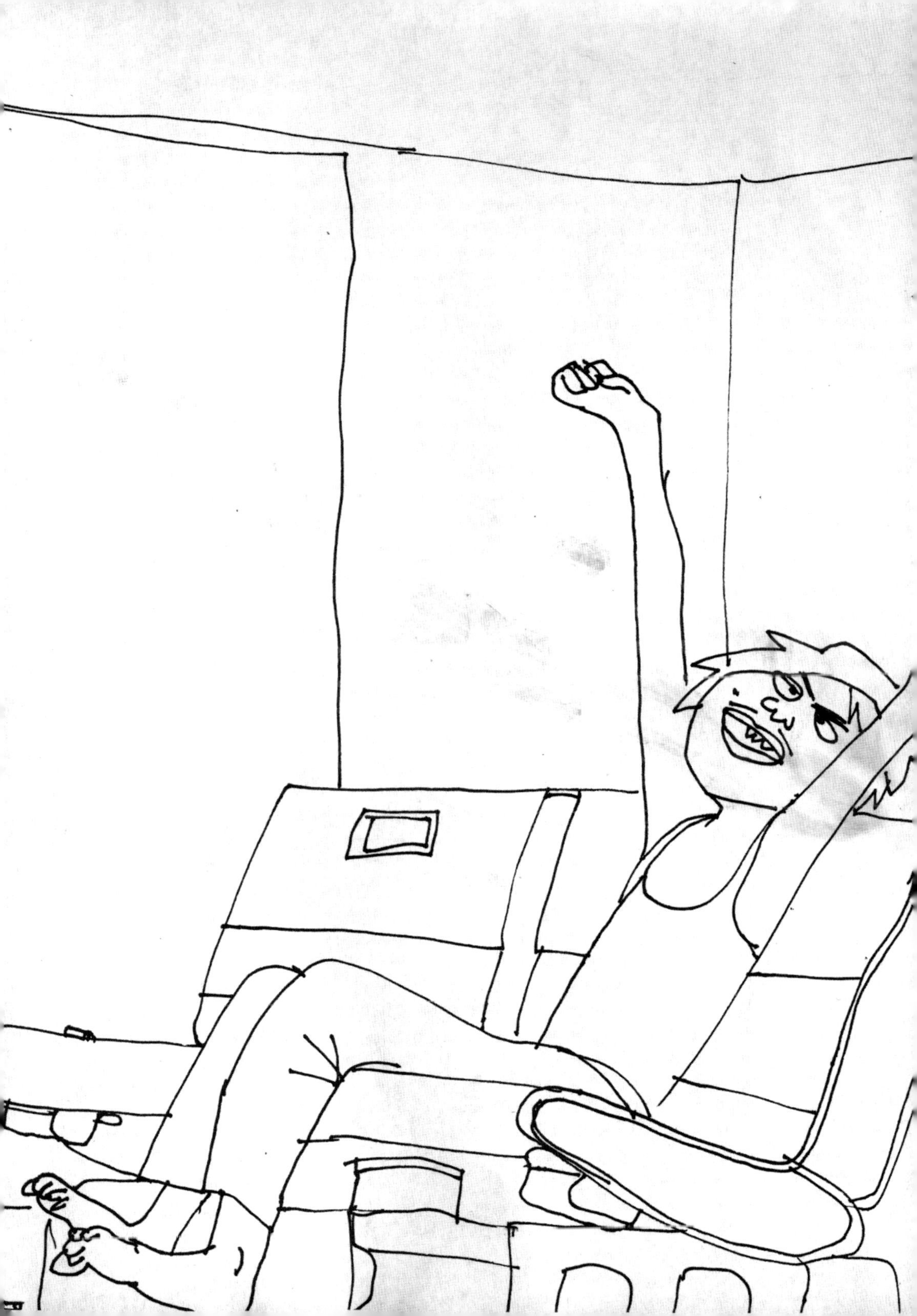

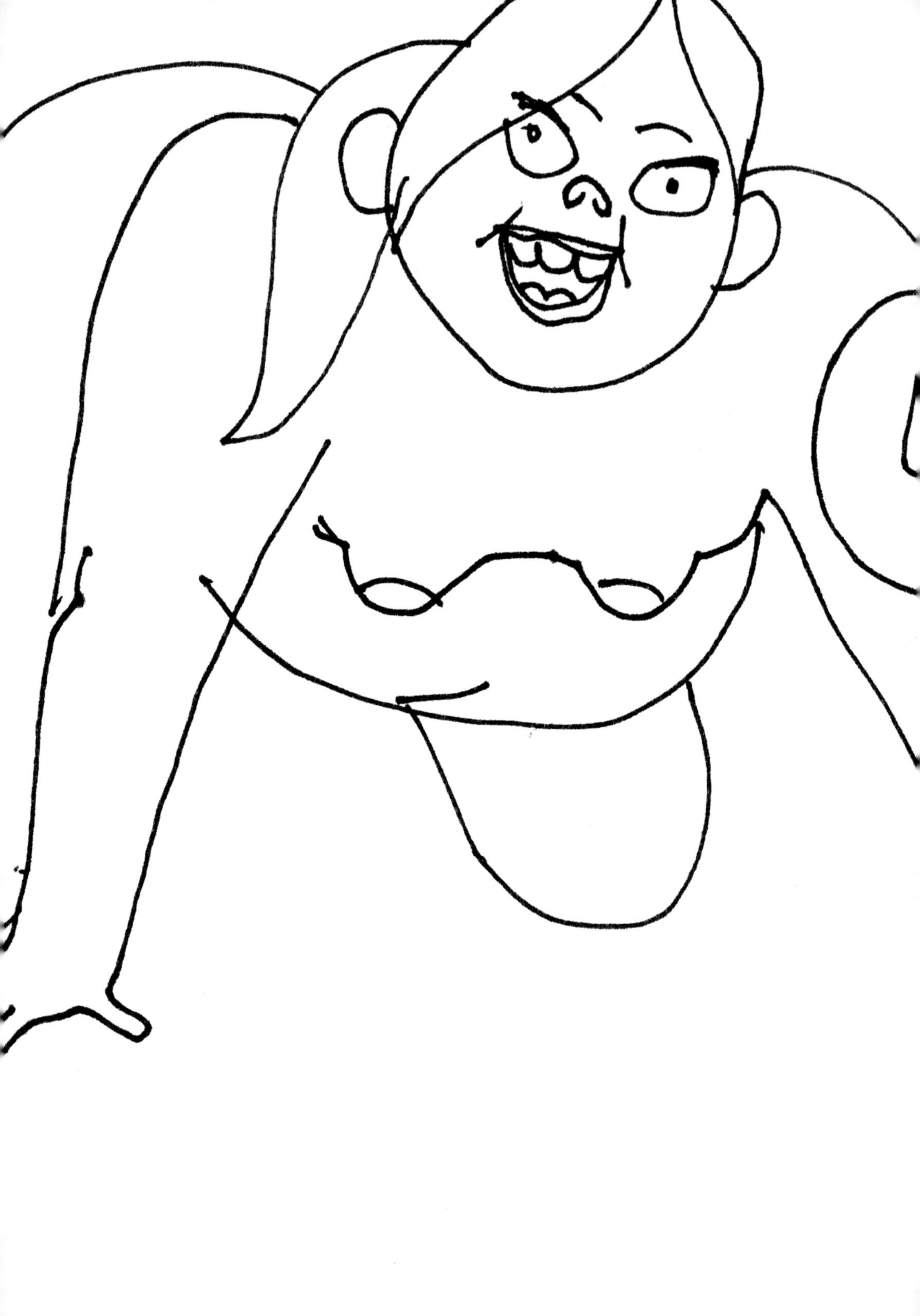

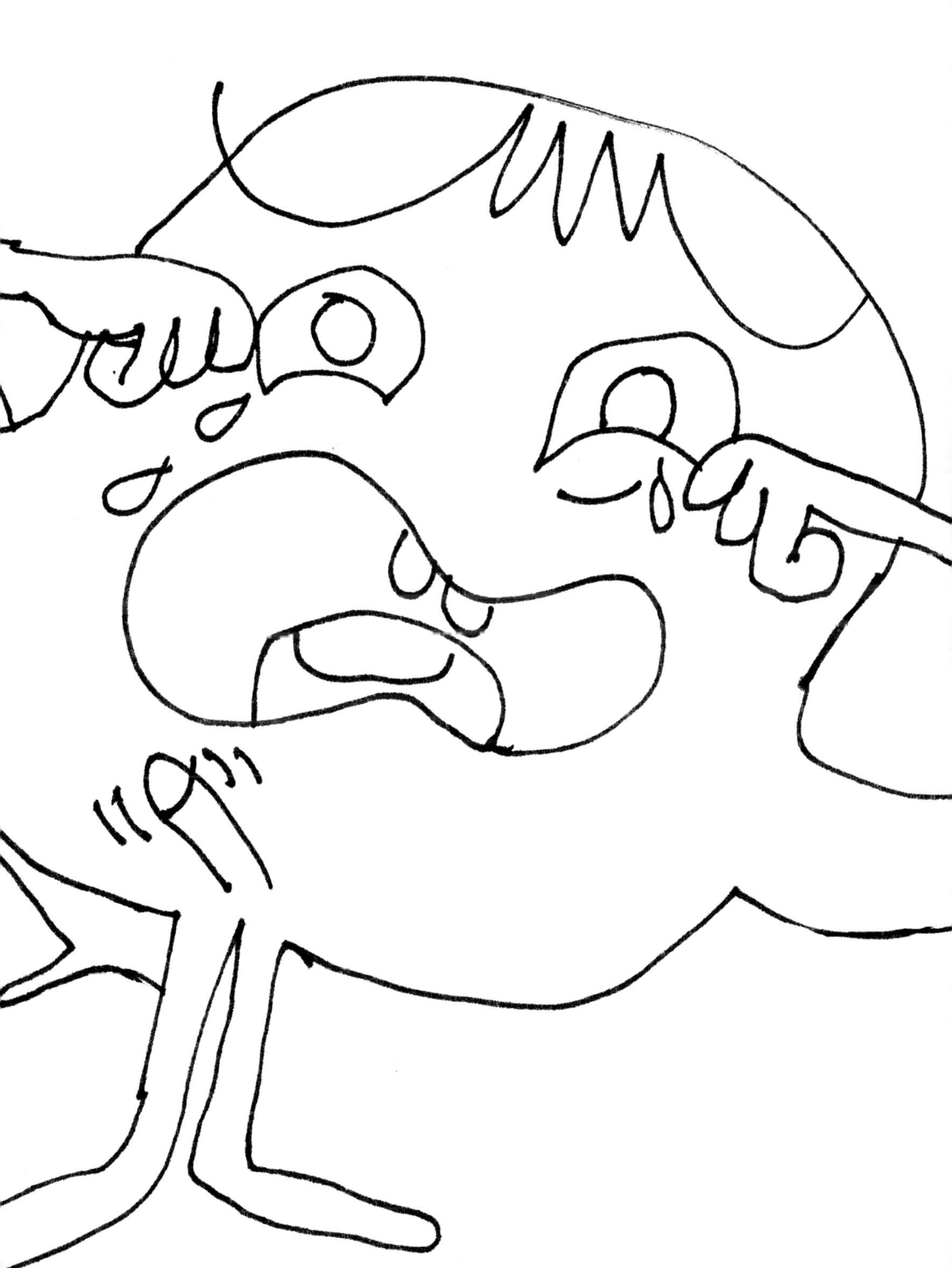

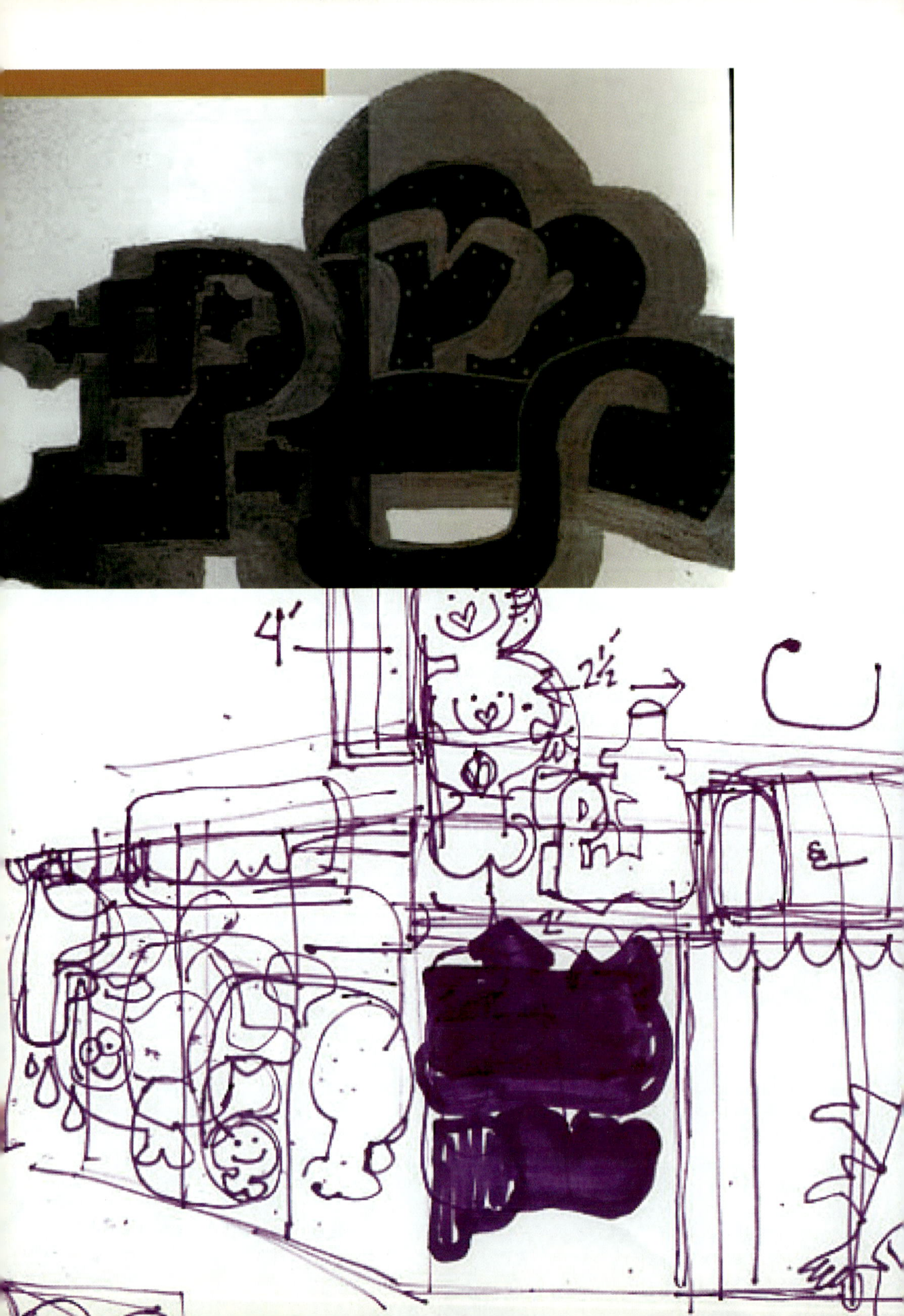
4′
2½

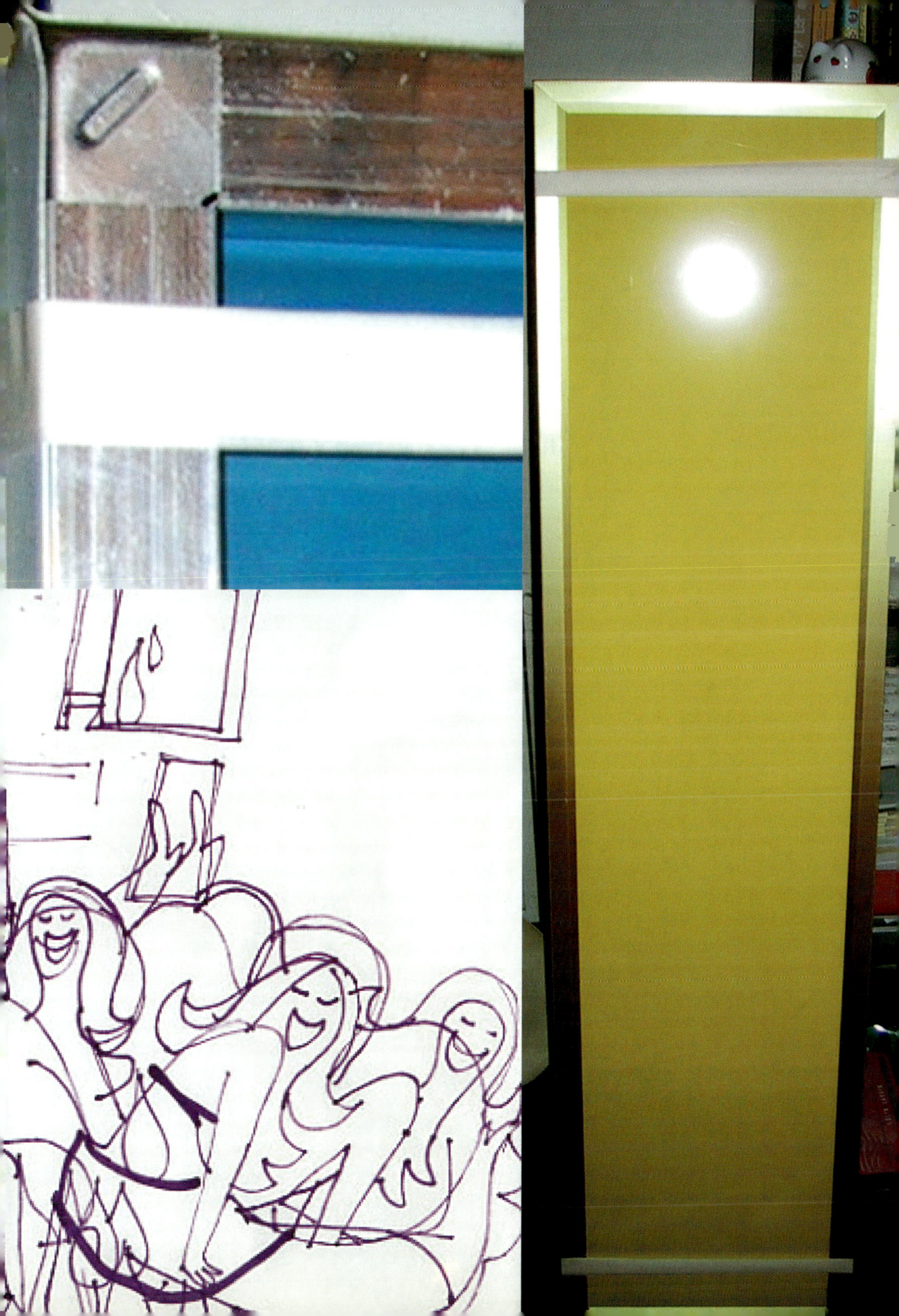

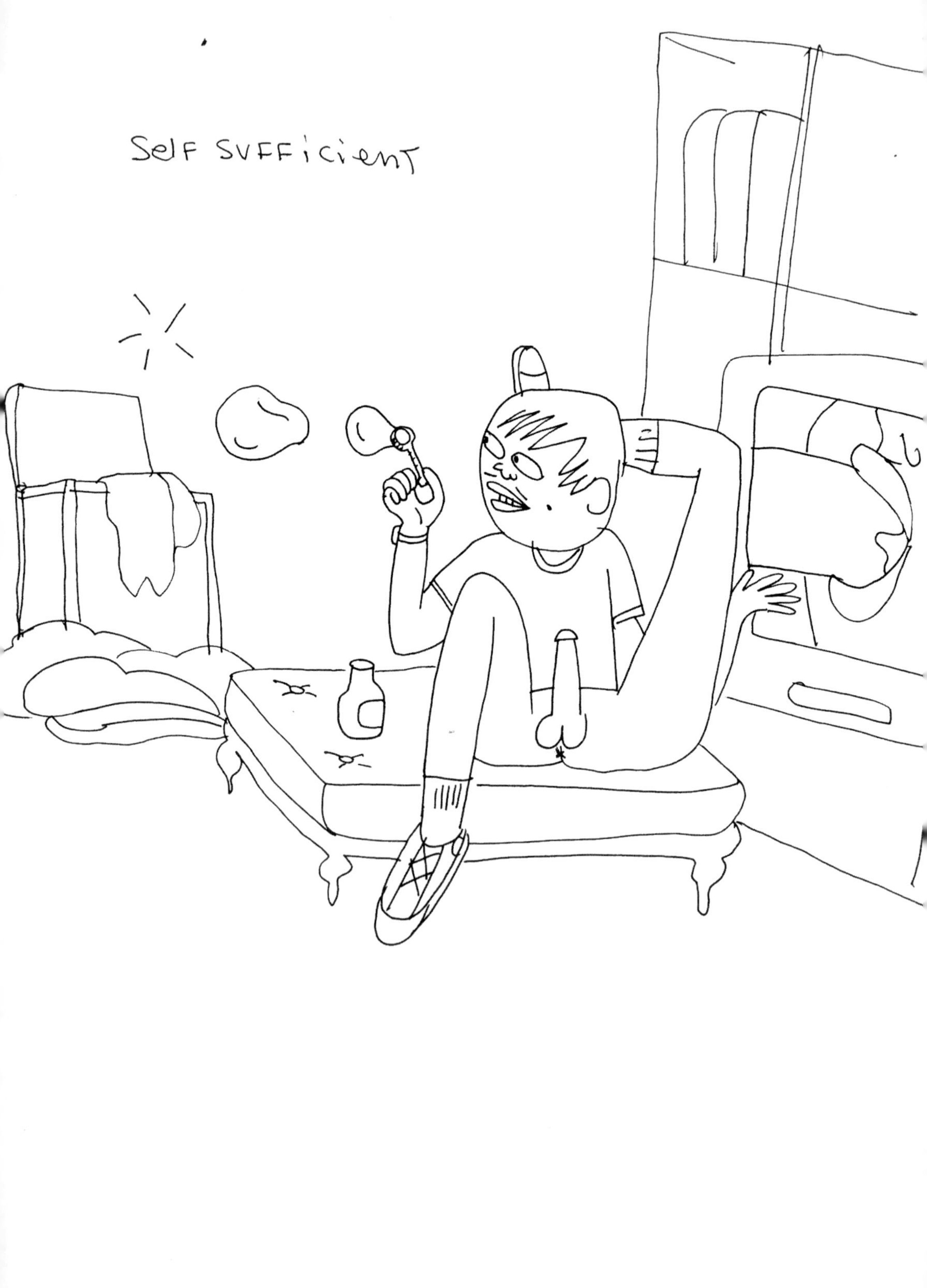
Self sufficient

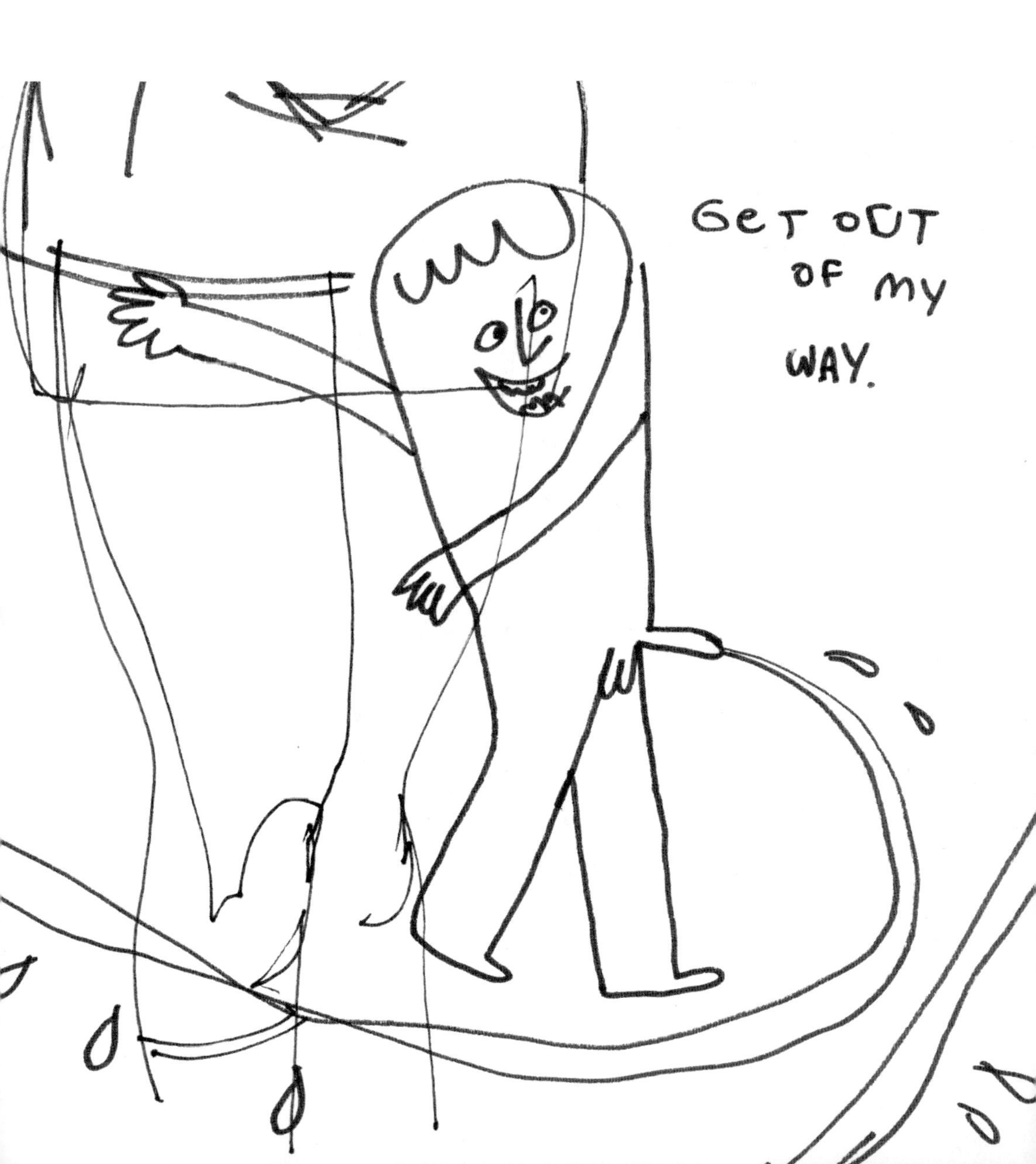
GET OUT
OF MY
WAY.

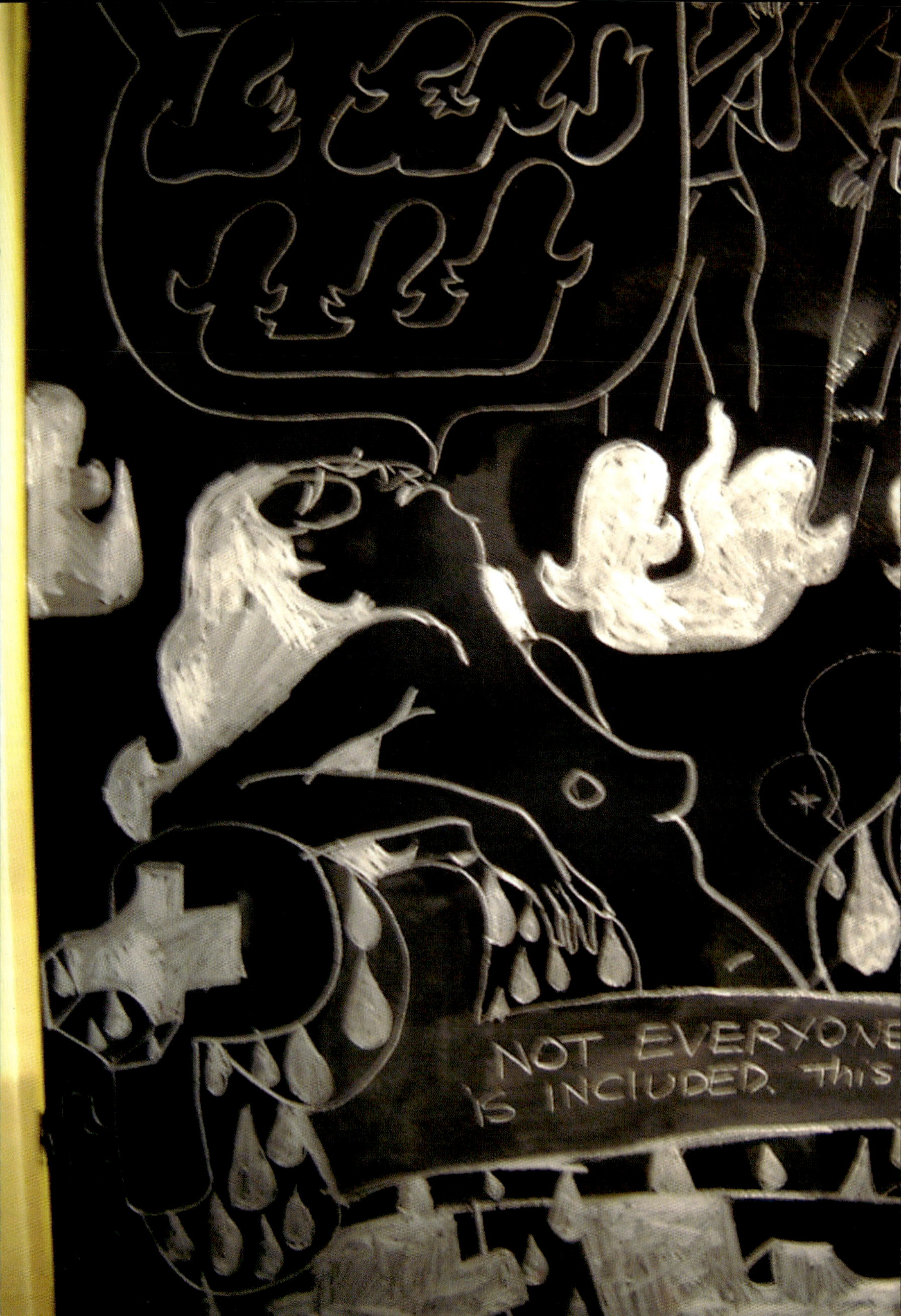
NOT EVERYONE
IS INCLUDED. THIS

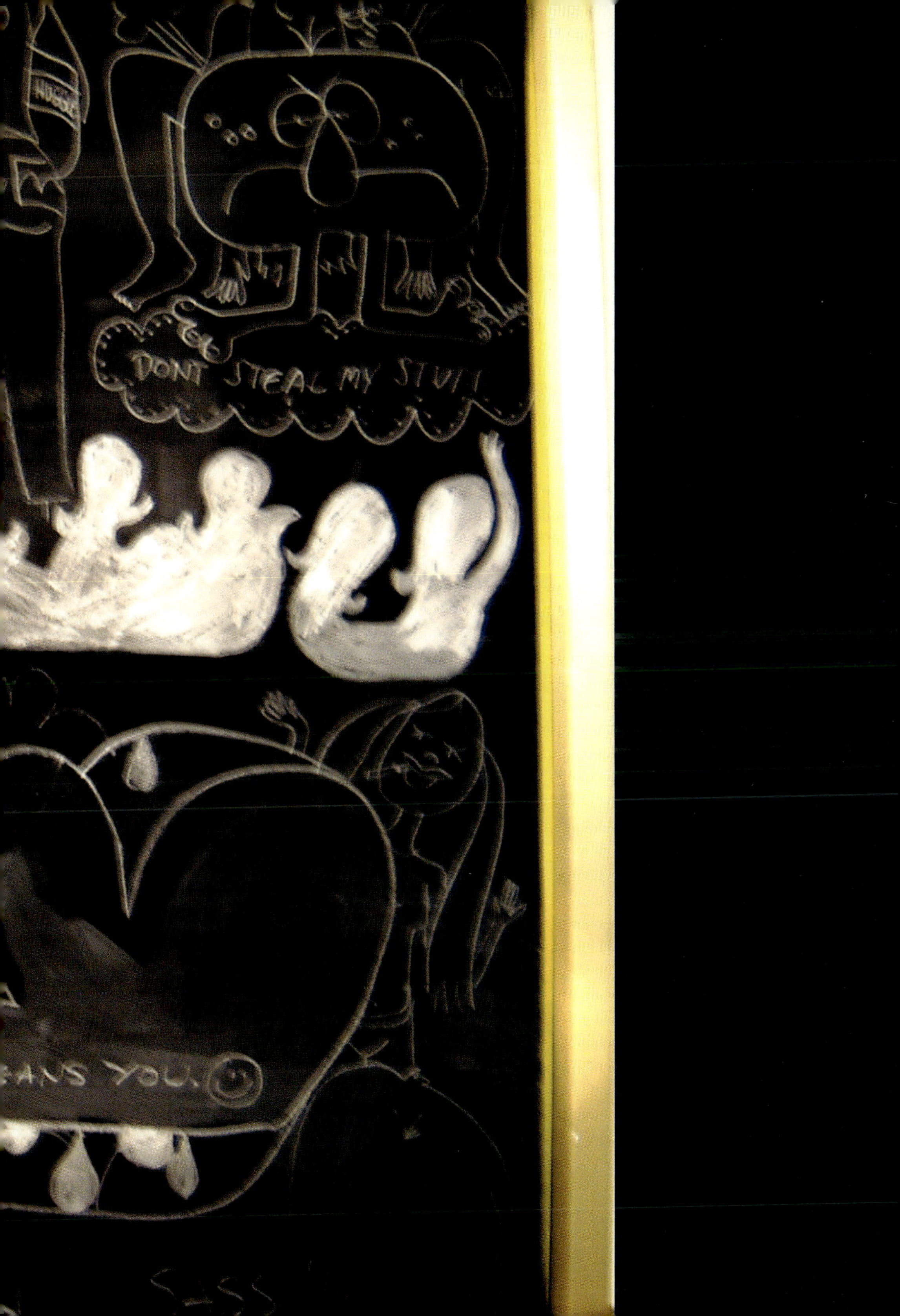
DONT STEAL MY
YOU.

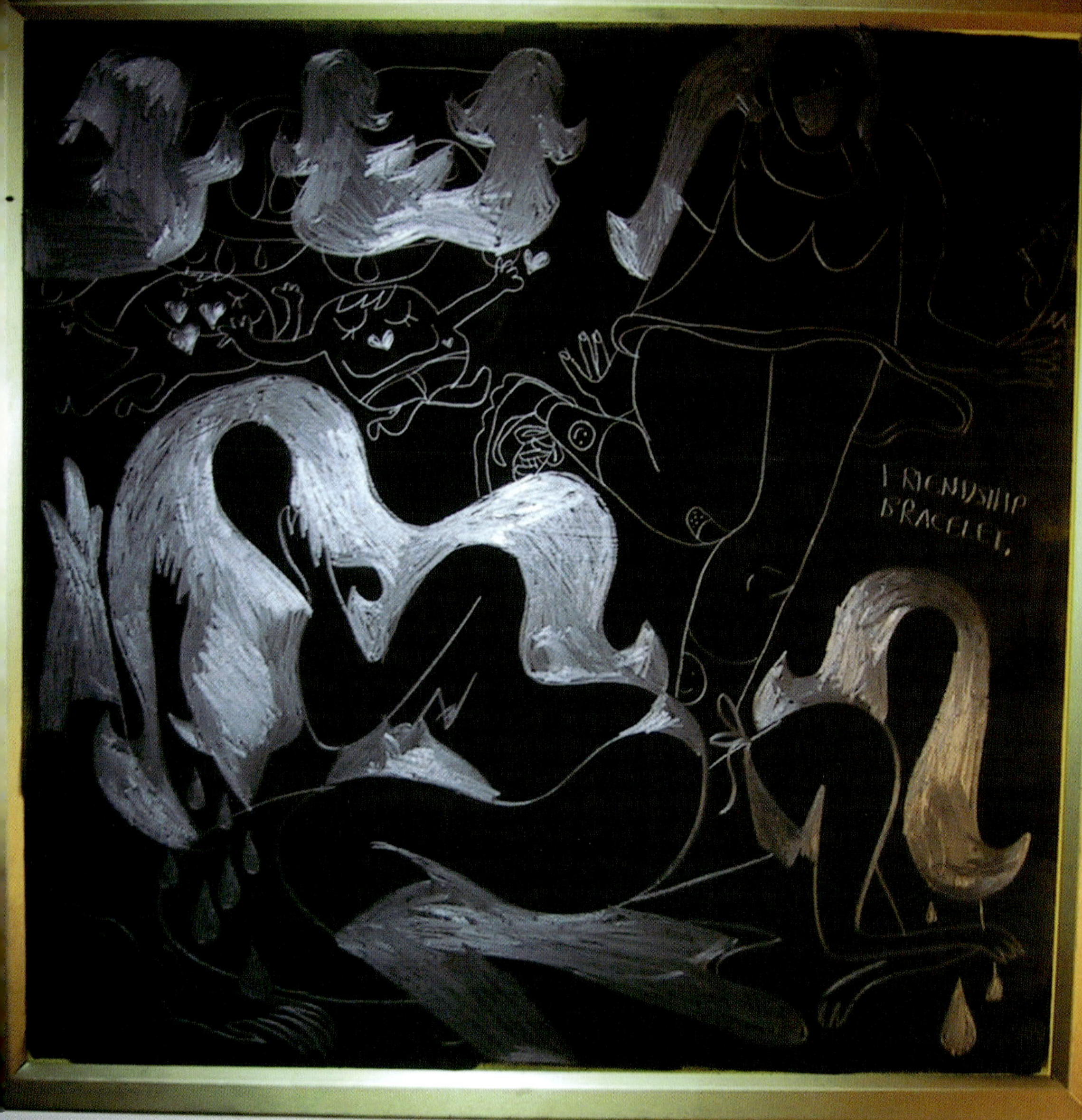
FRIENDSHIP
BRACELET,

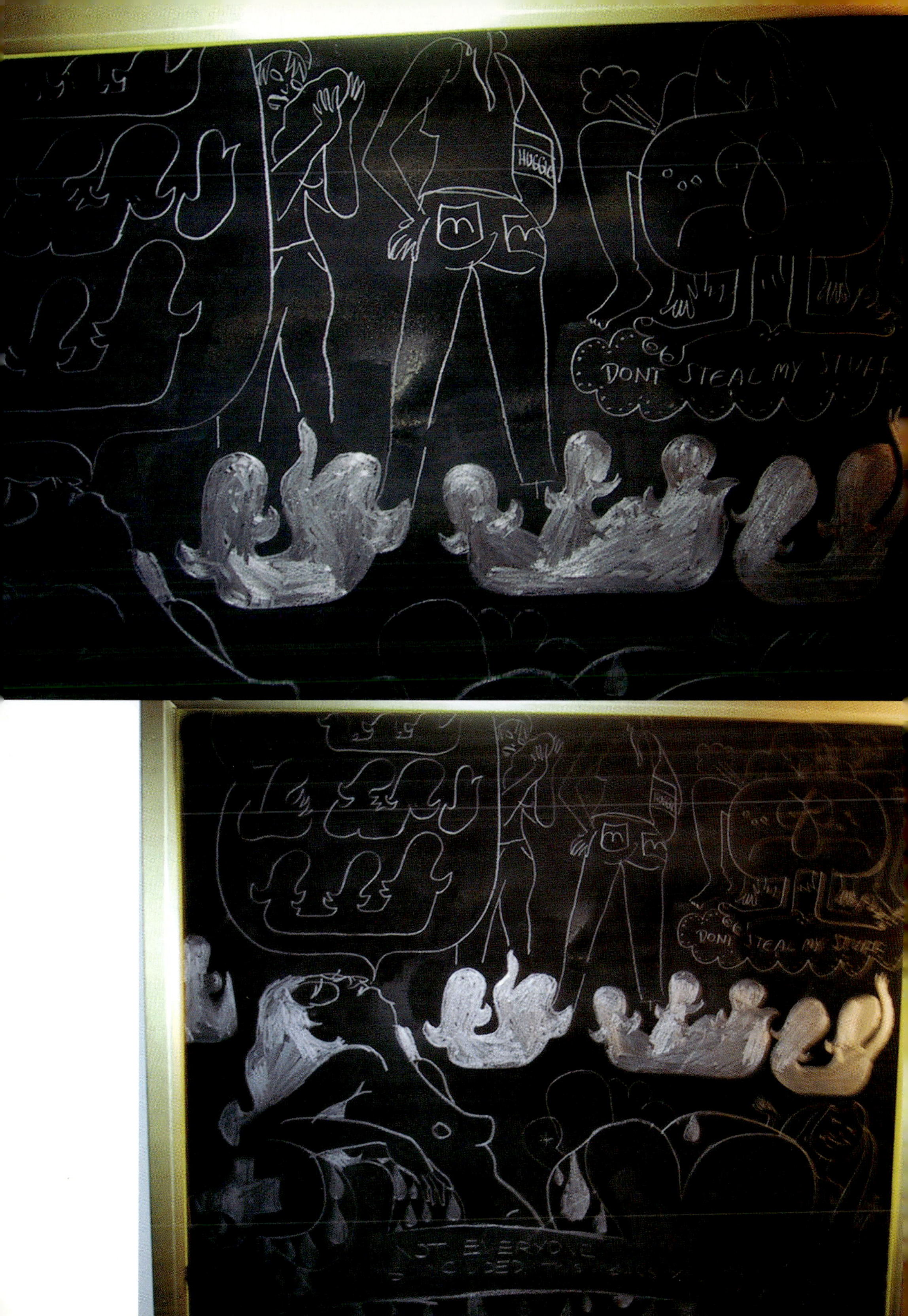
HUGGIE
DONT STEAL MY STUFF
NOT EVERYONE

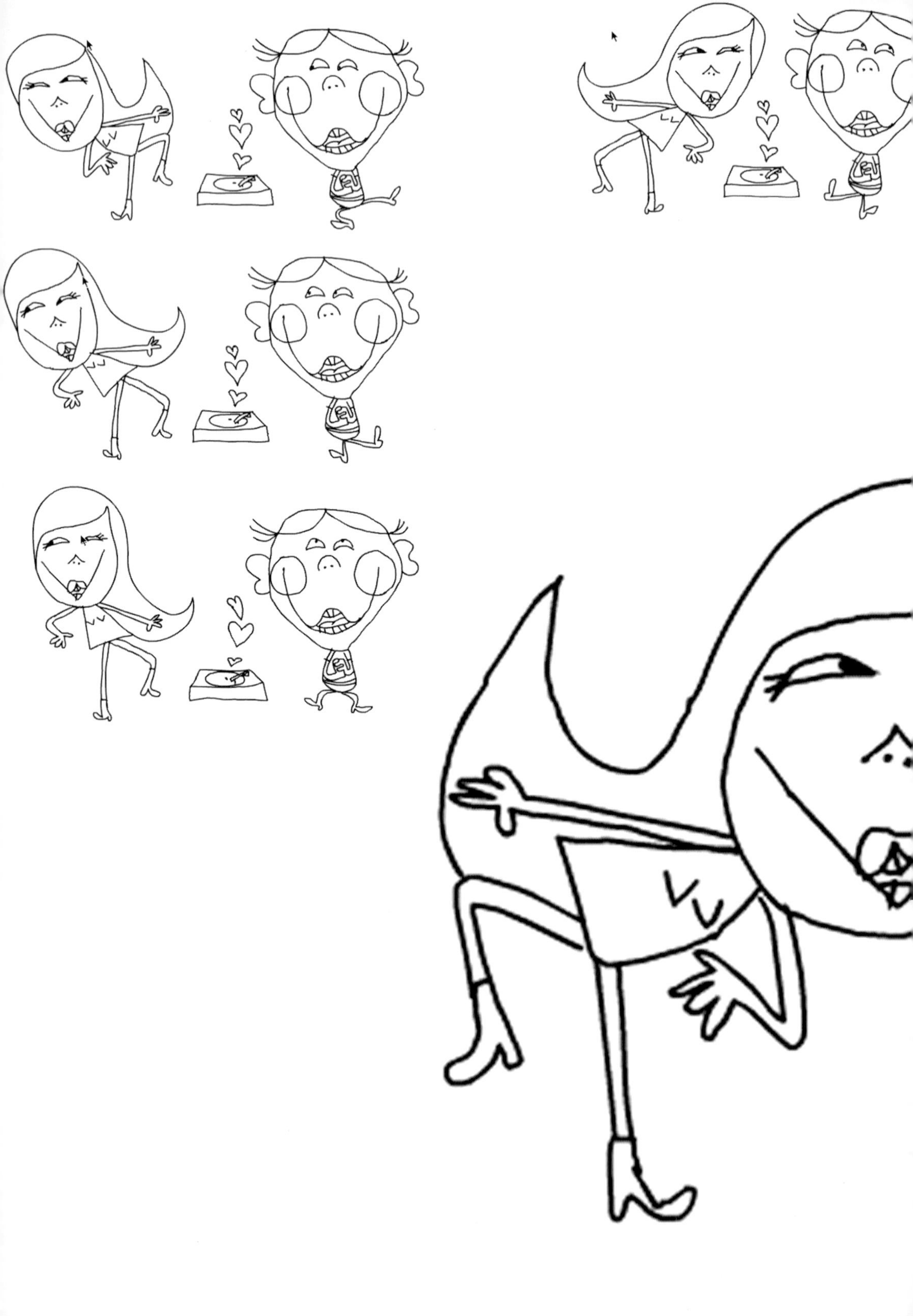

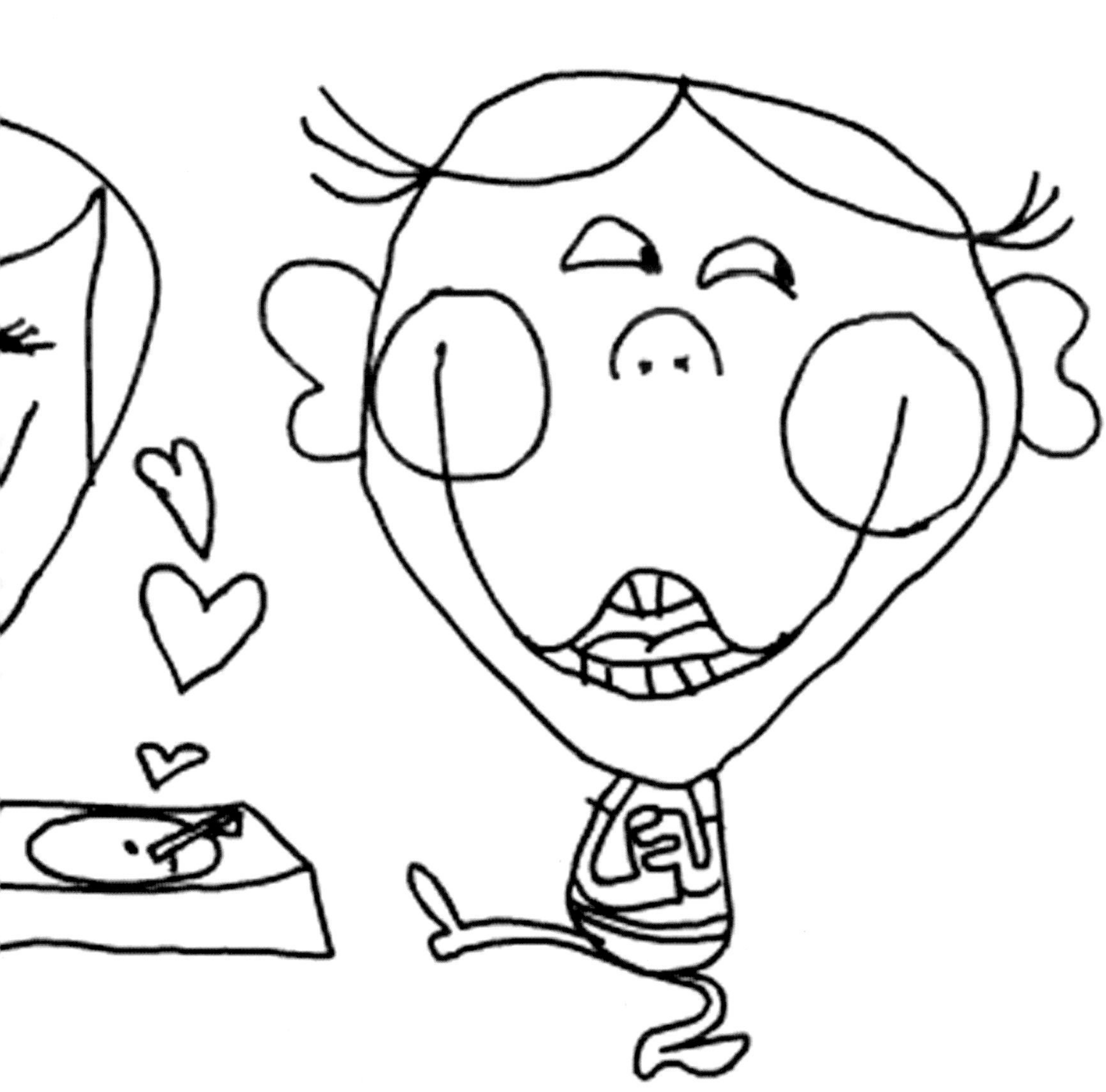

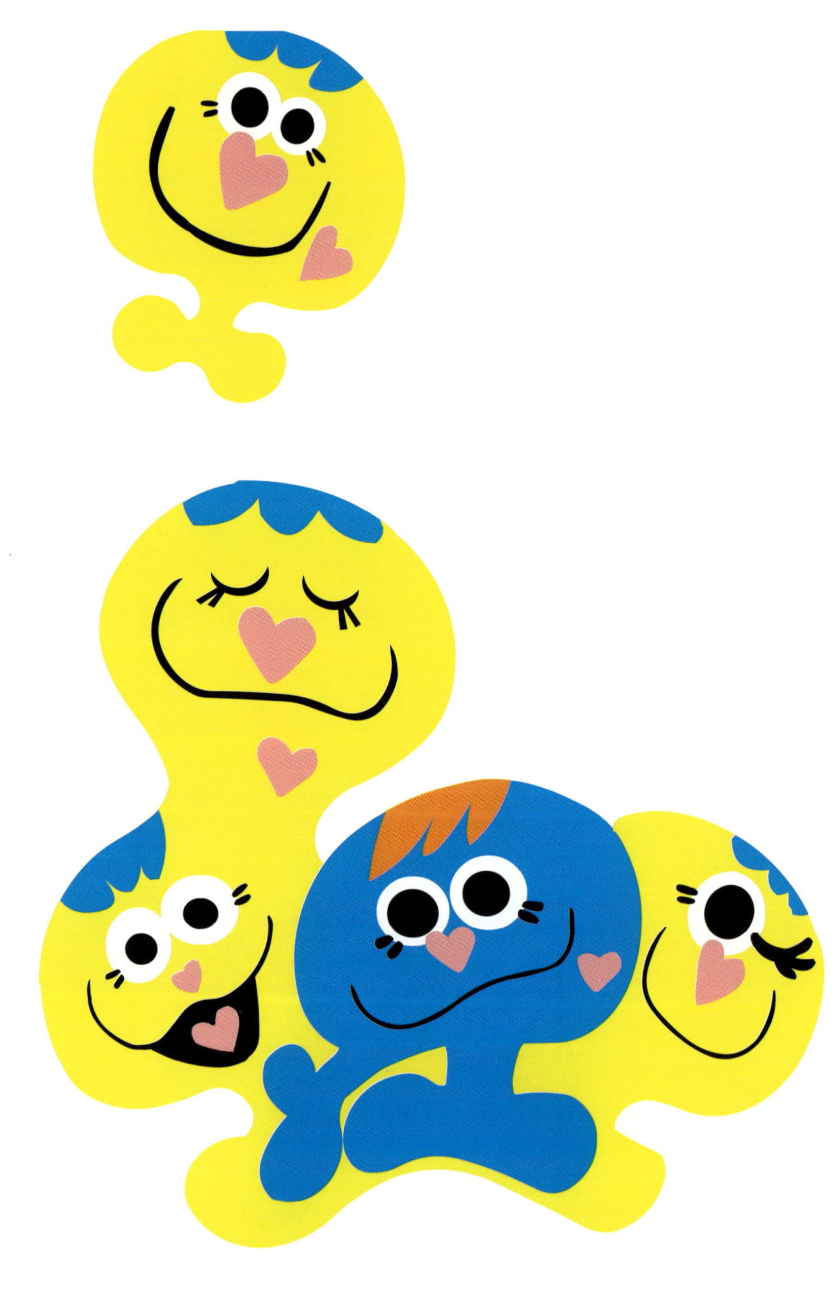

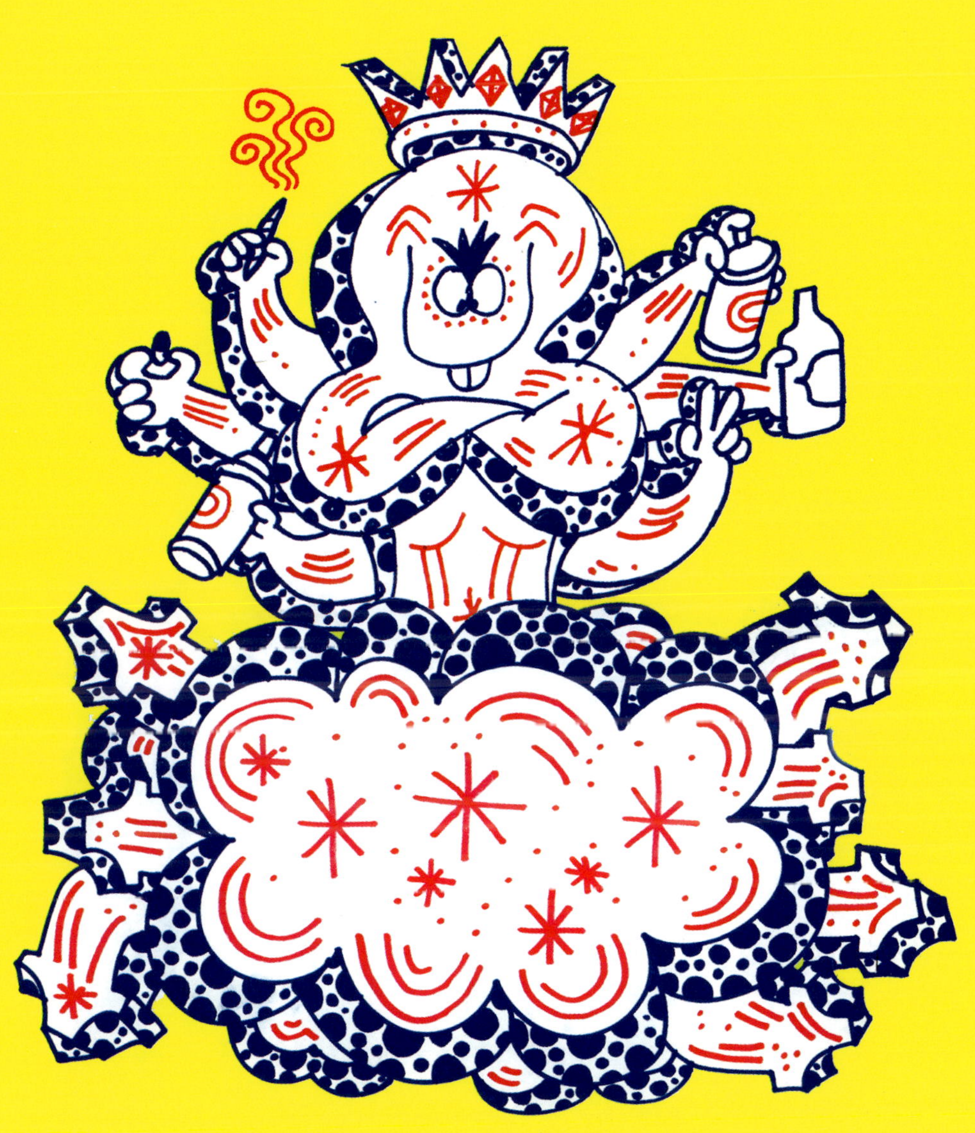

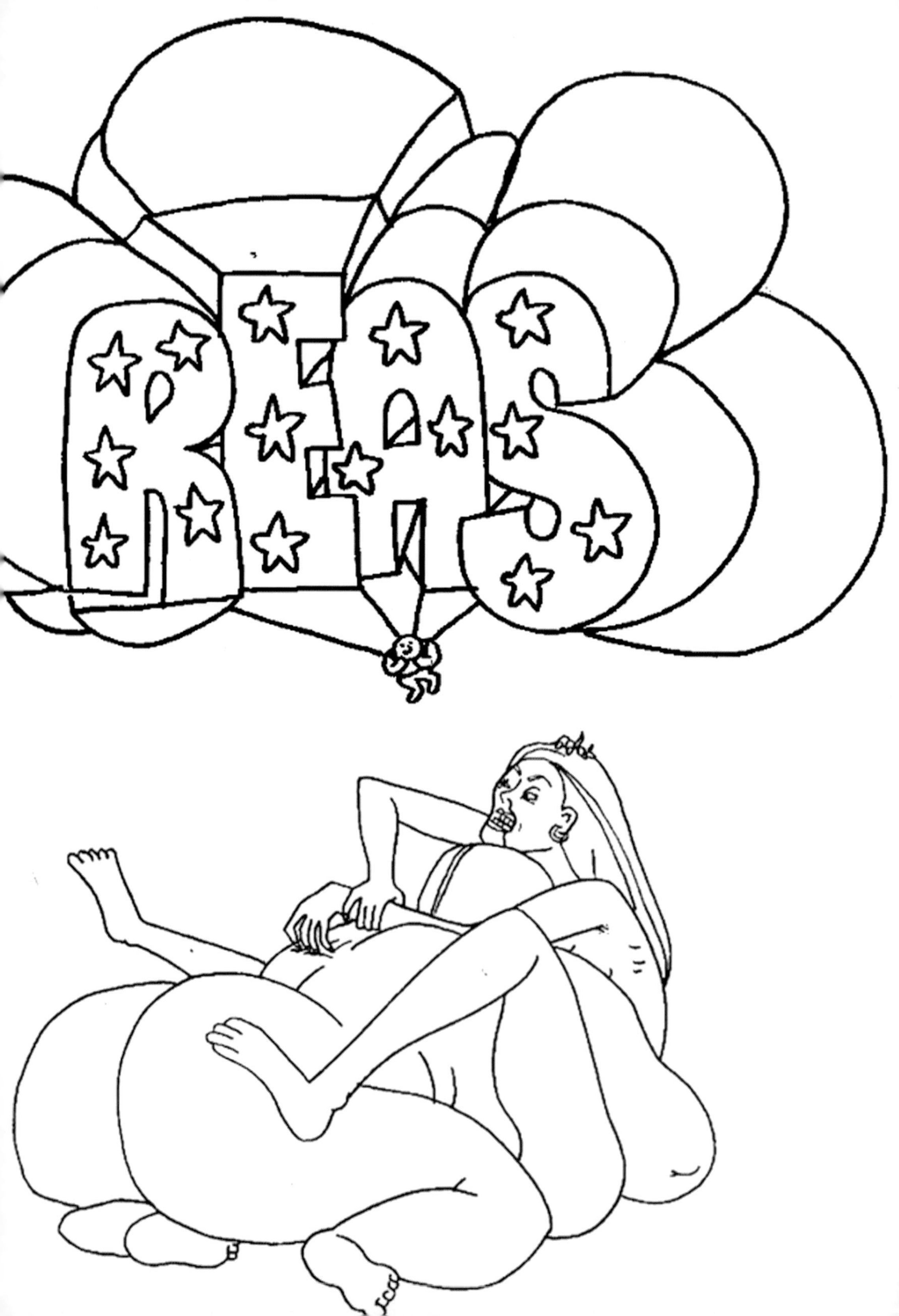

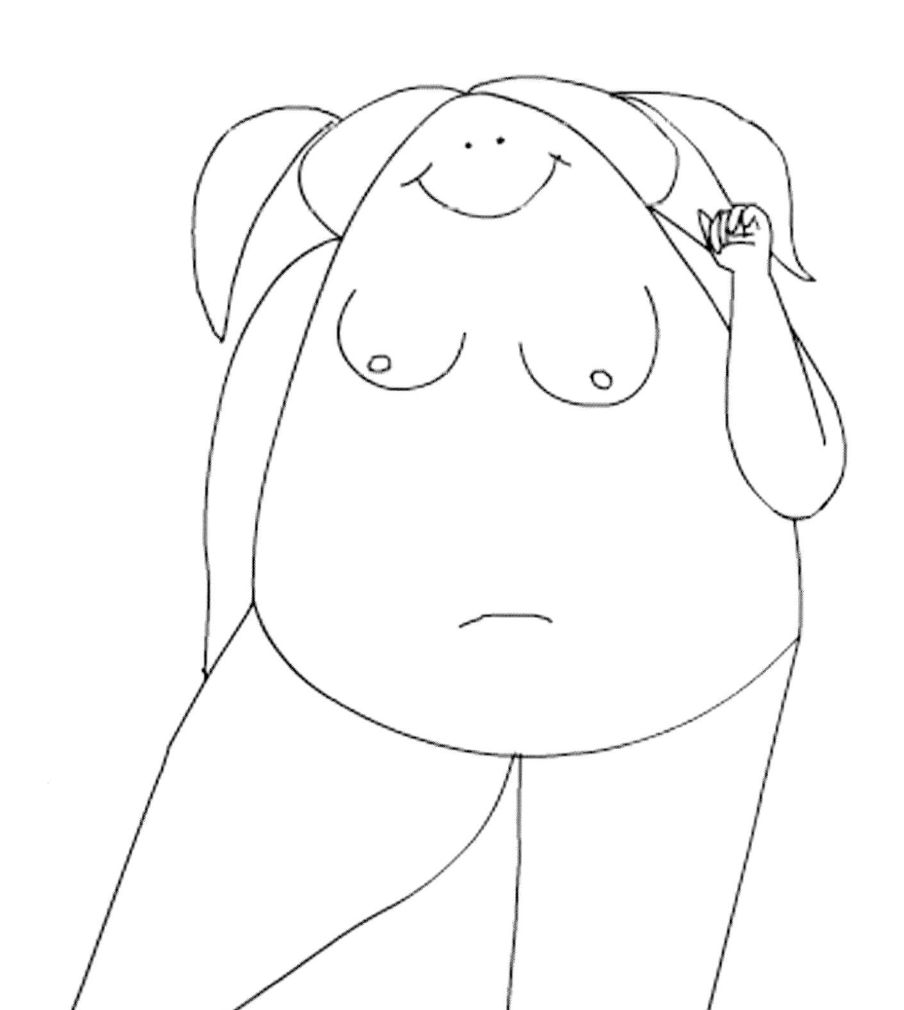

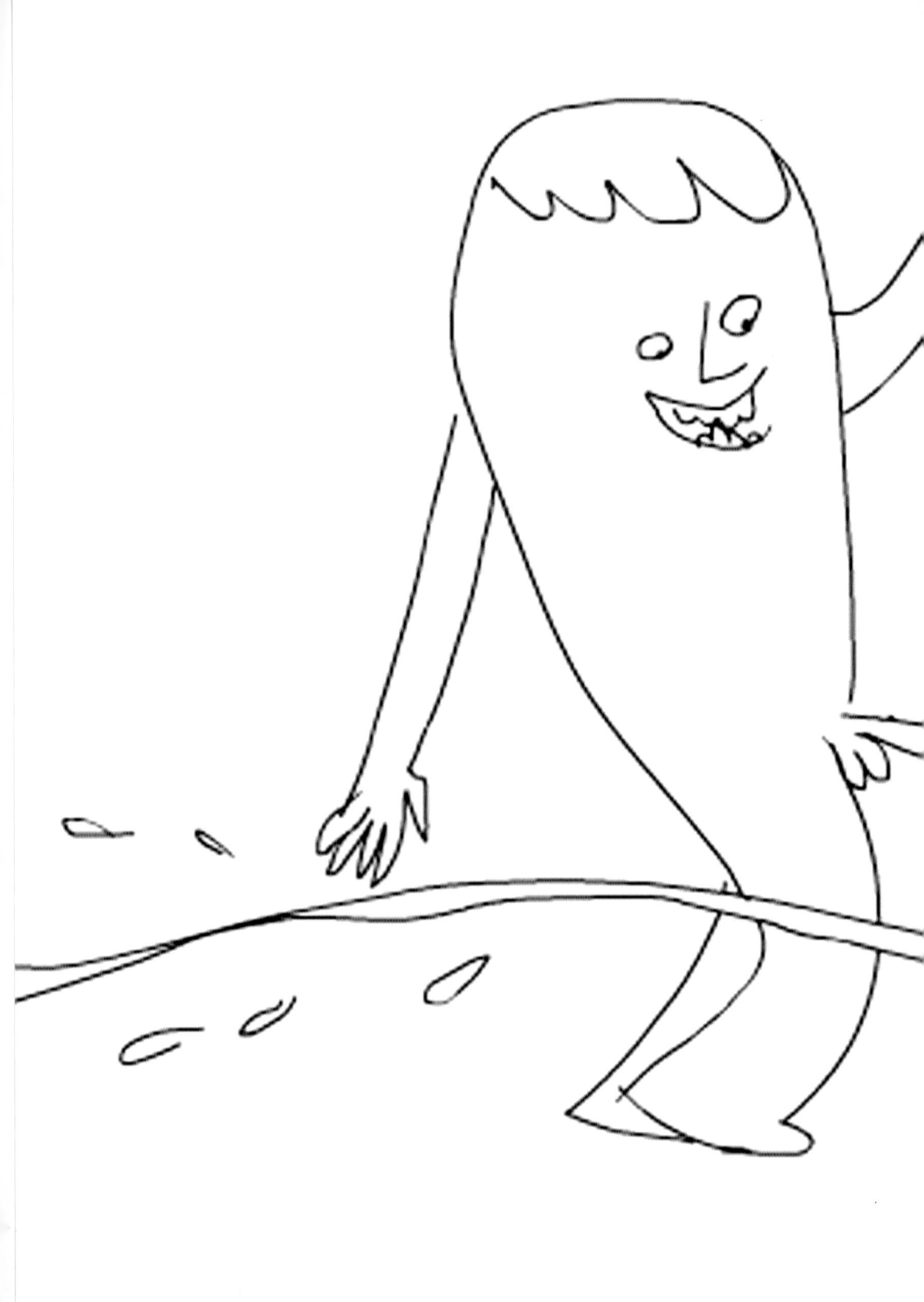

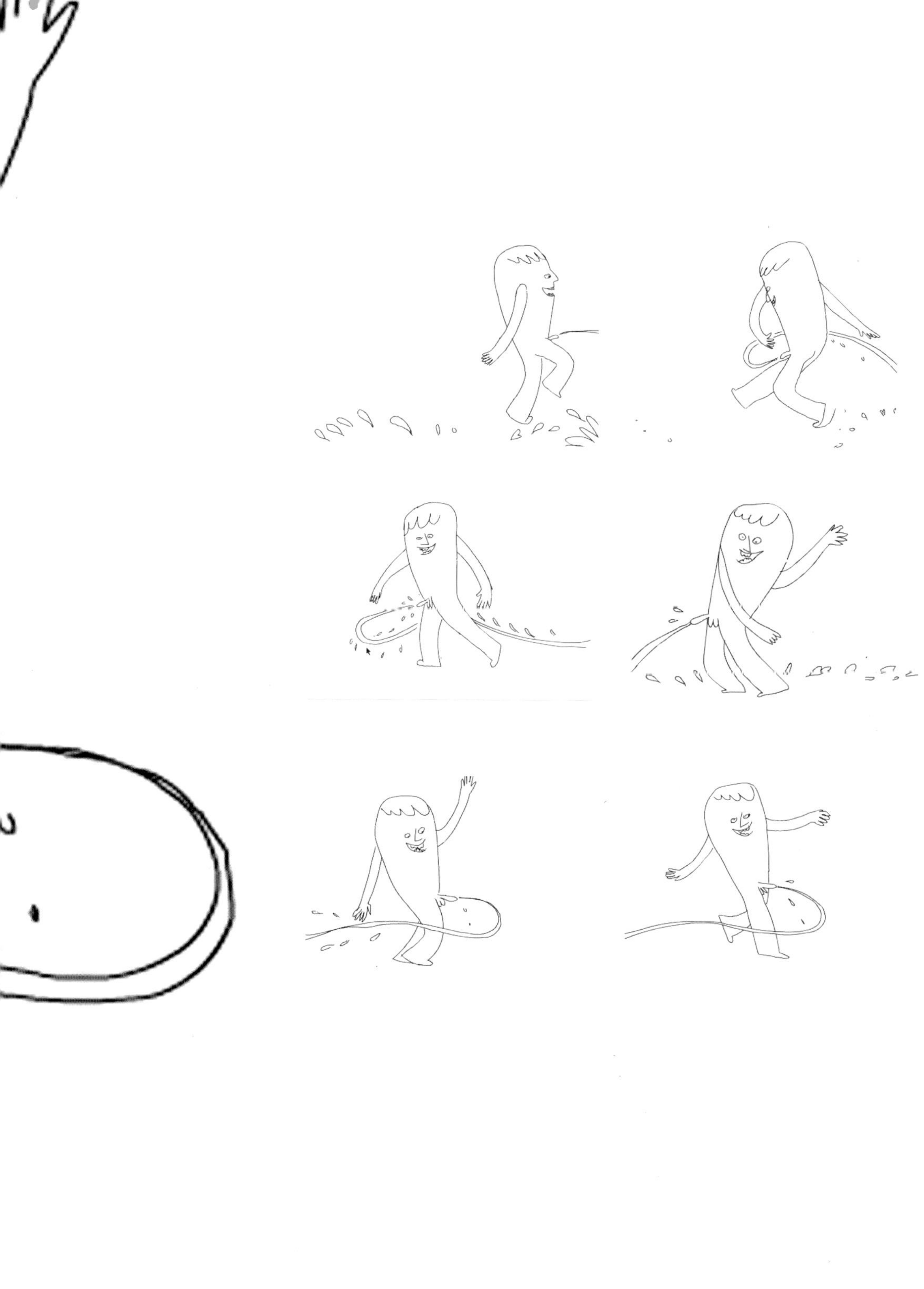

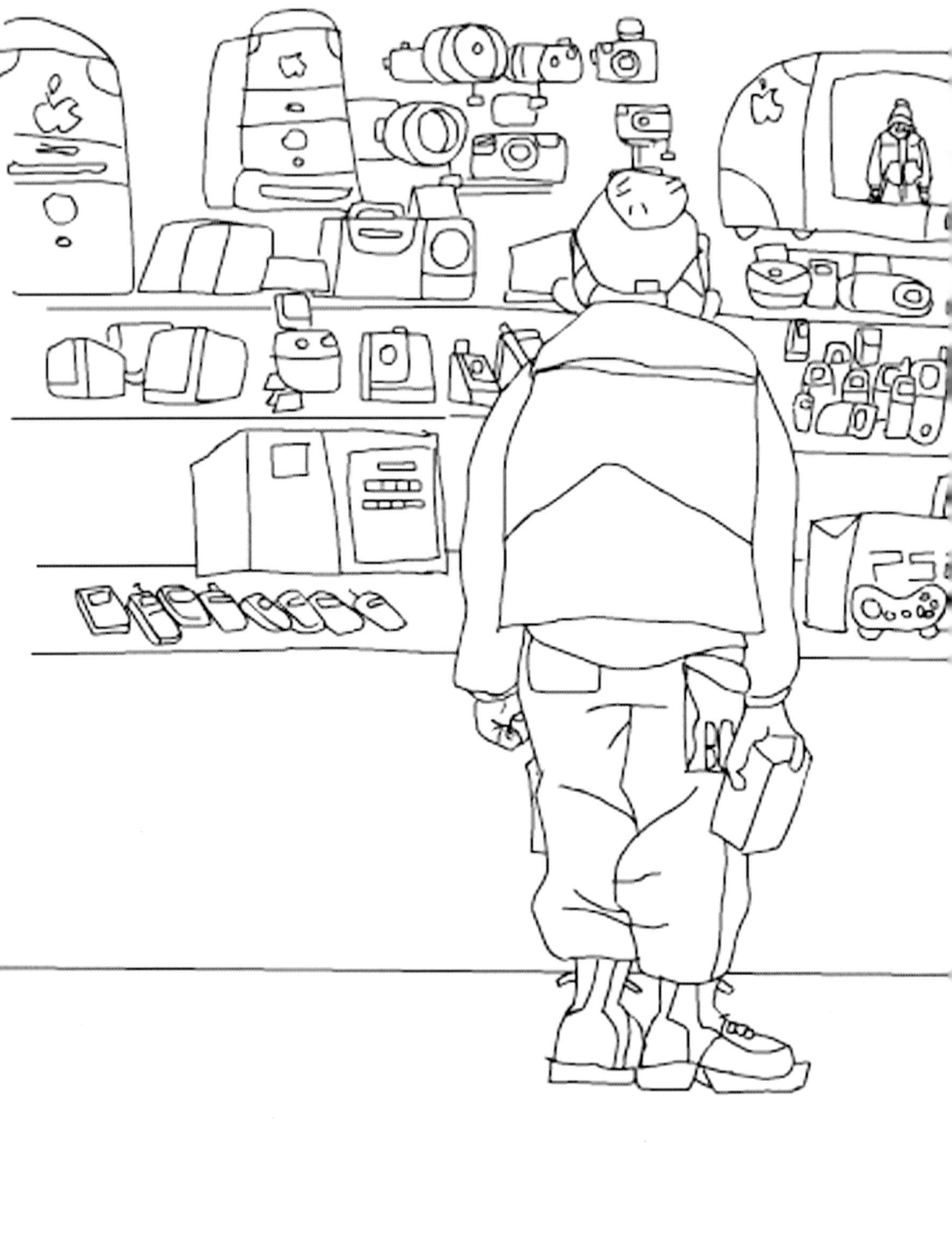

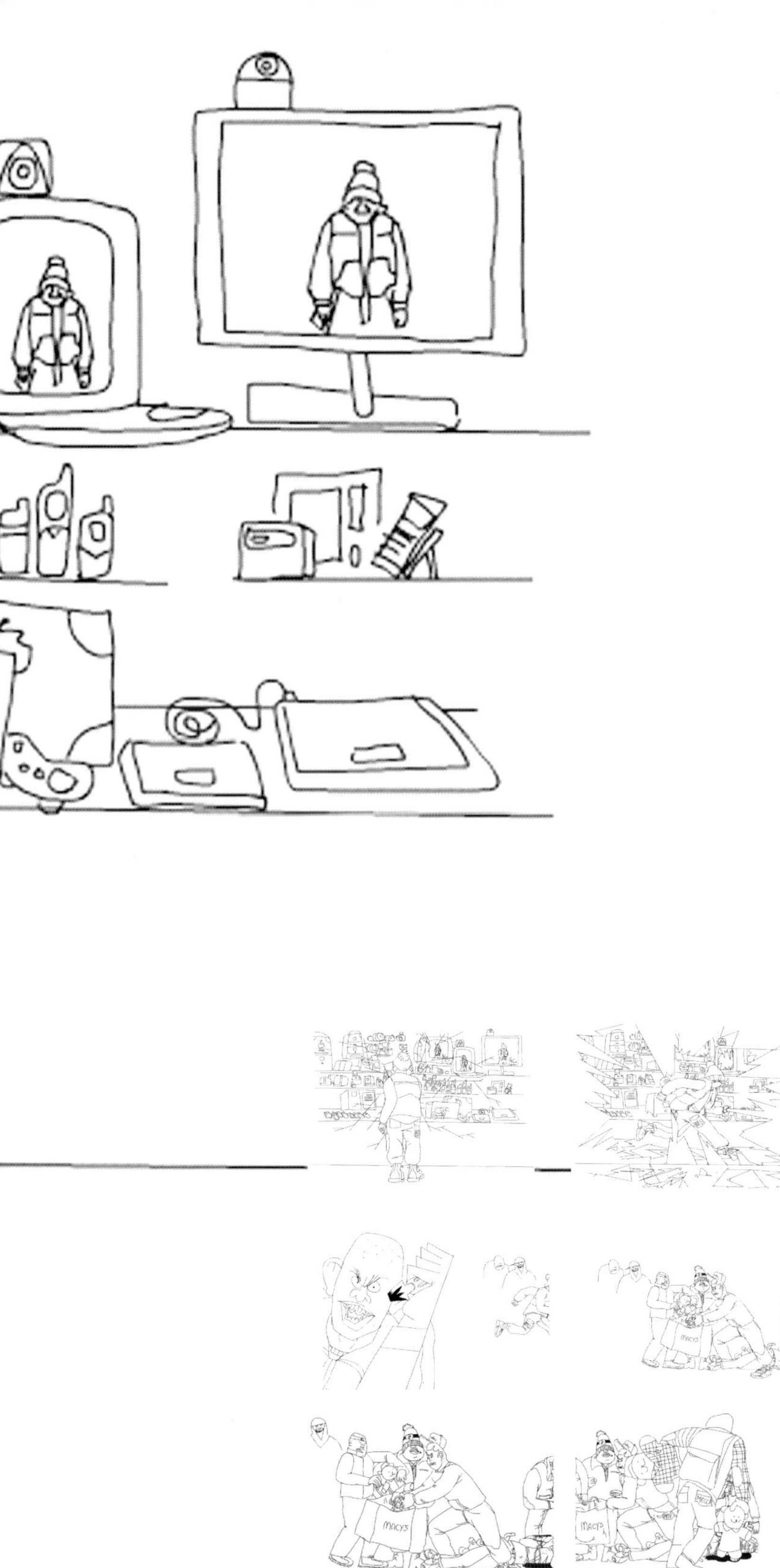

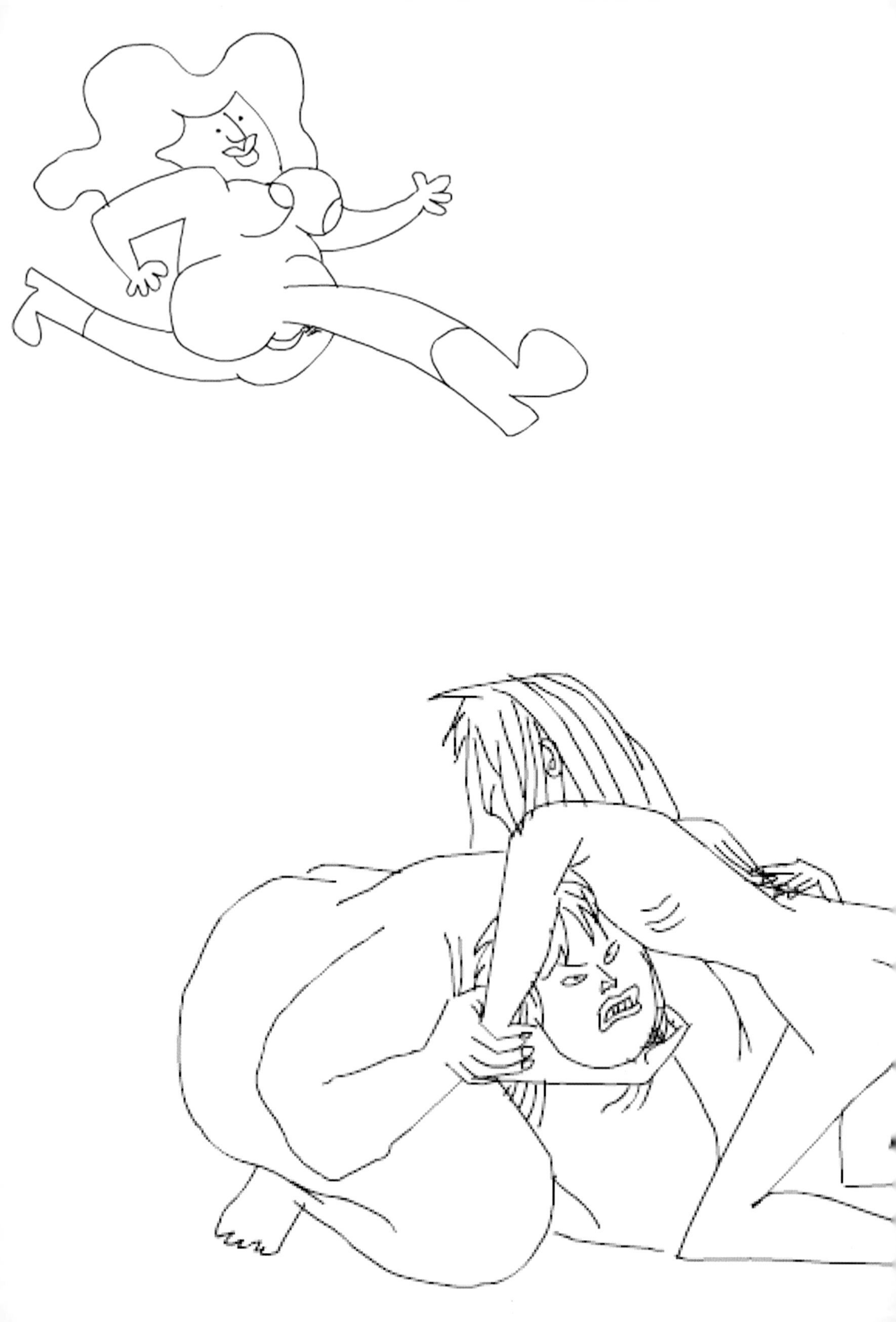

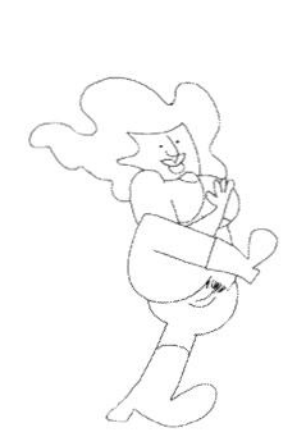
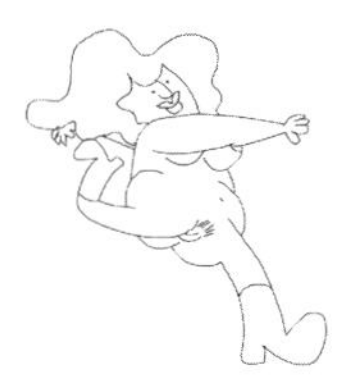
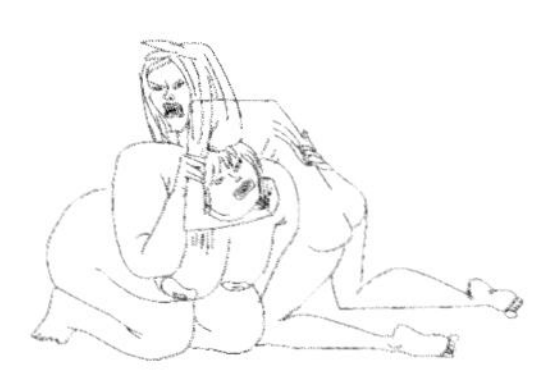
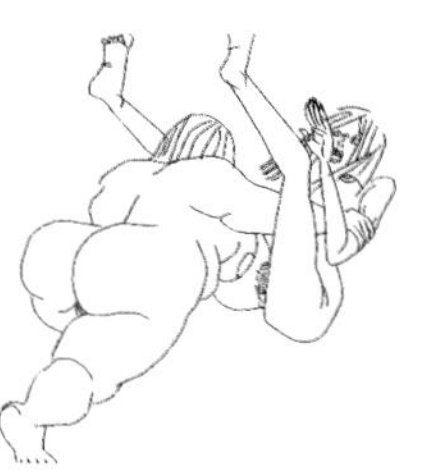
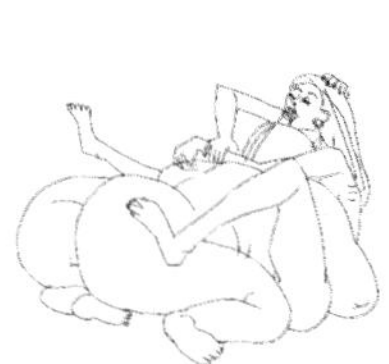
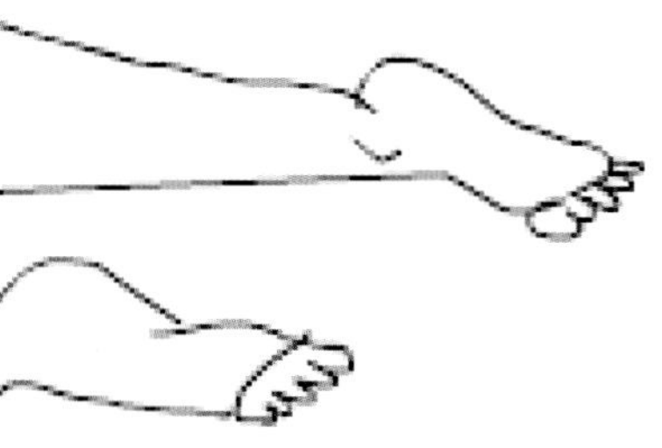

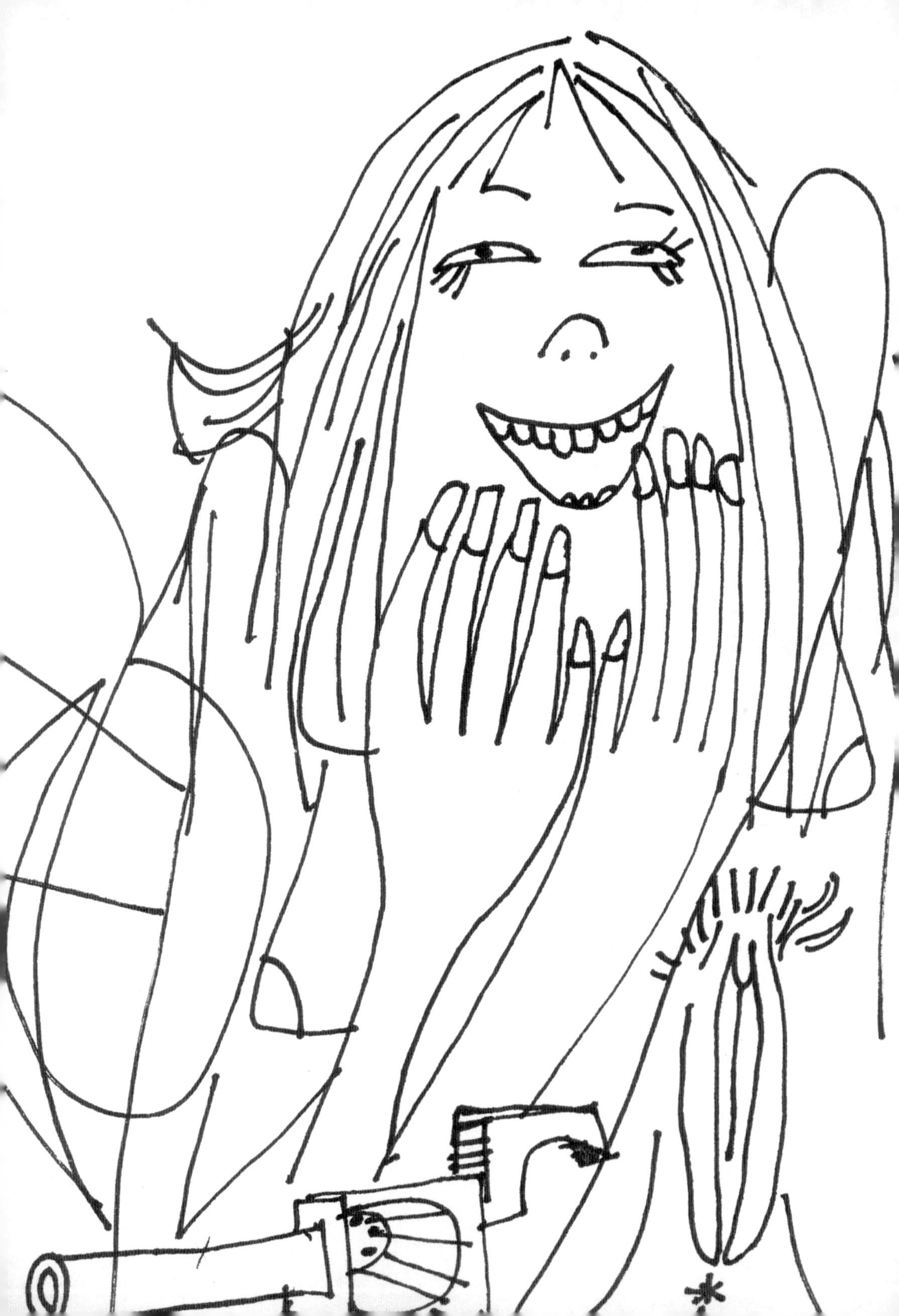

IM HAPPY.
Thank GOD TO BE HERE.

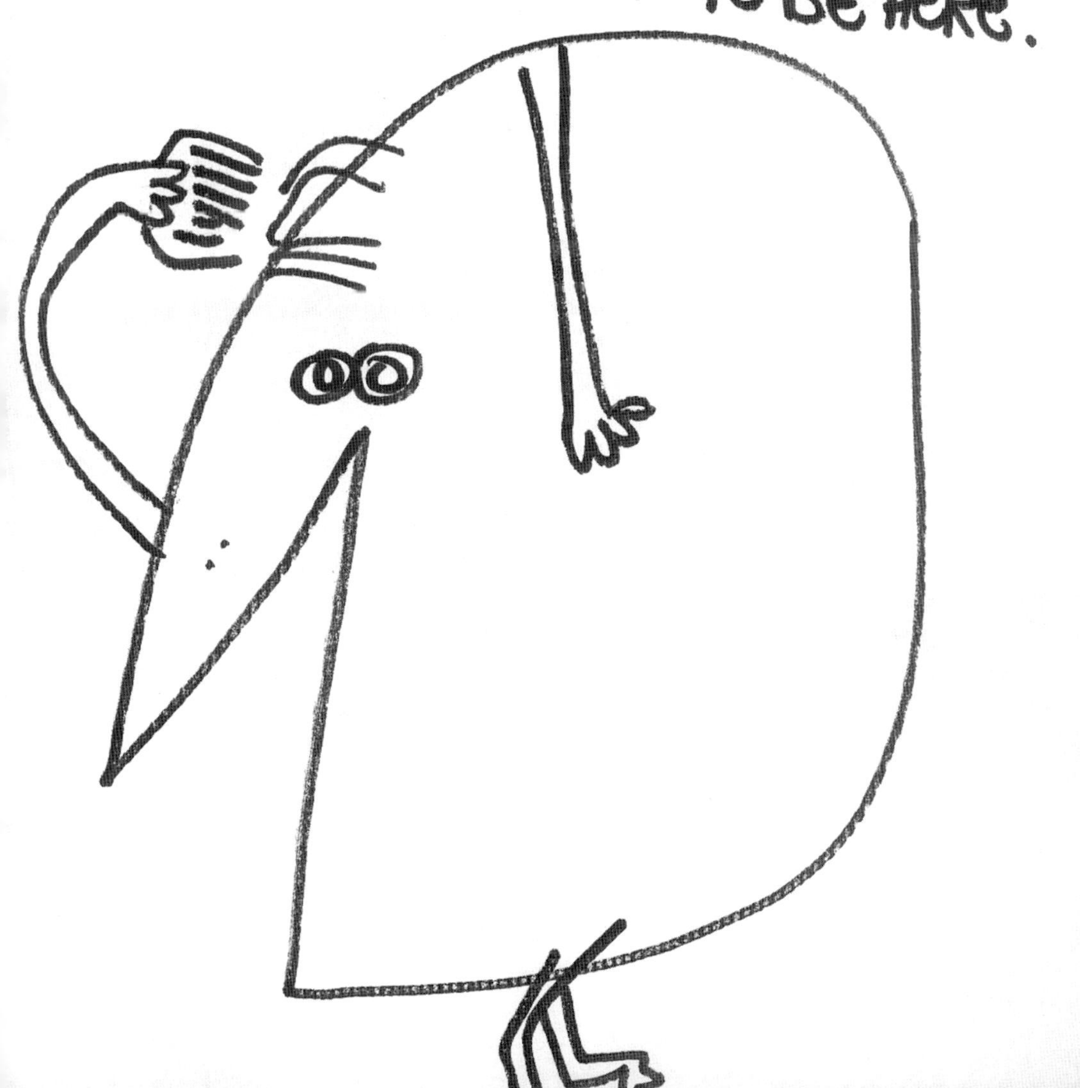

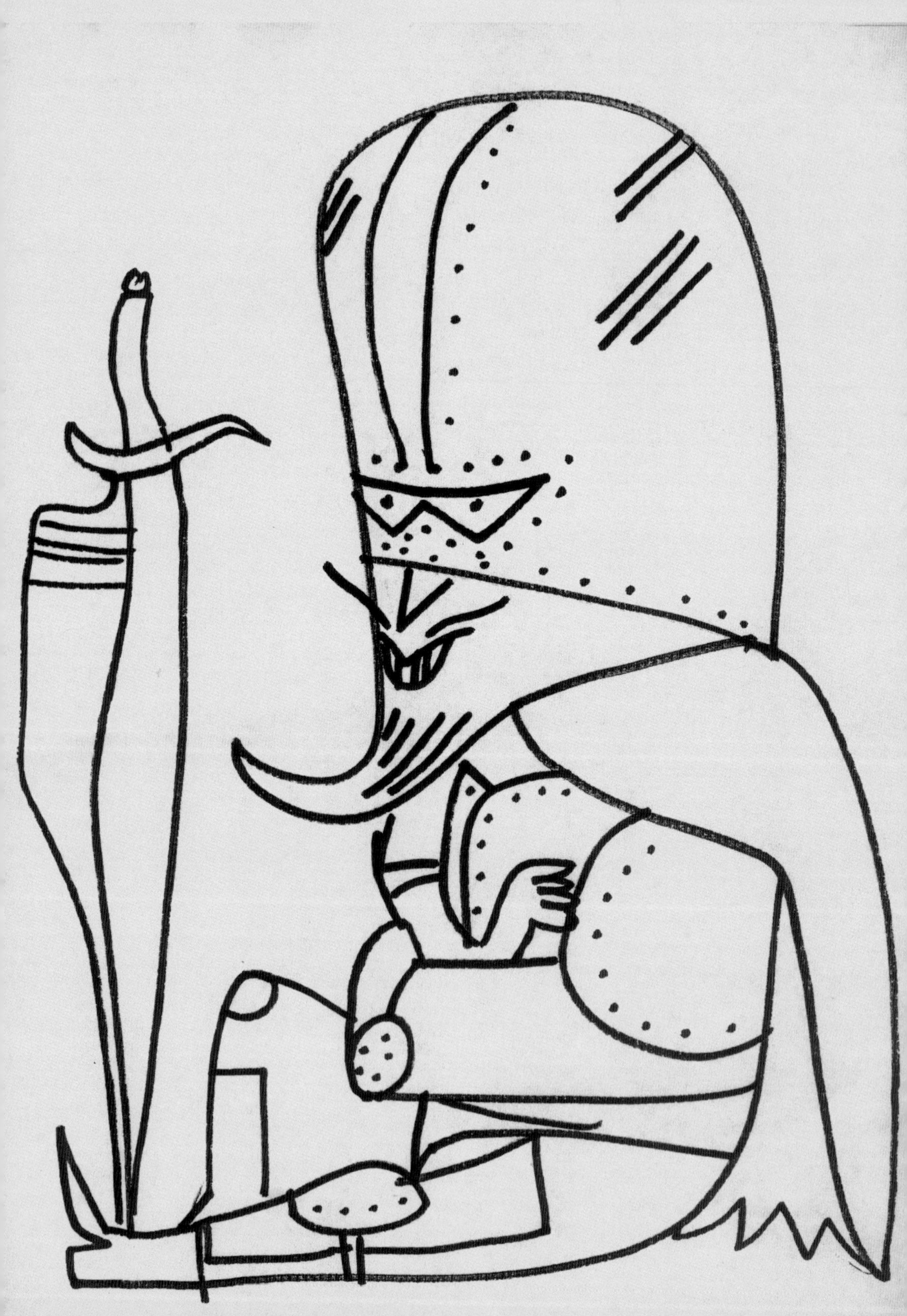

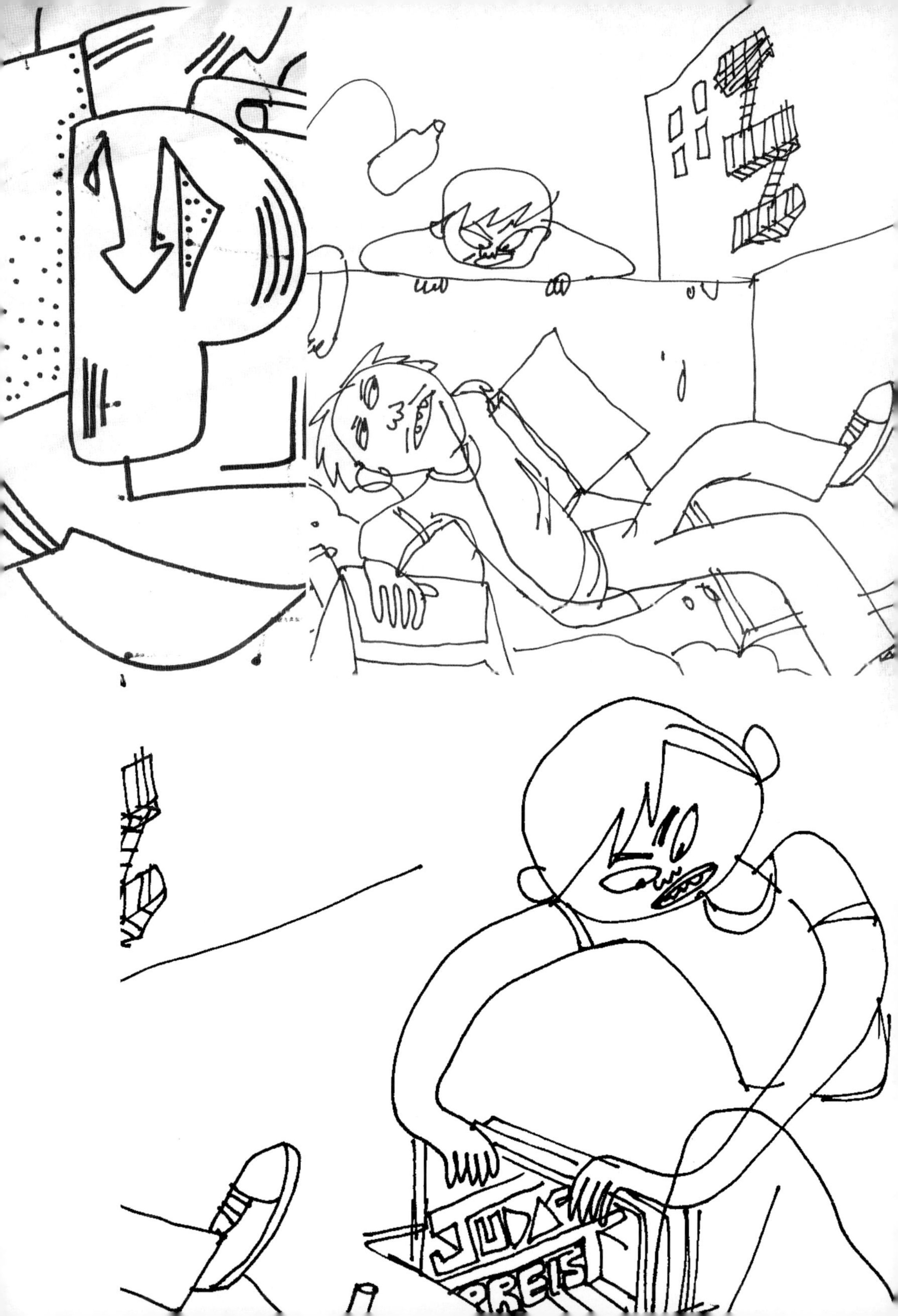
JUDA
PREIS

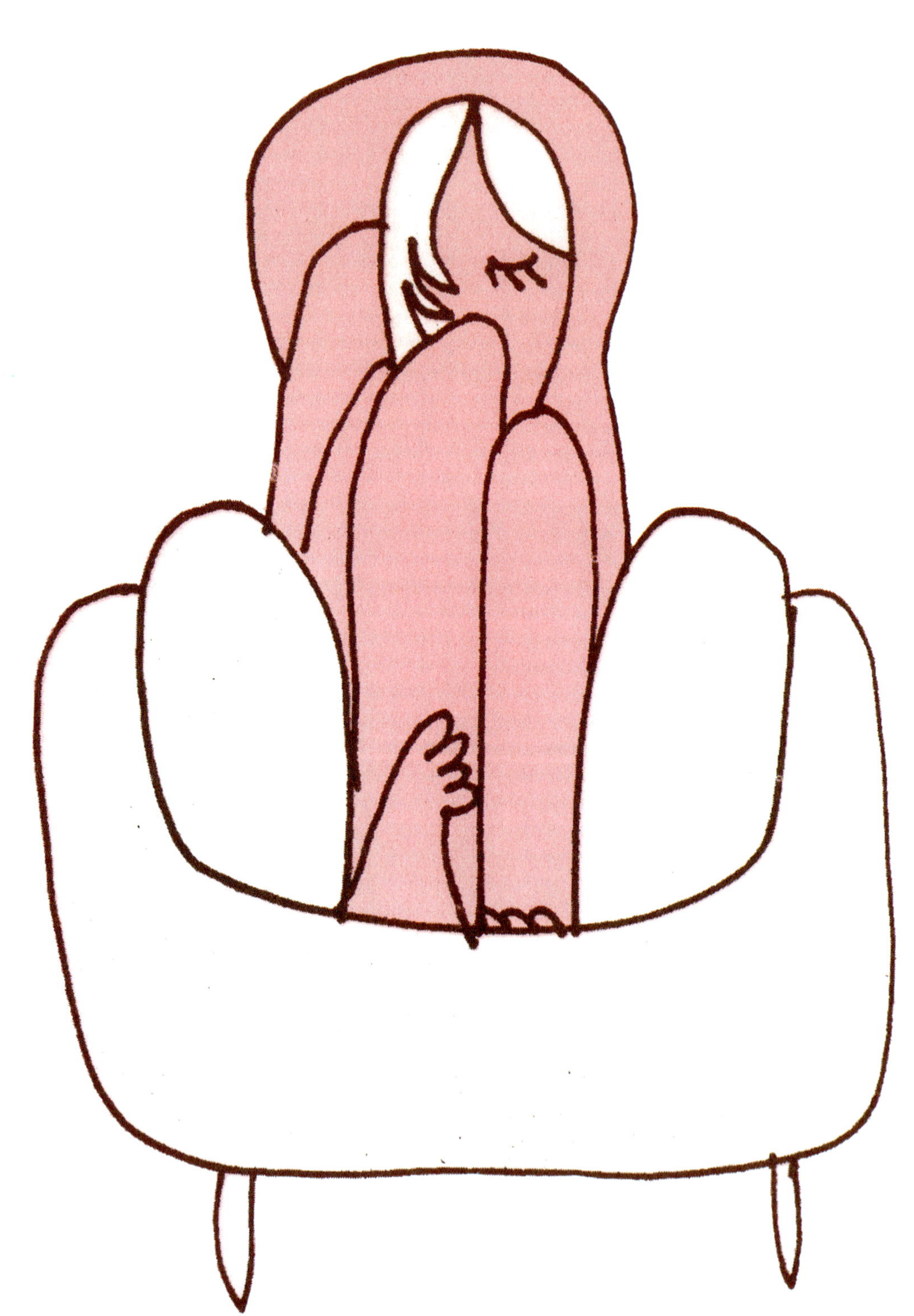

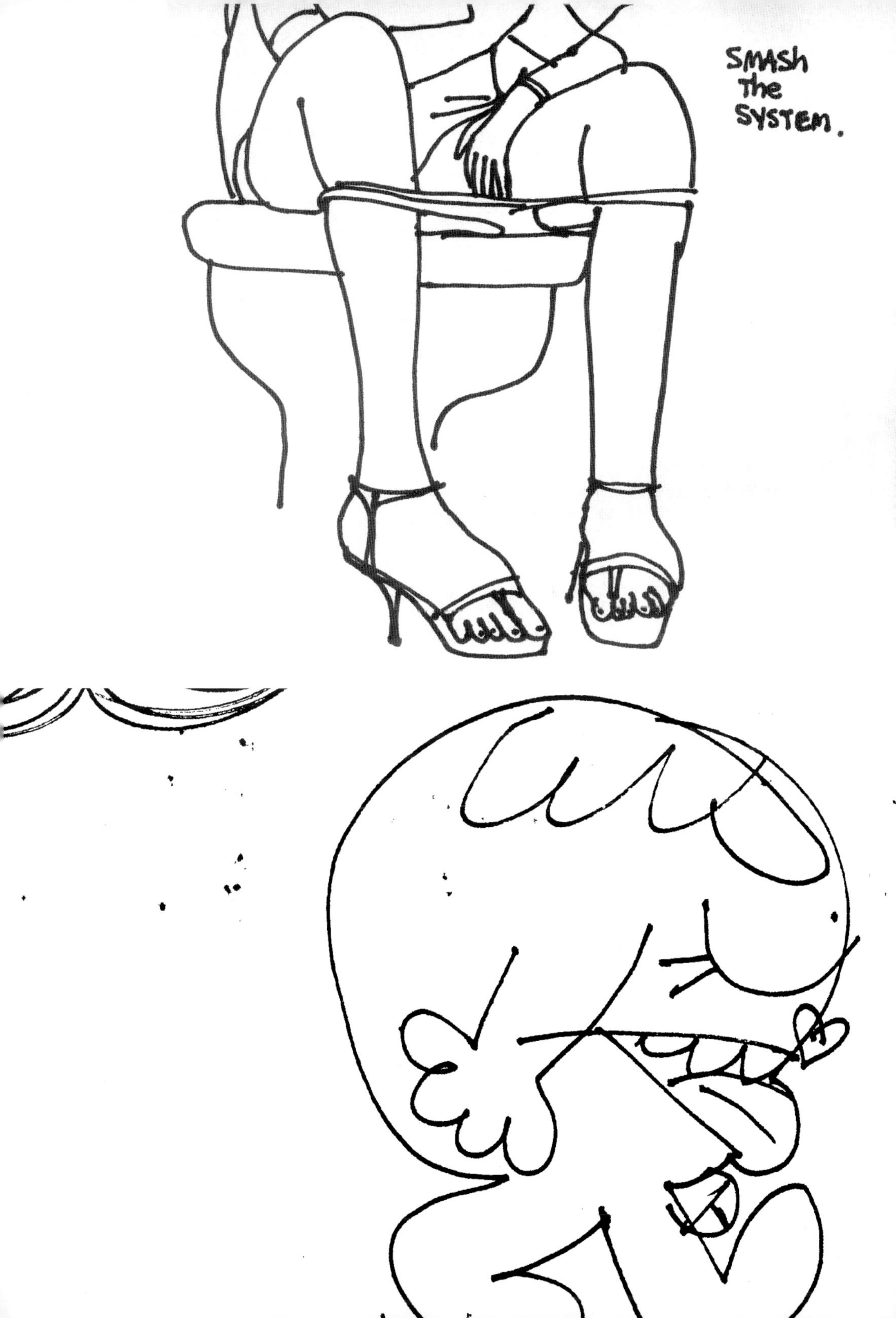
SMASH The SYSTEM.

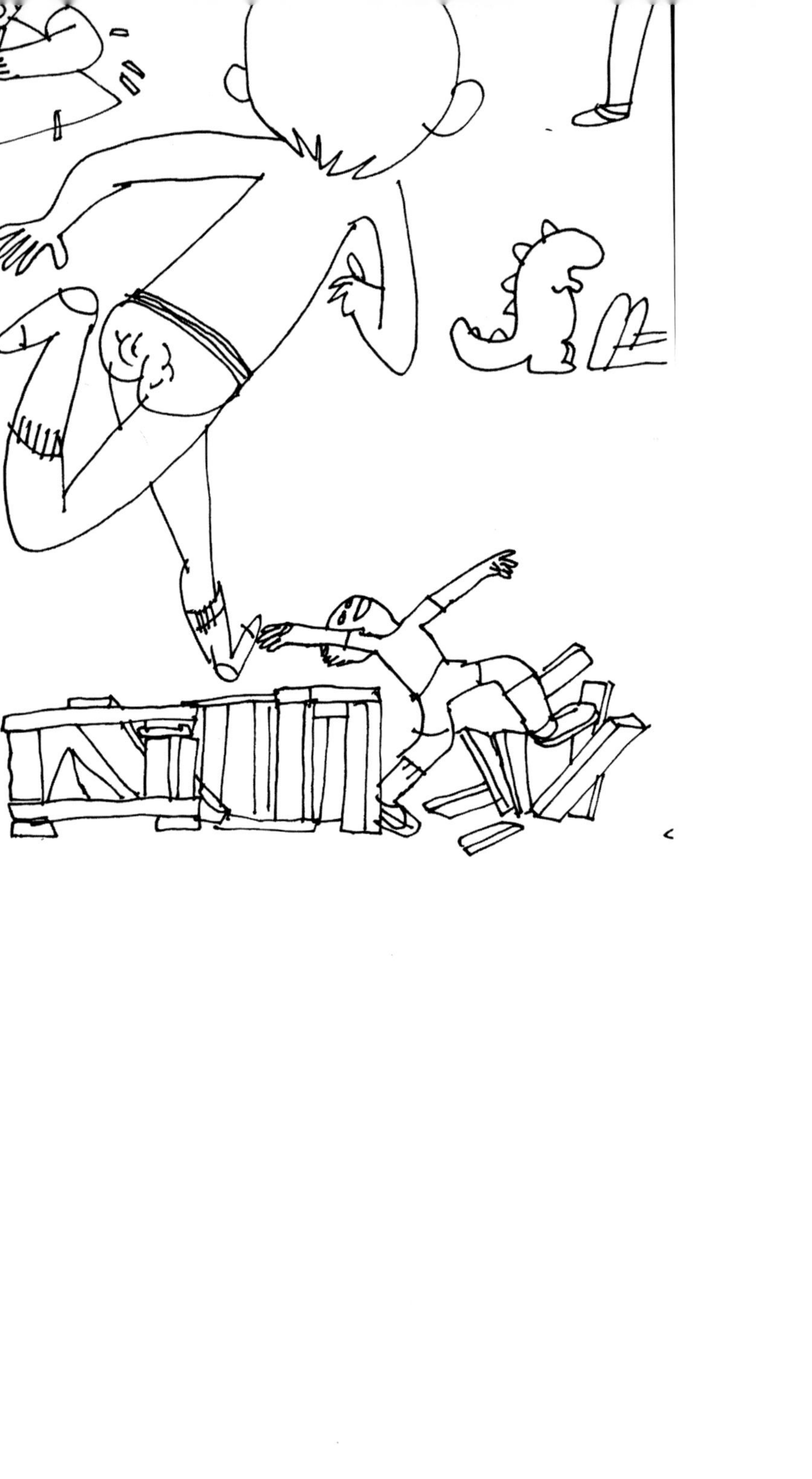

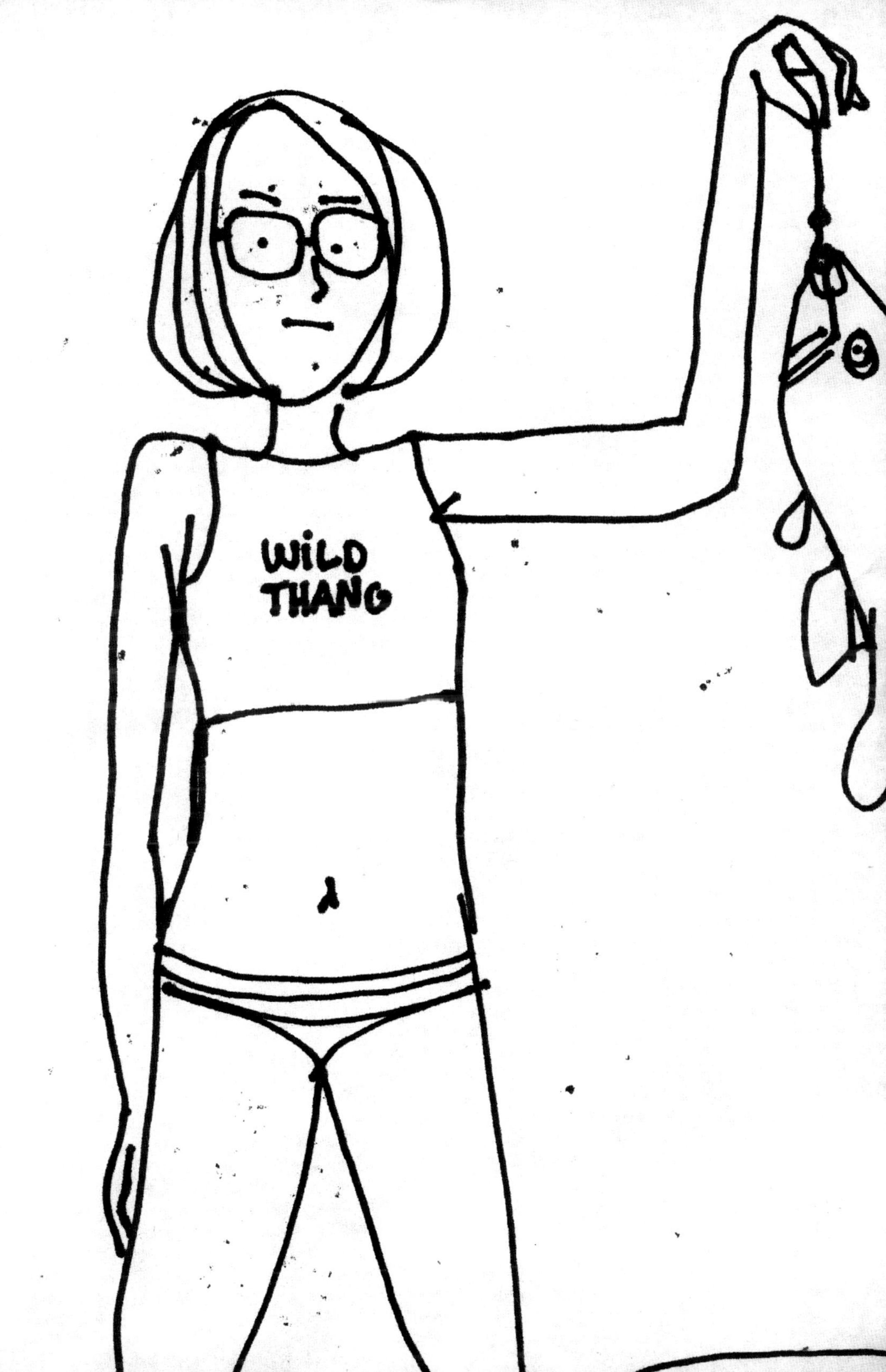
WILD
THANG

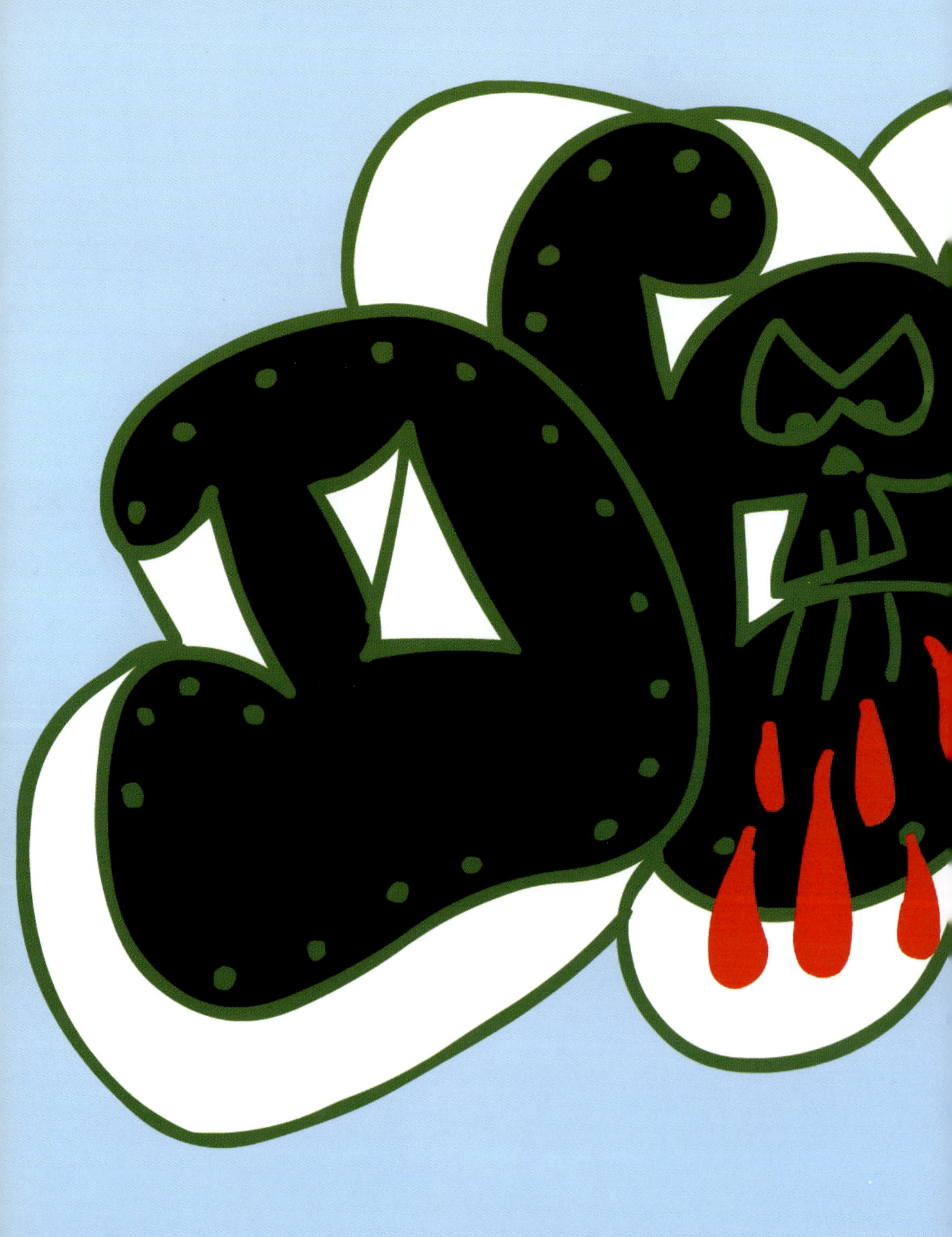

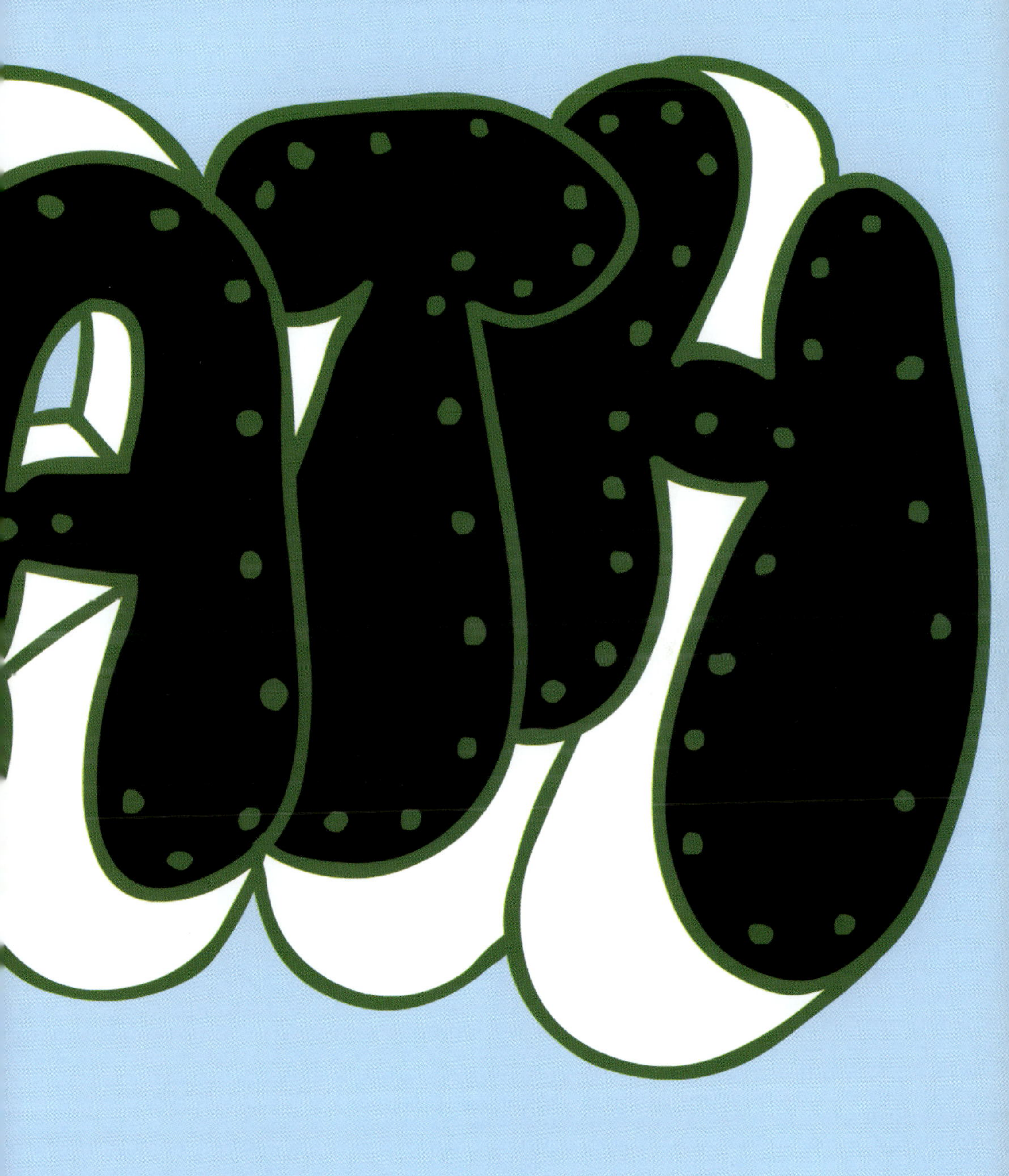

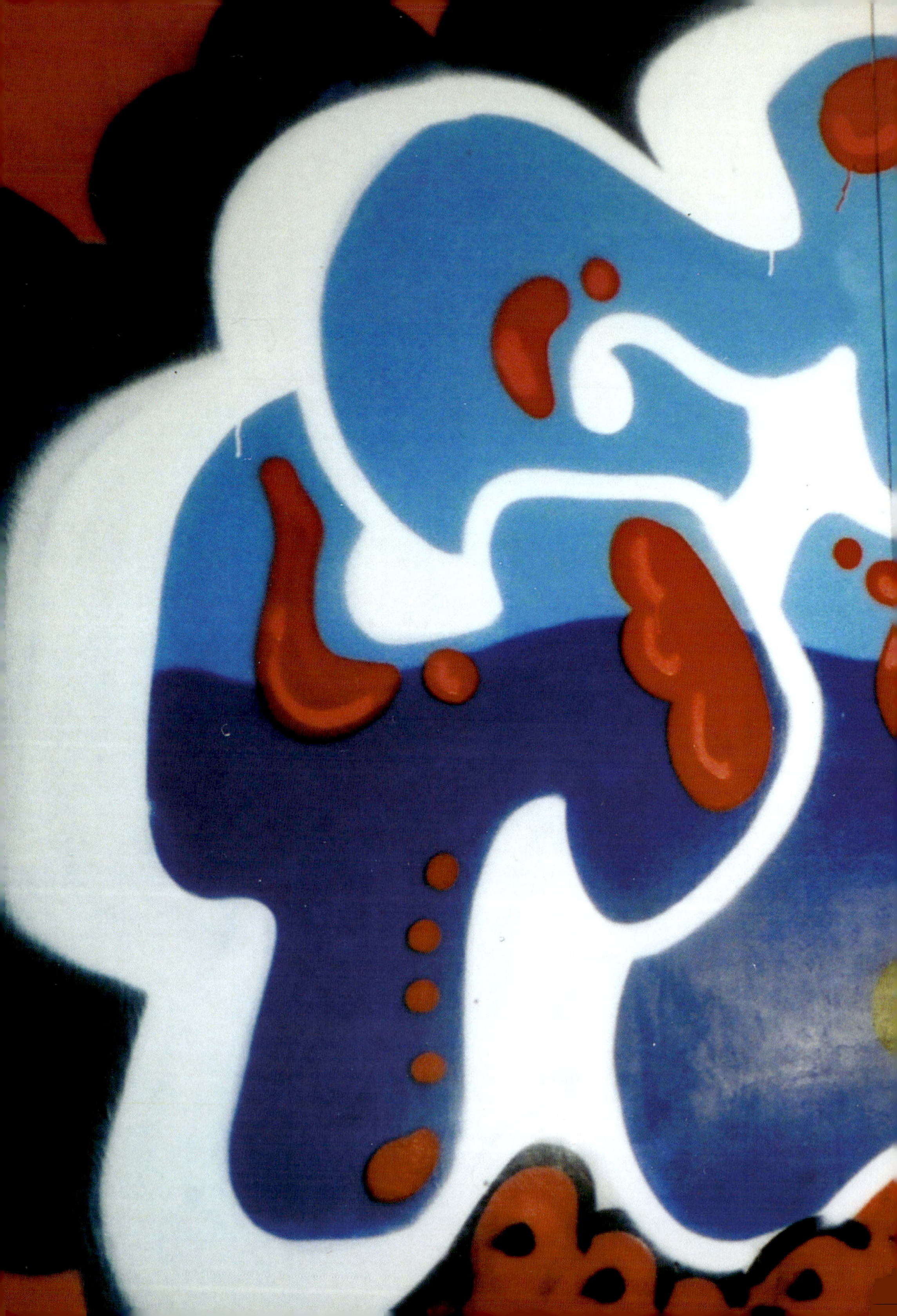

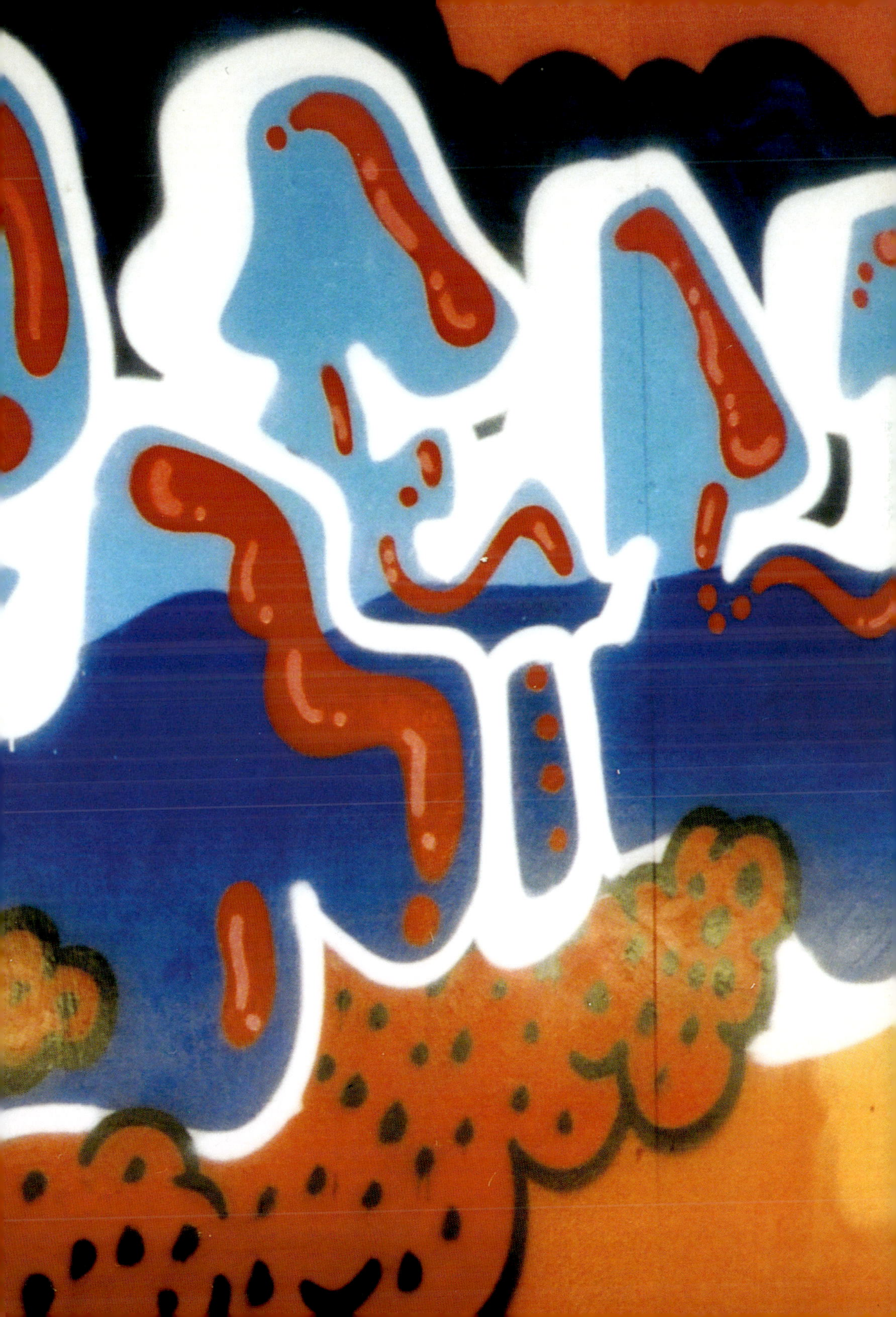

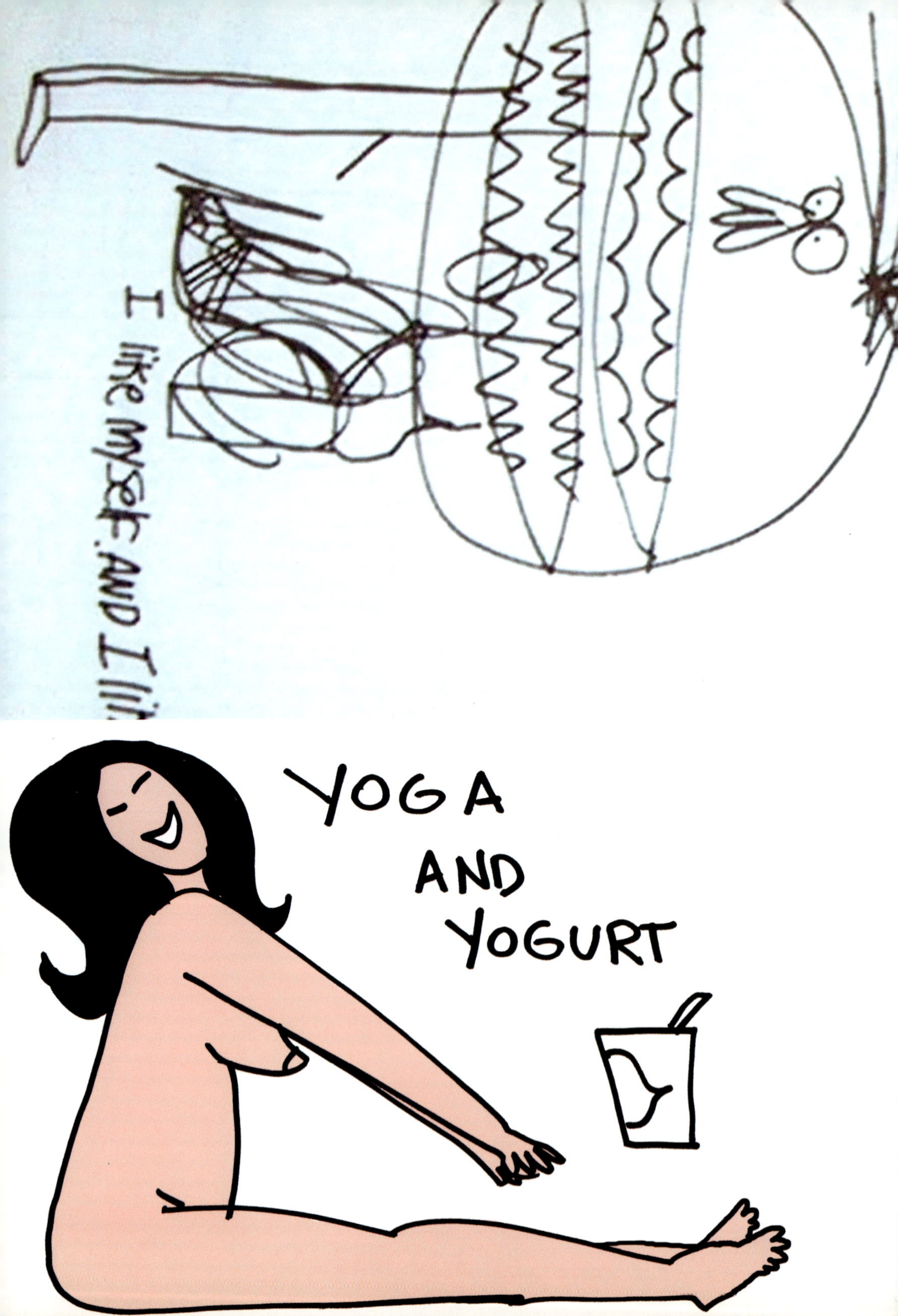
I like mySeLF. AND I
YOGA
AND
YOGURT

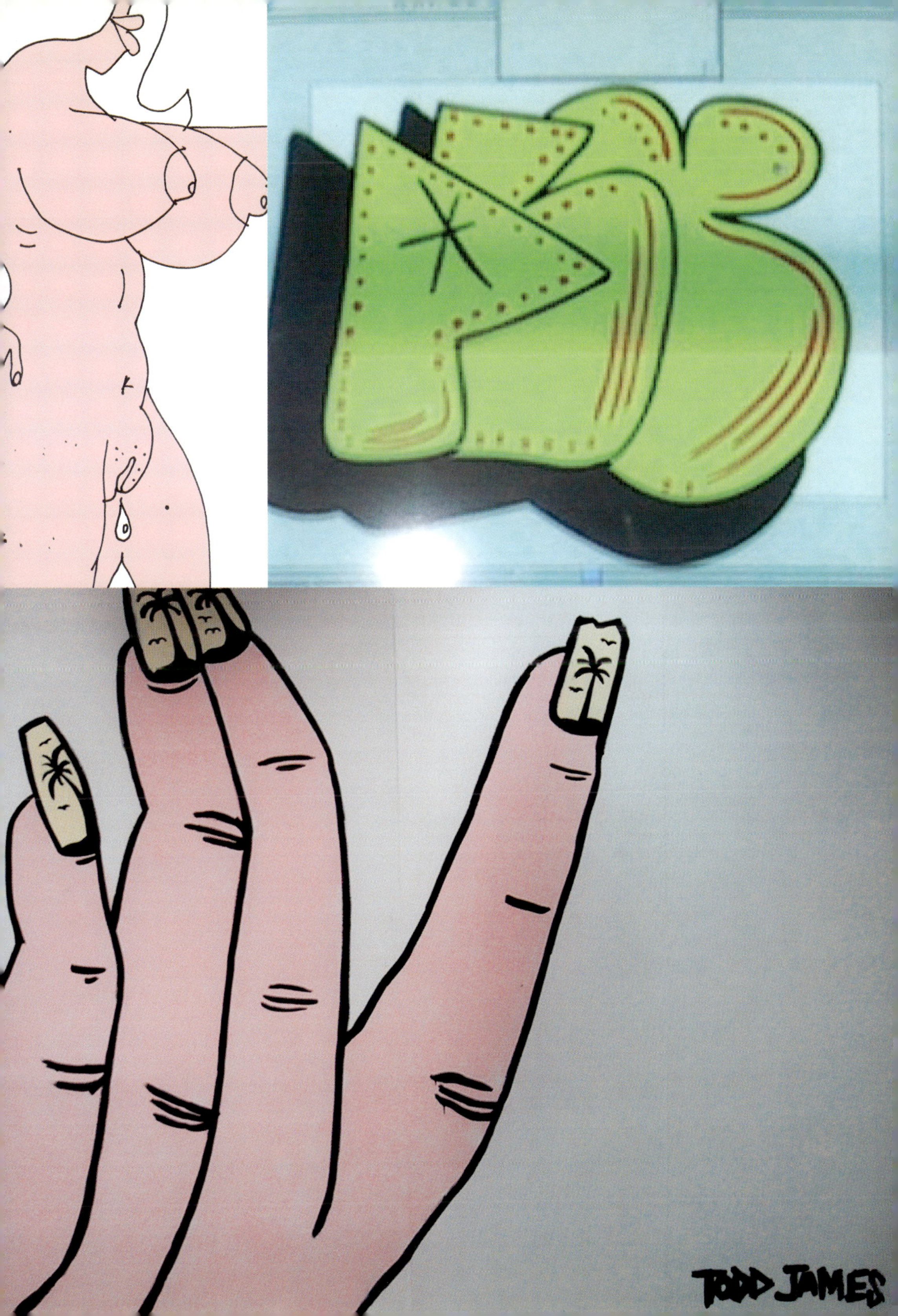
TODD JAMES

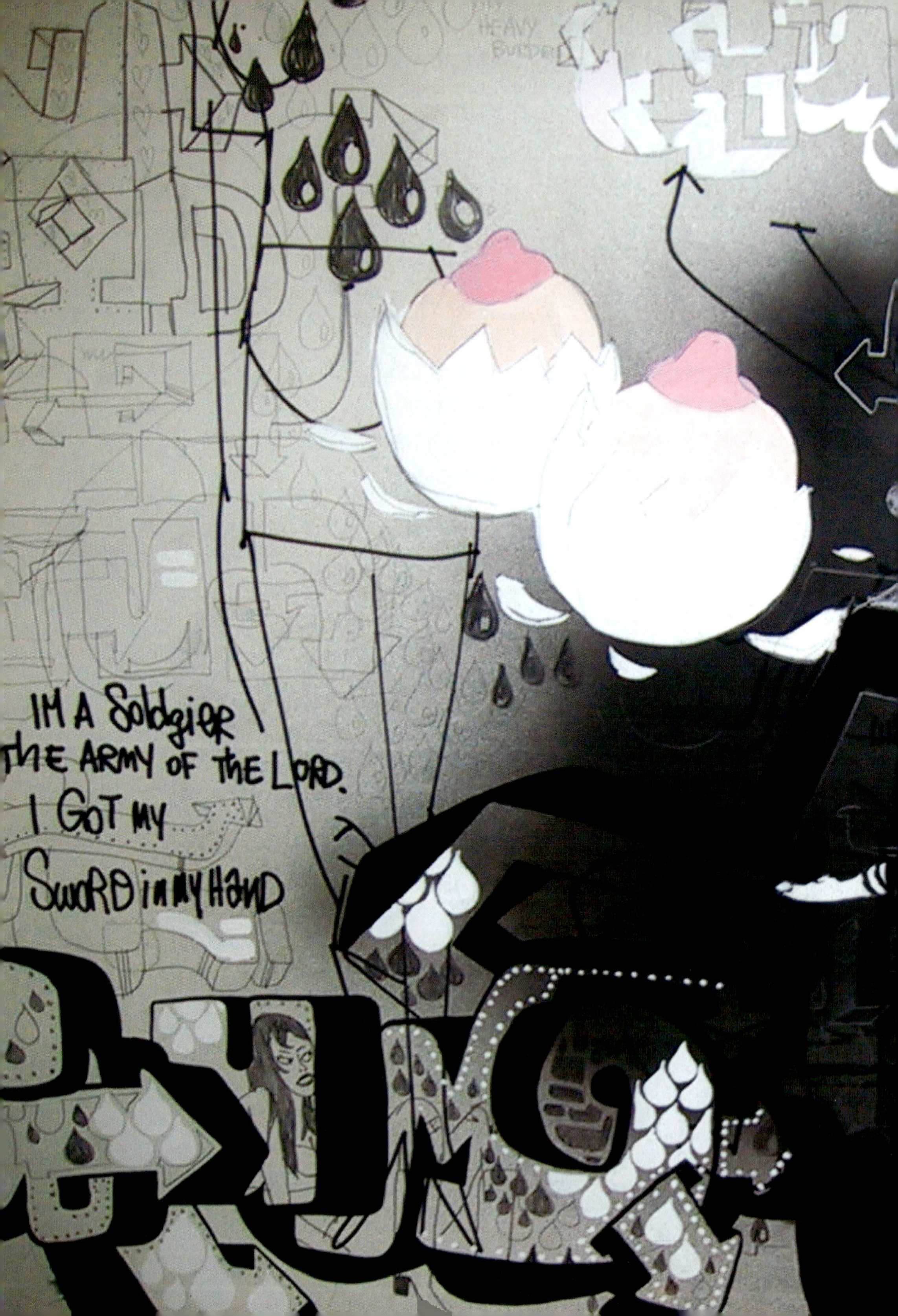
IM A Soldgier
THE ARMY OF THE LORD.
I GOT MY
SWORD in my HAND

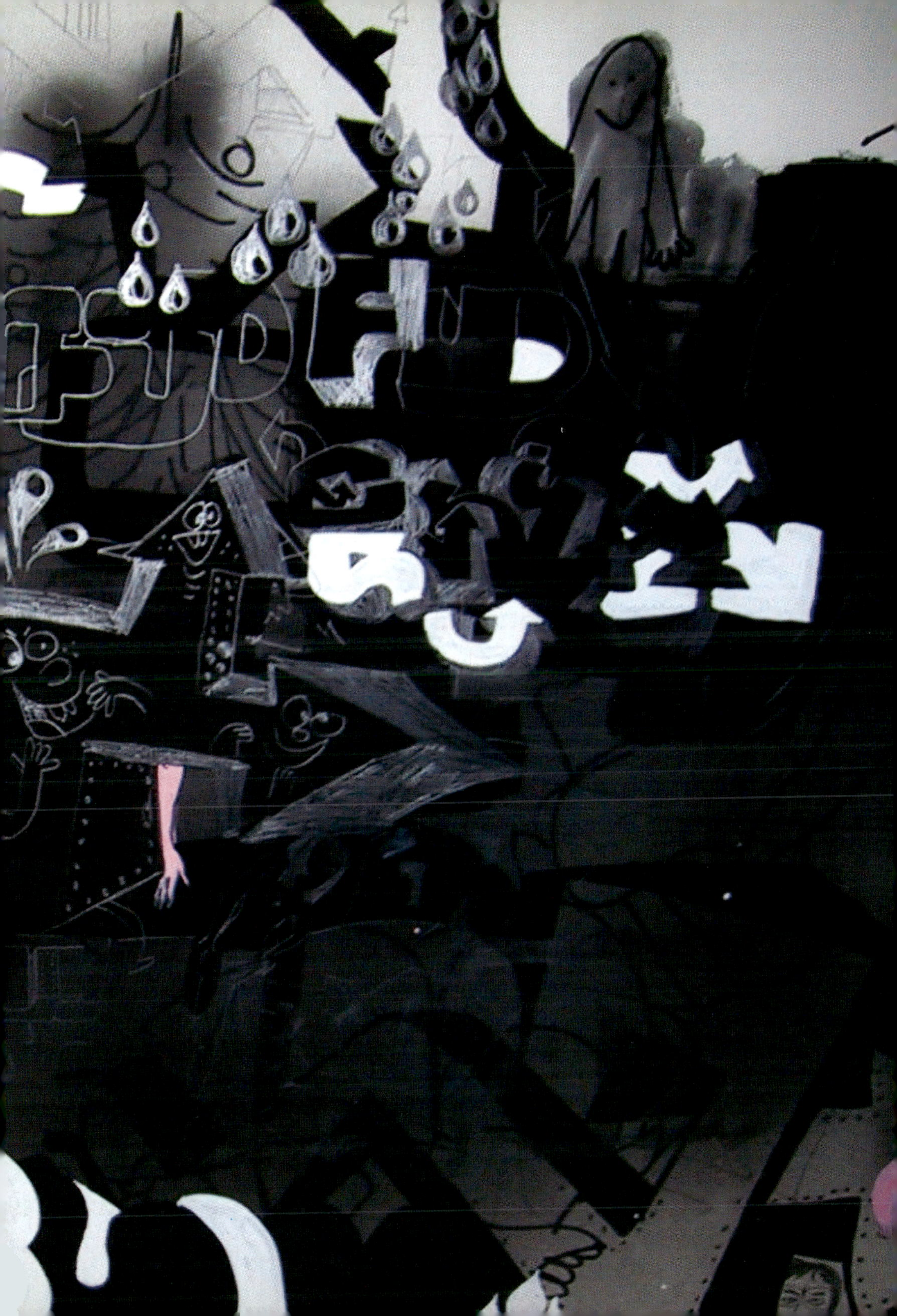

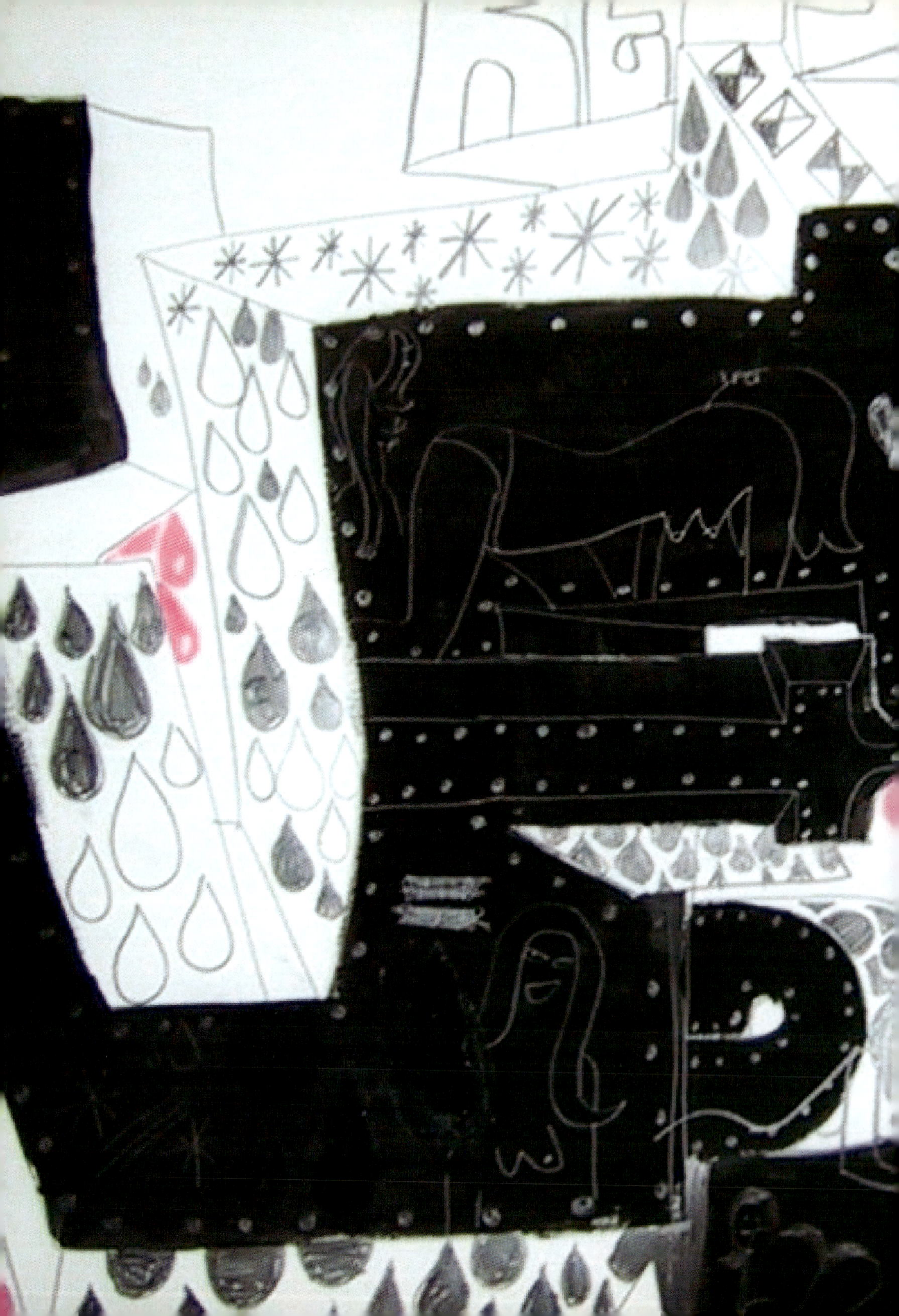

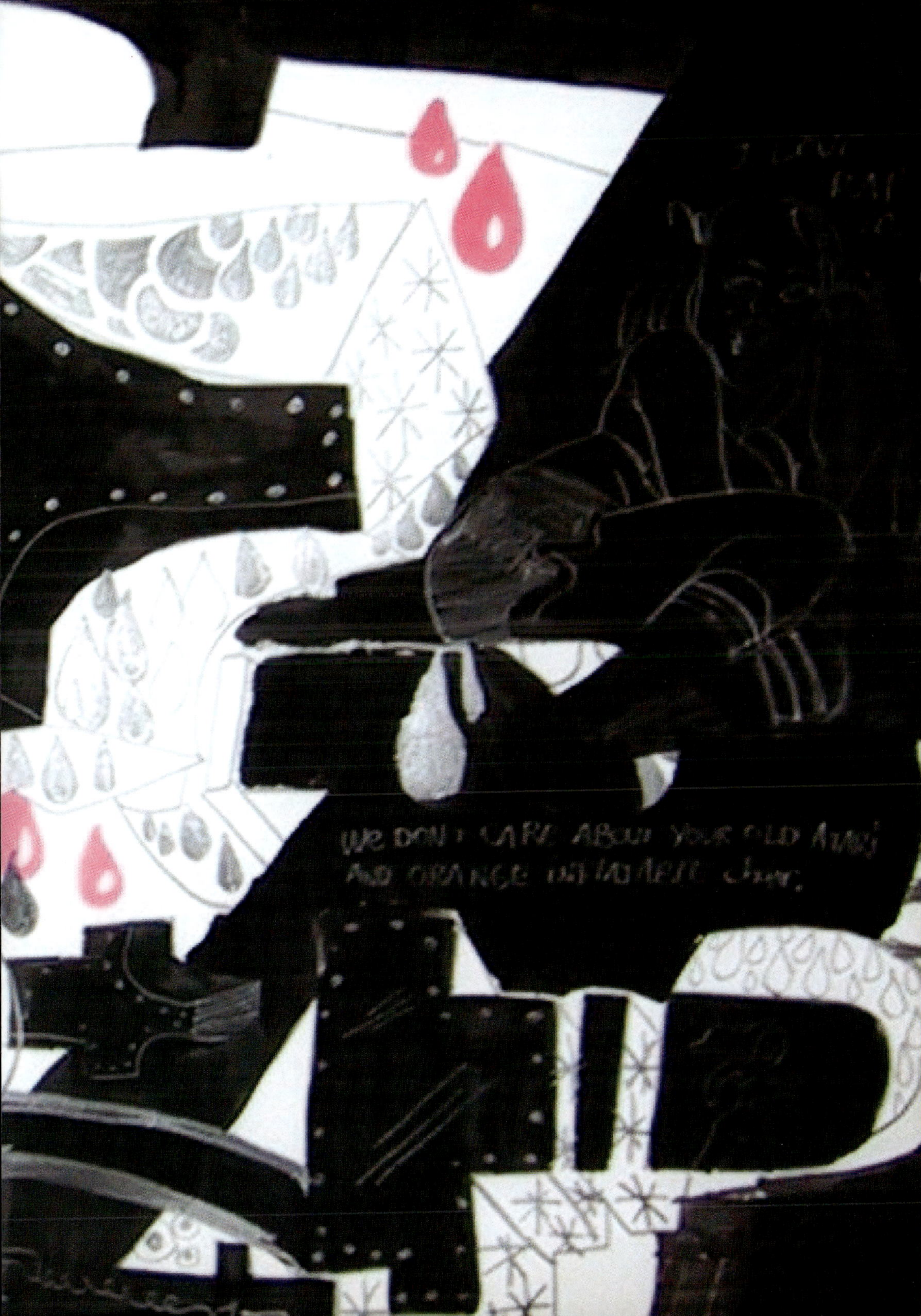
WE DON'T CARE ABOUT YOUR OLD AUNT

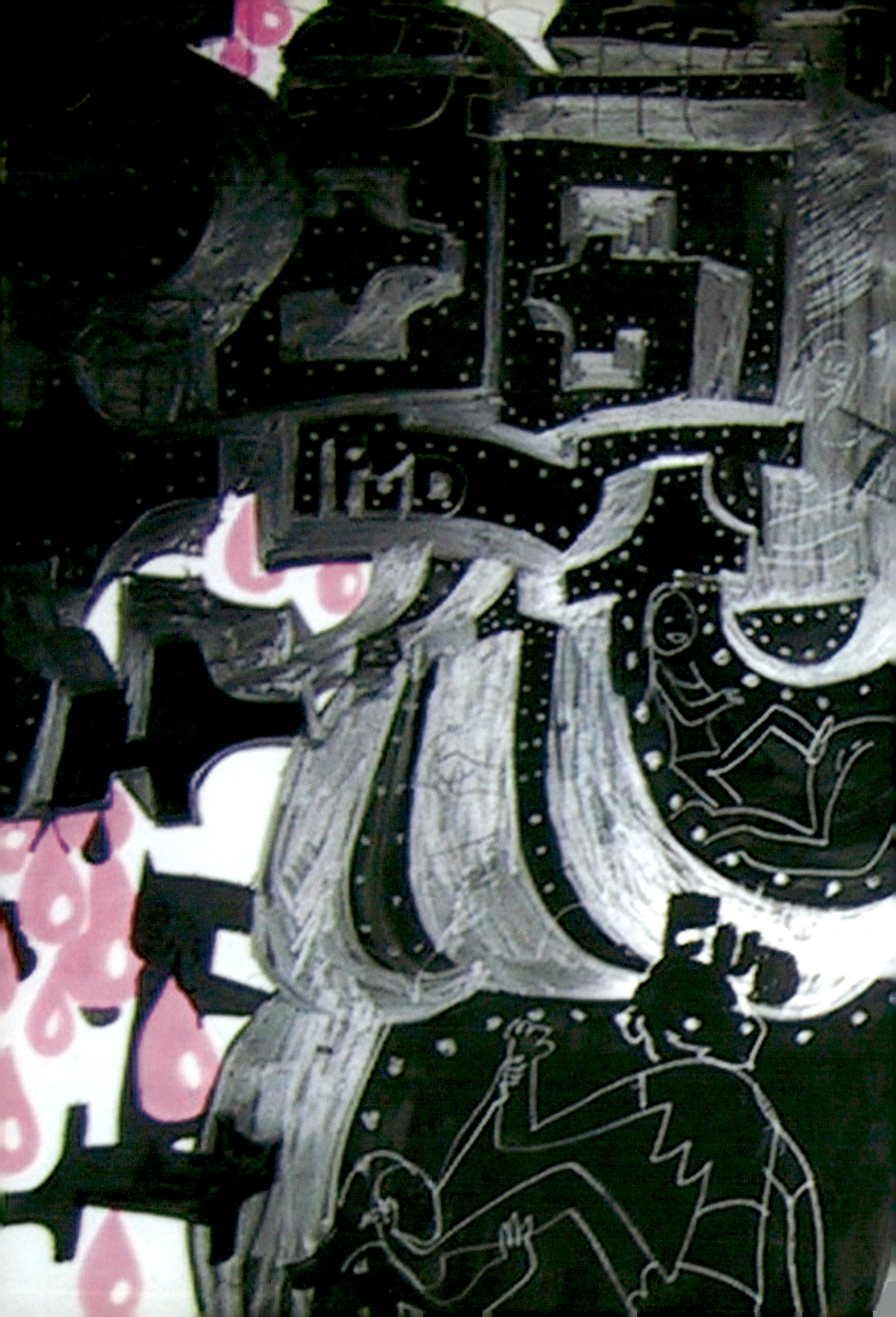

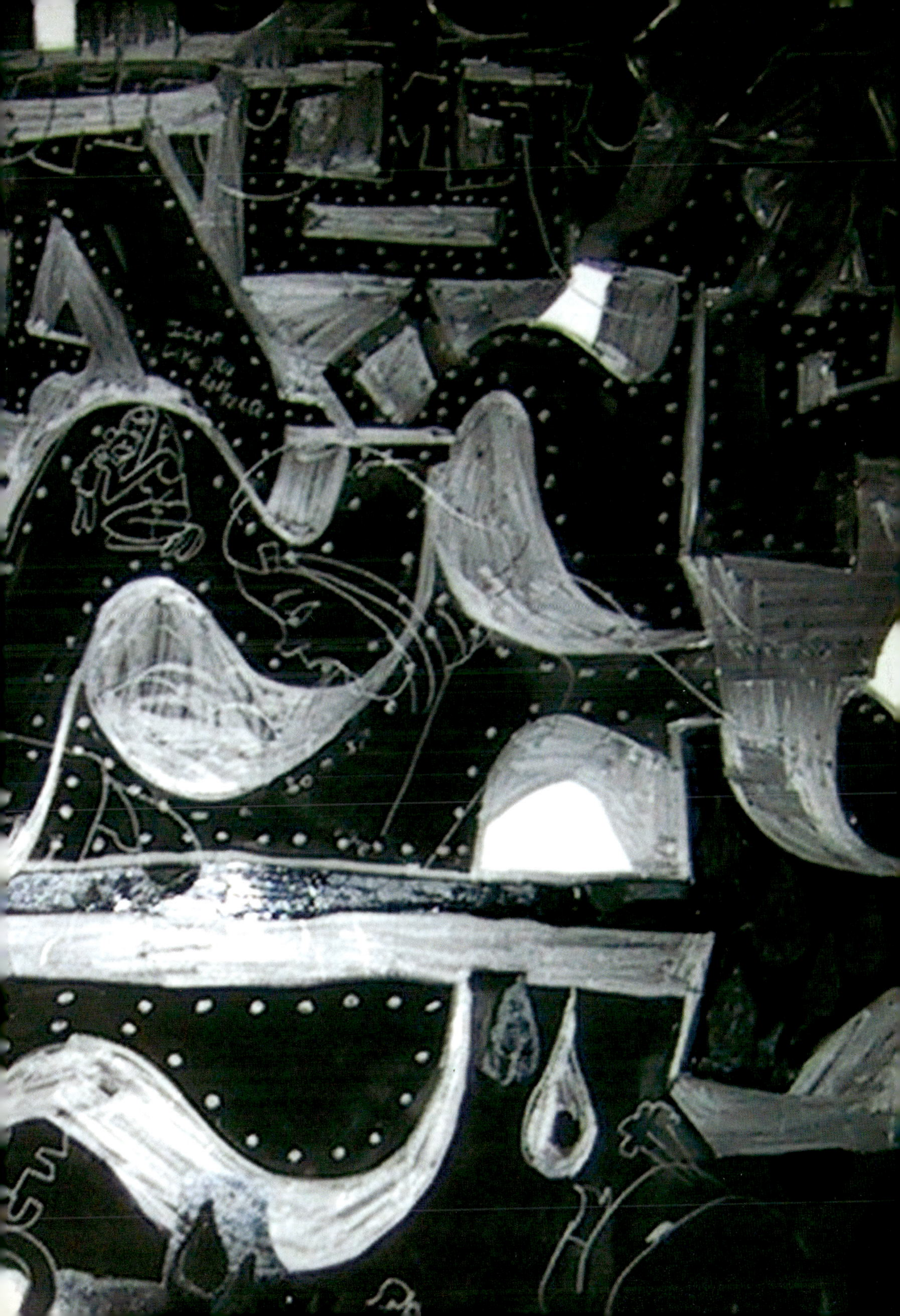

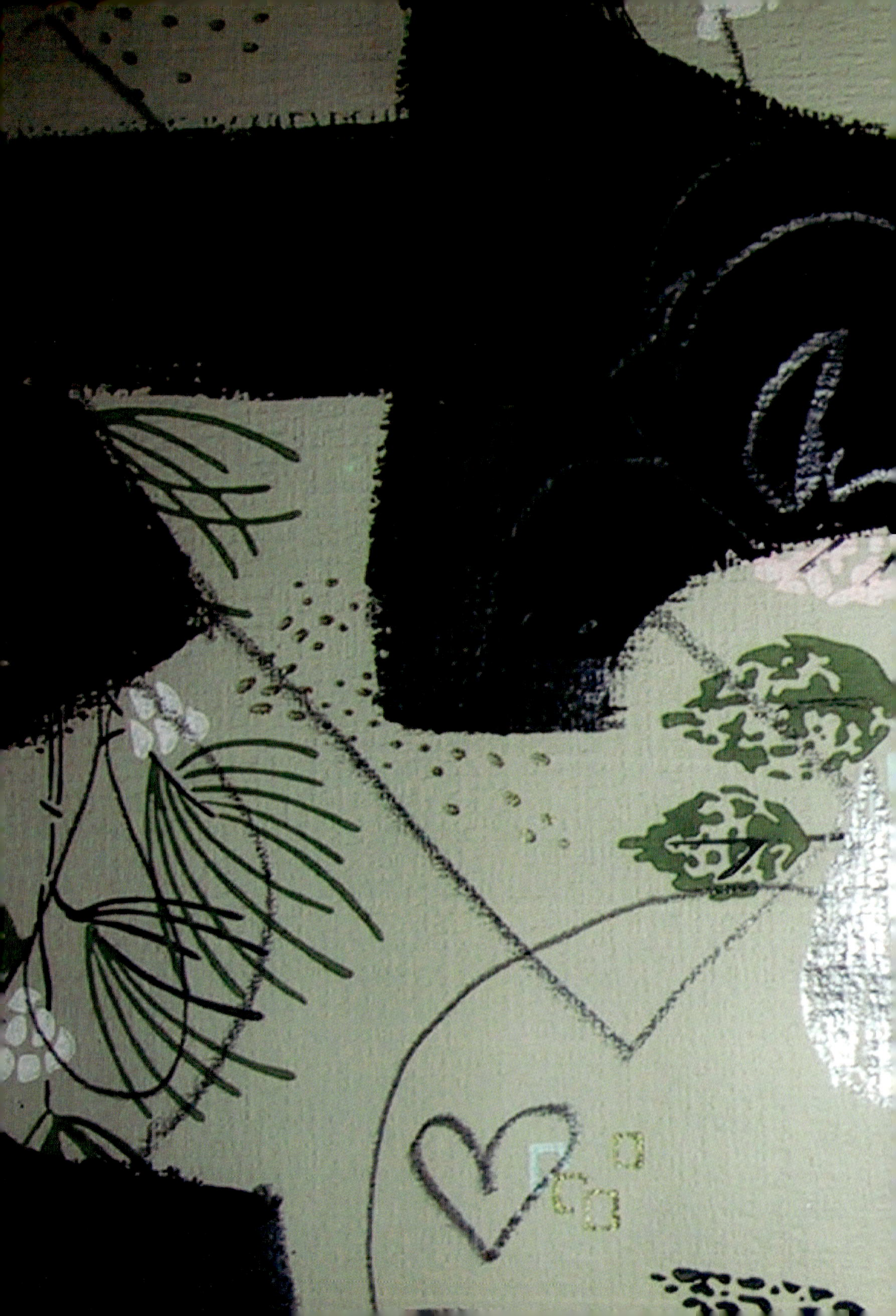

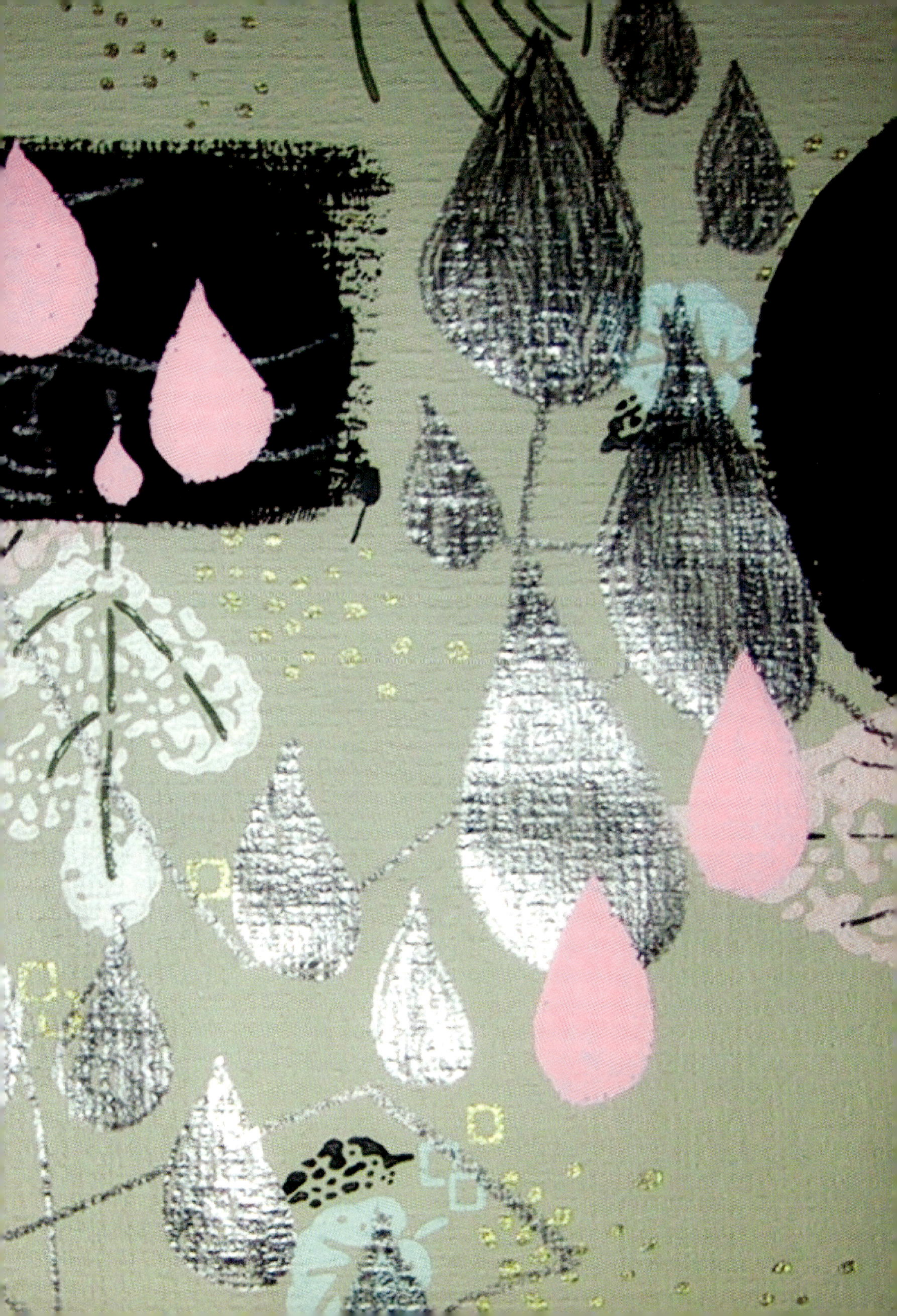

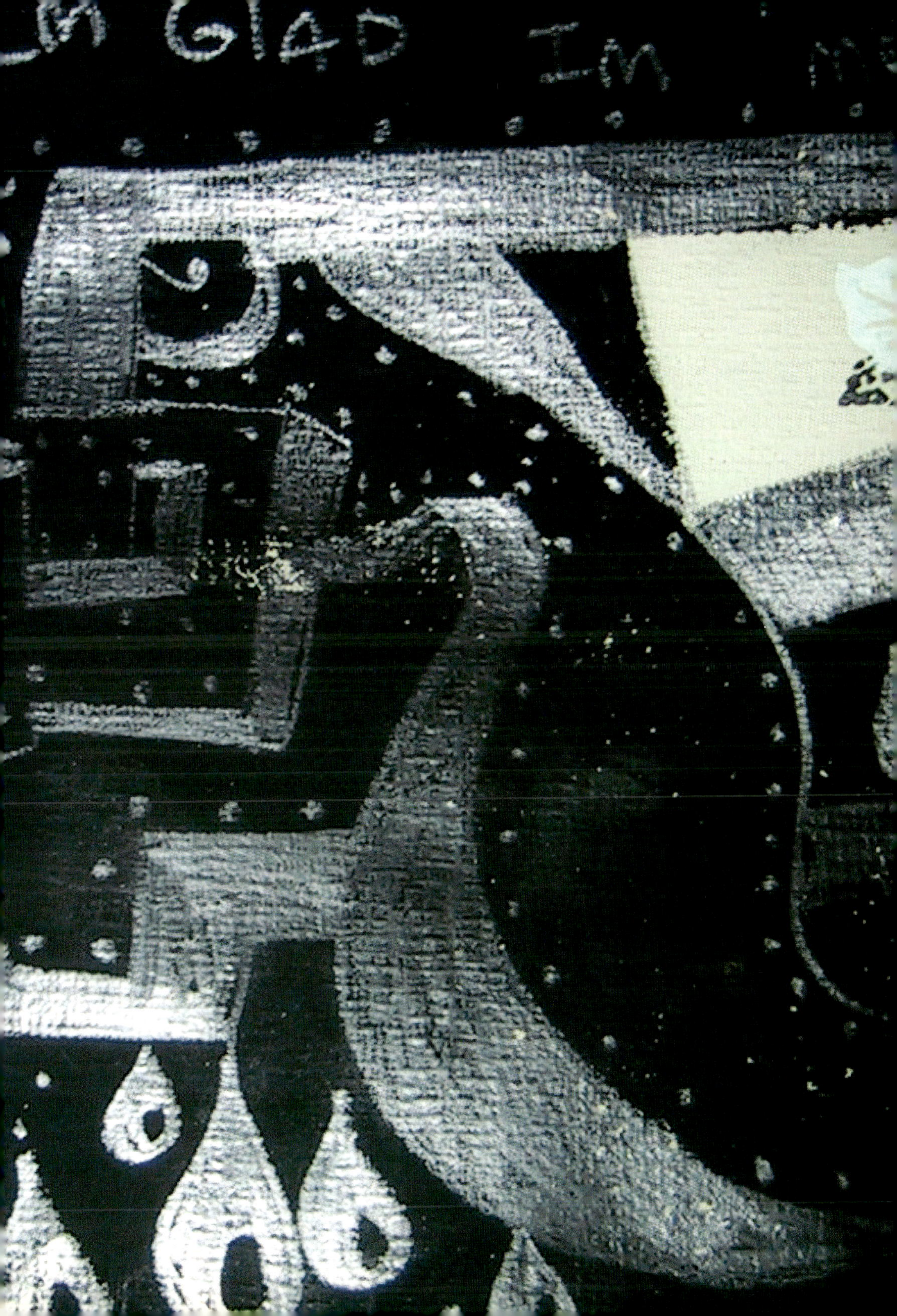
GlAD IM

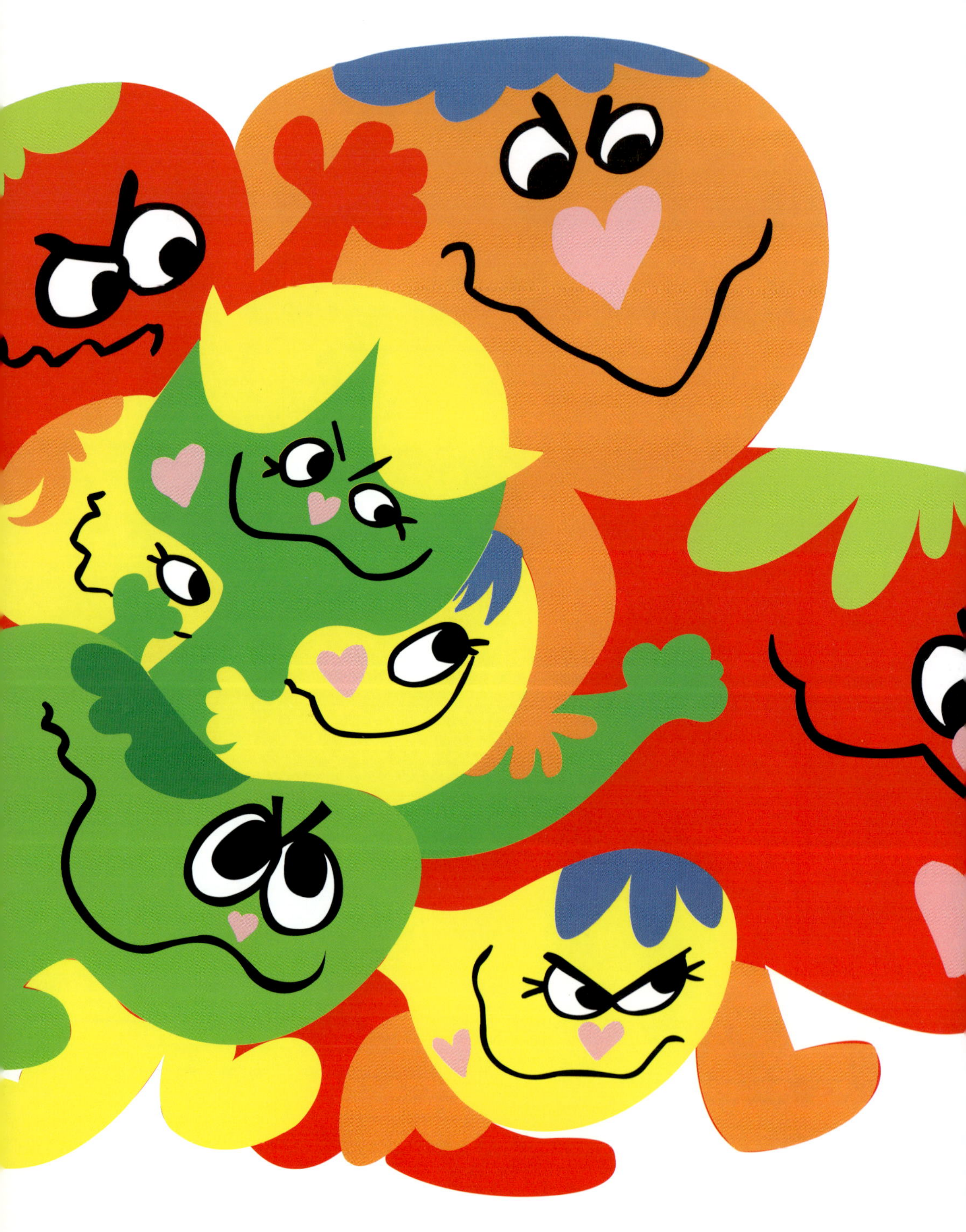

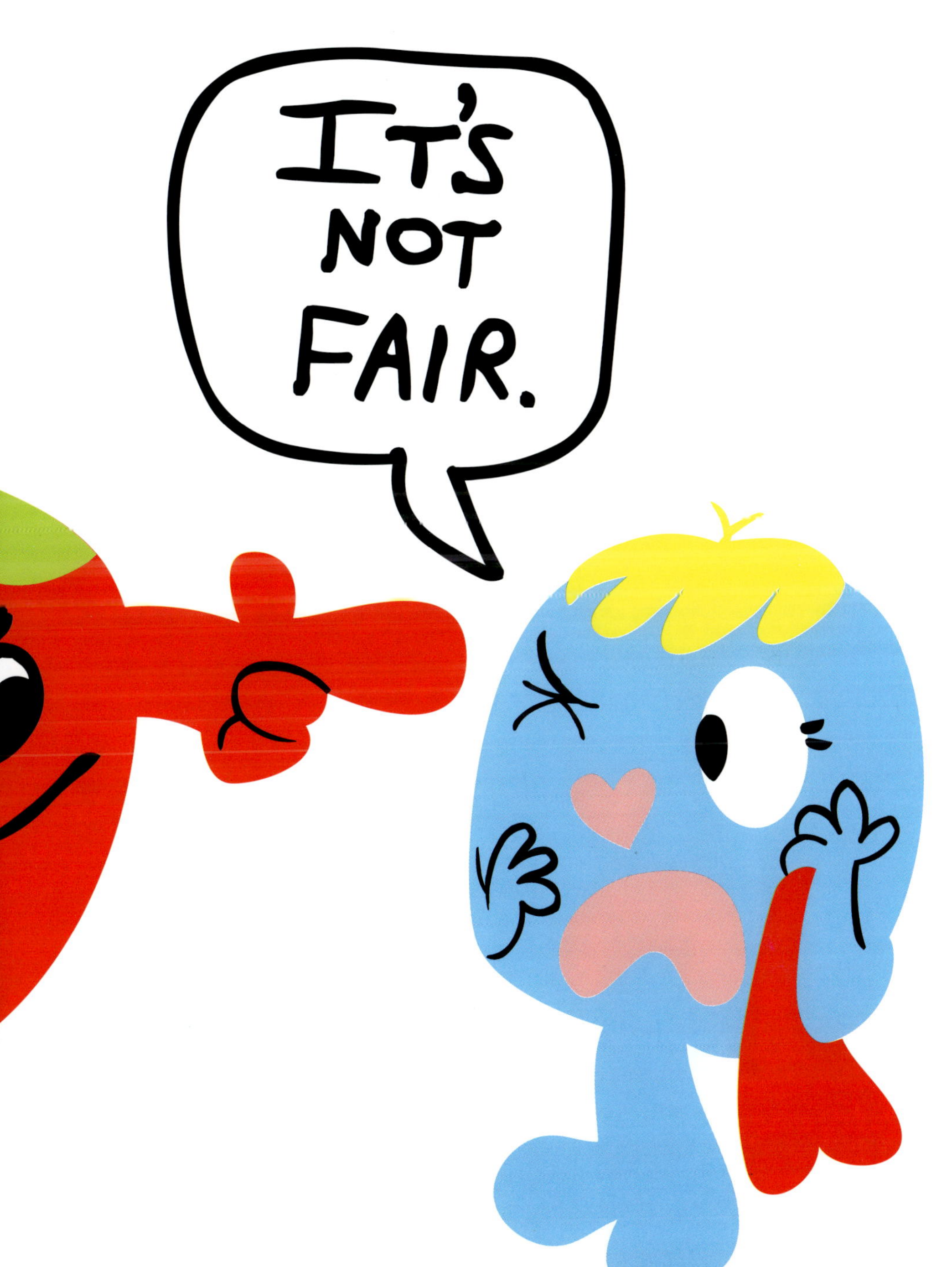
IT'S NOT FAIR.

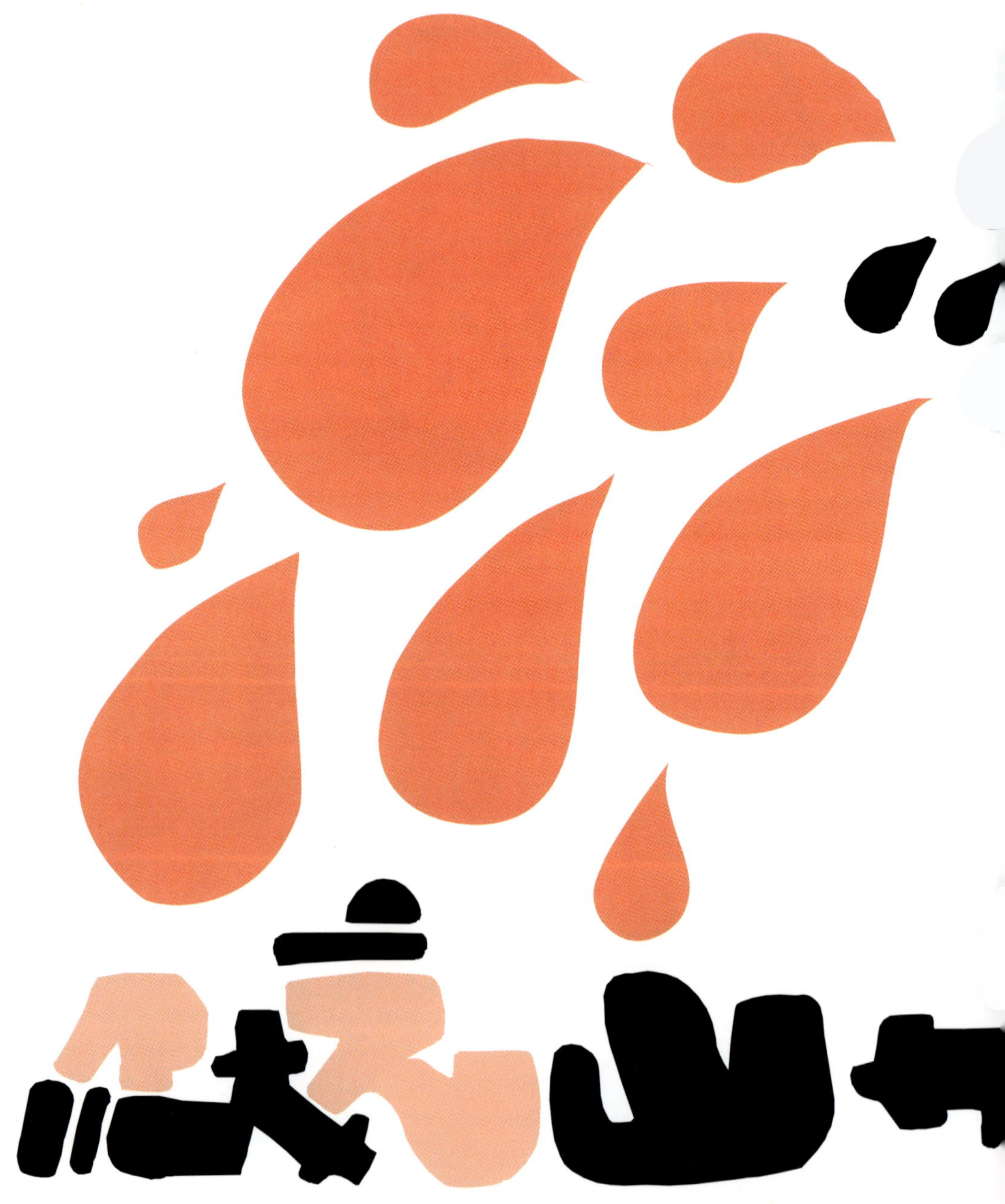

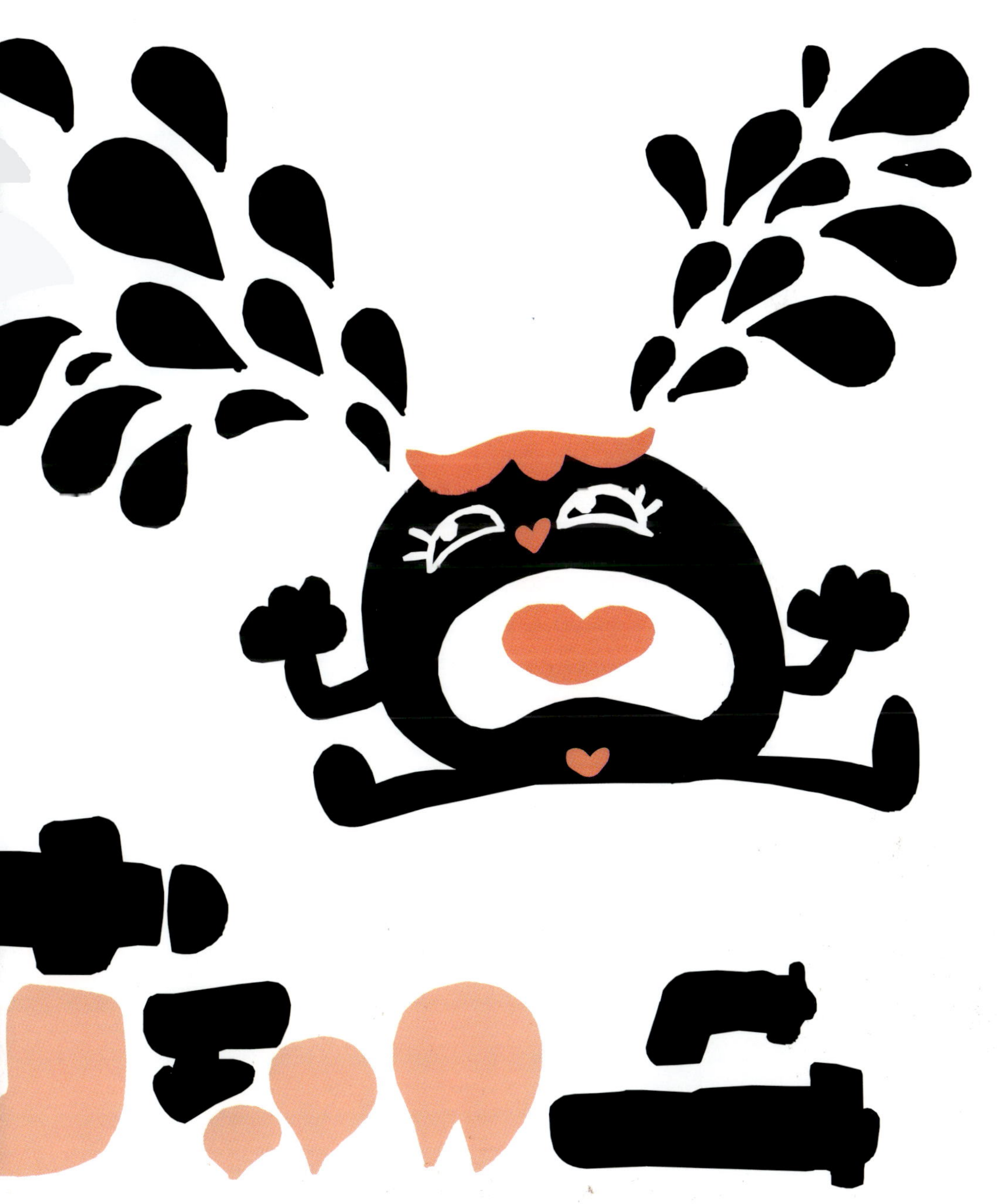

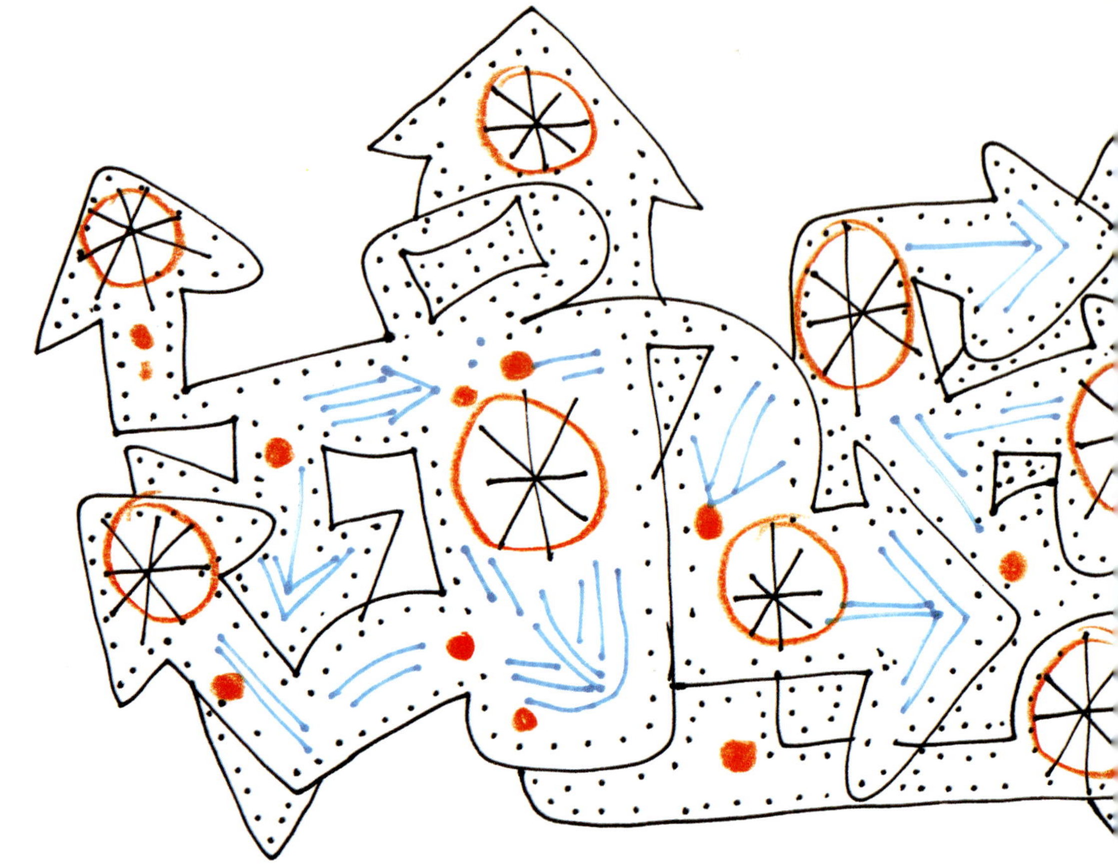

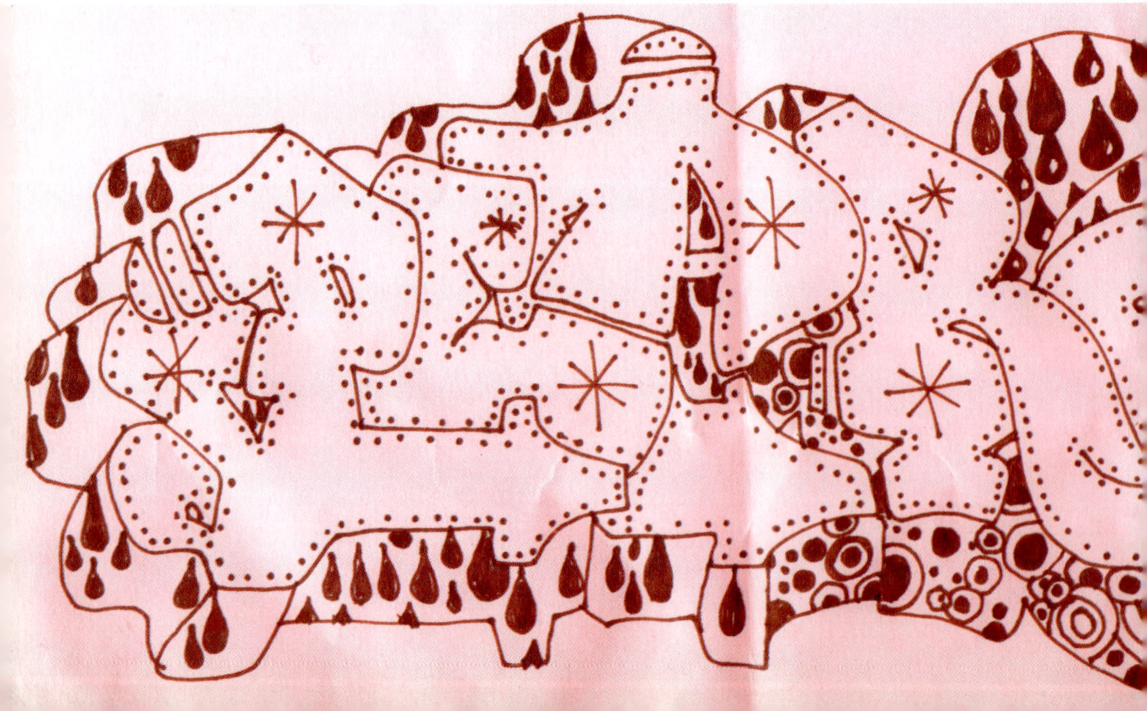

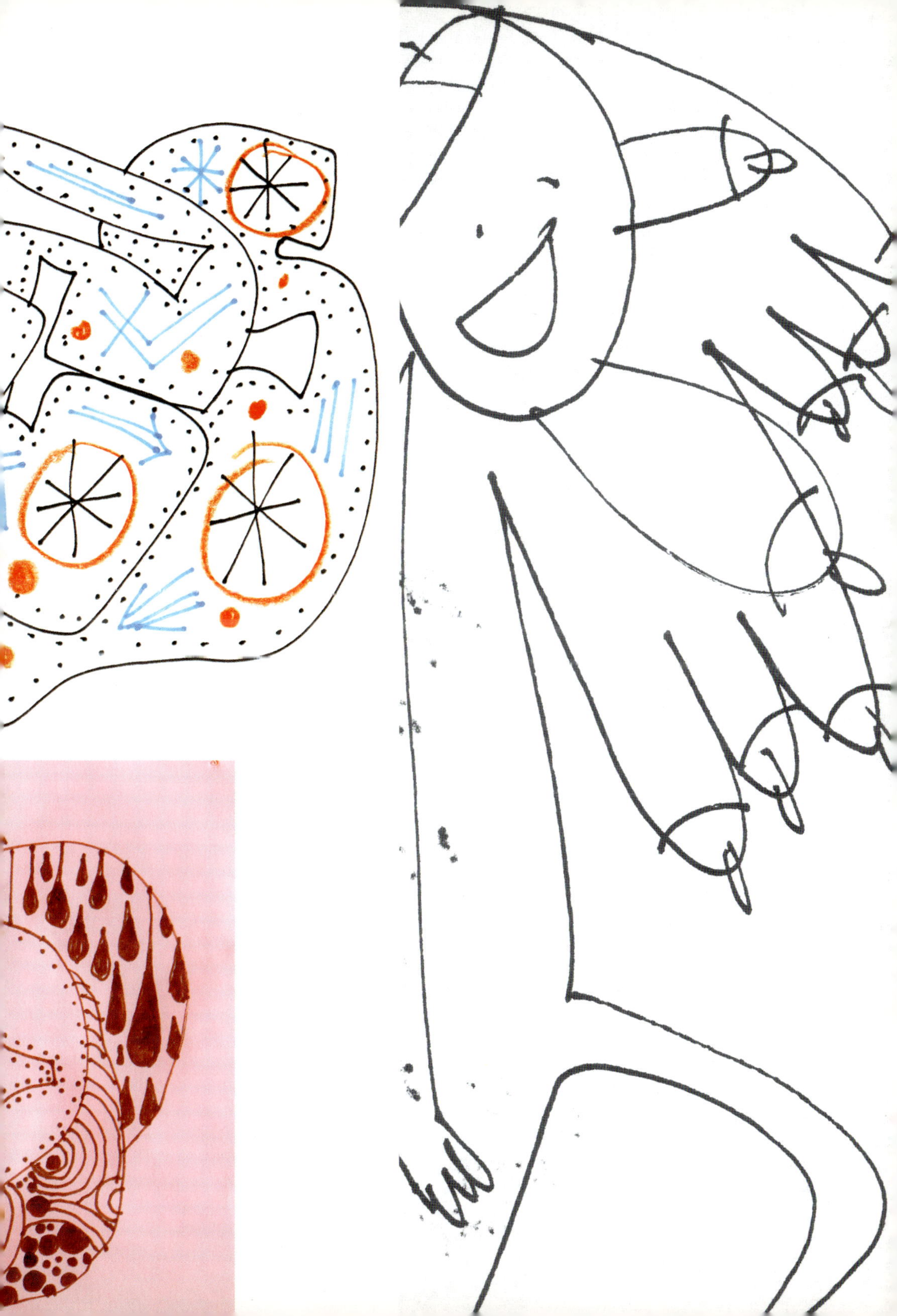

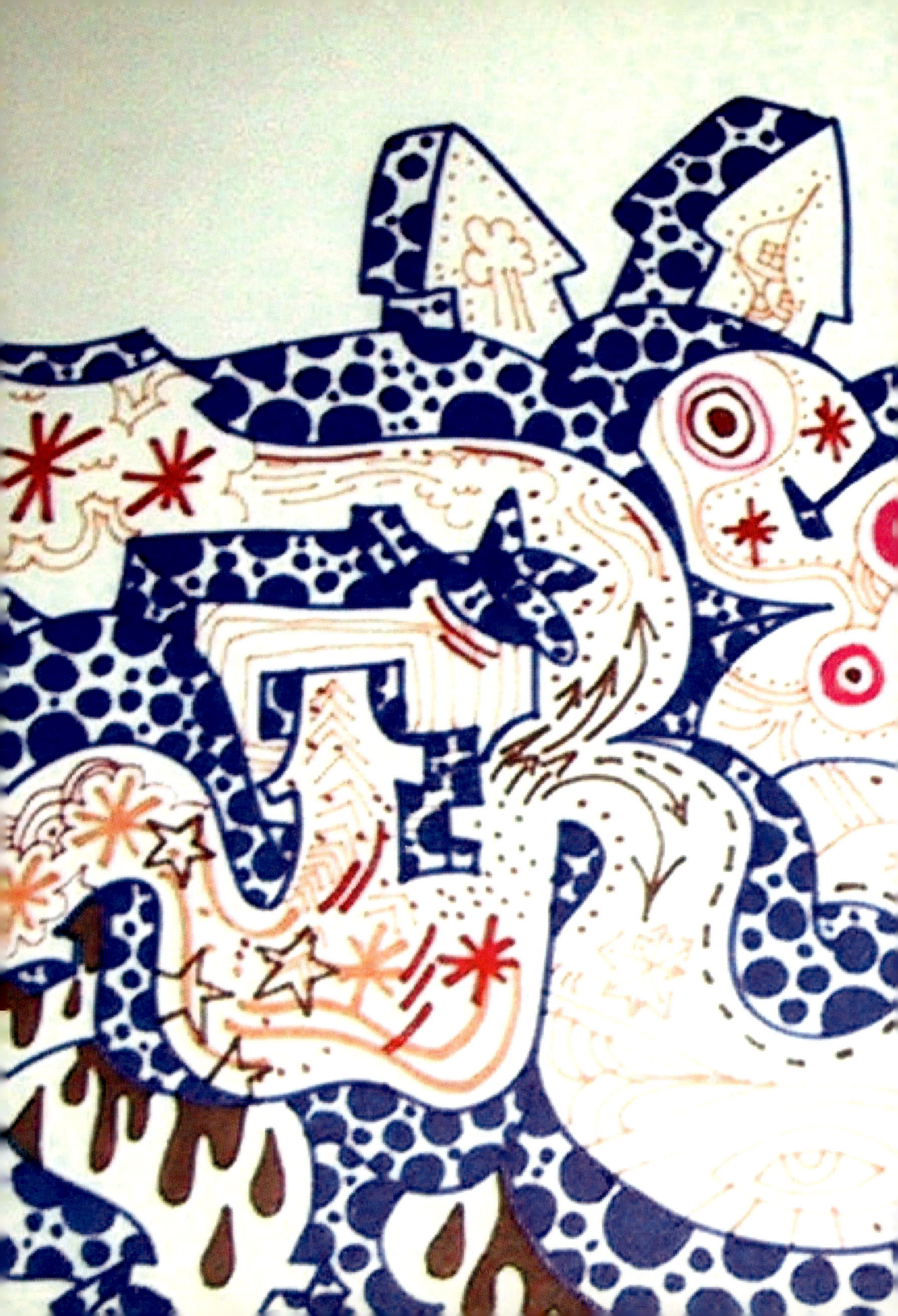

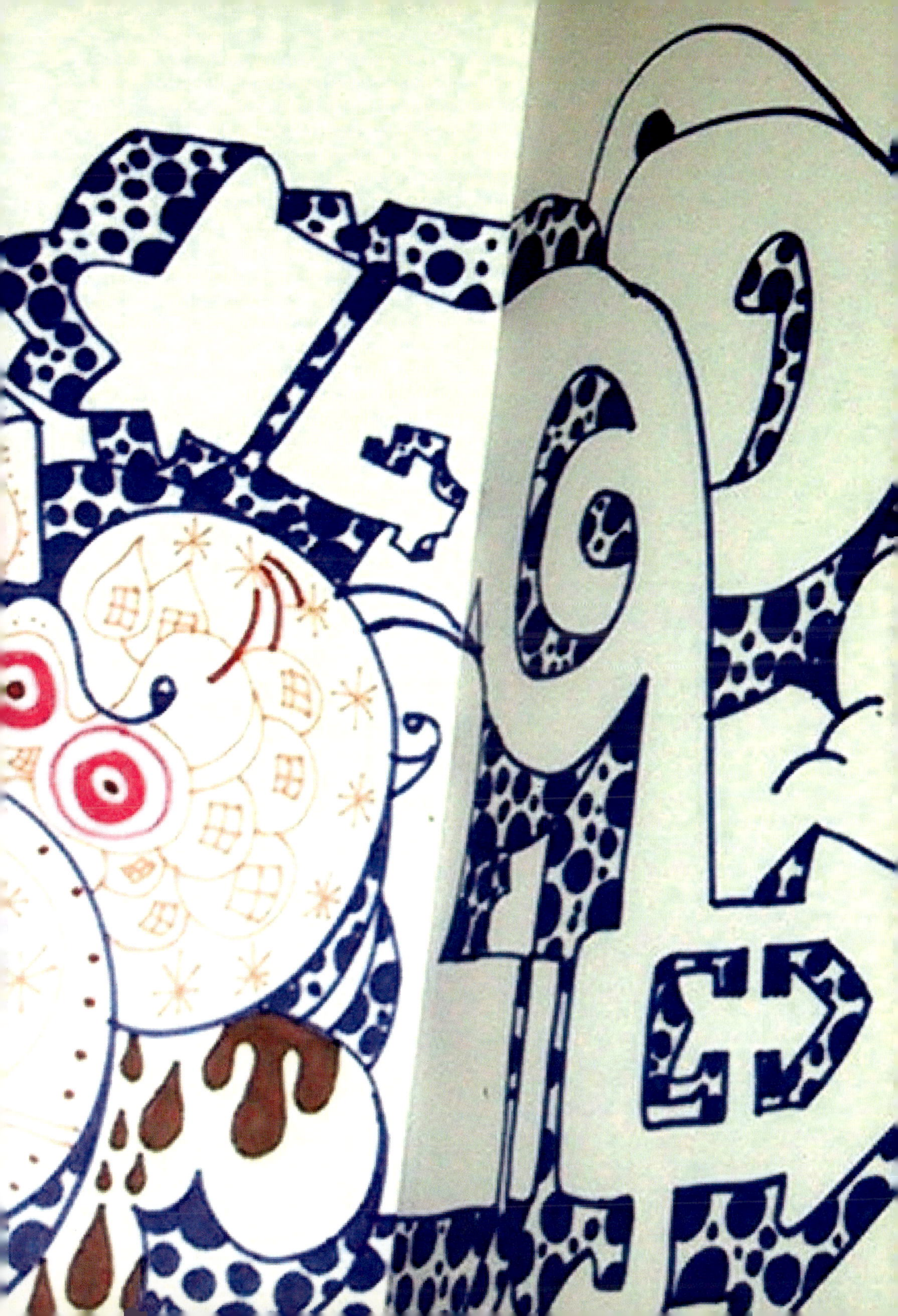

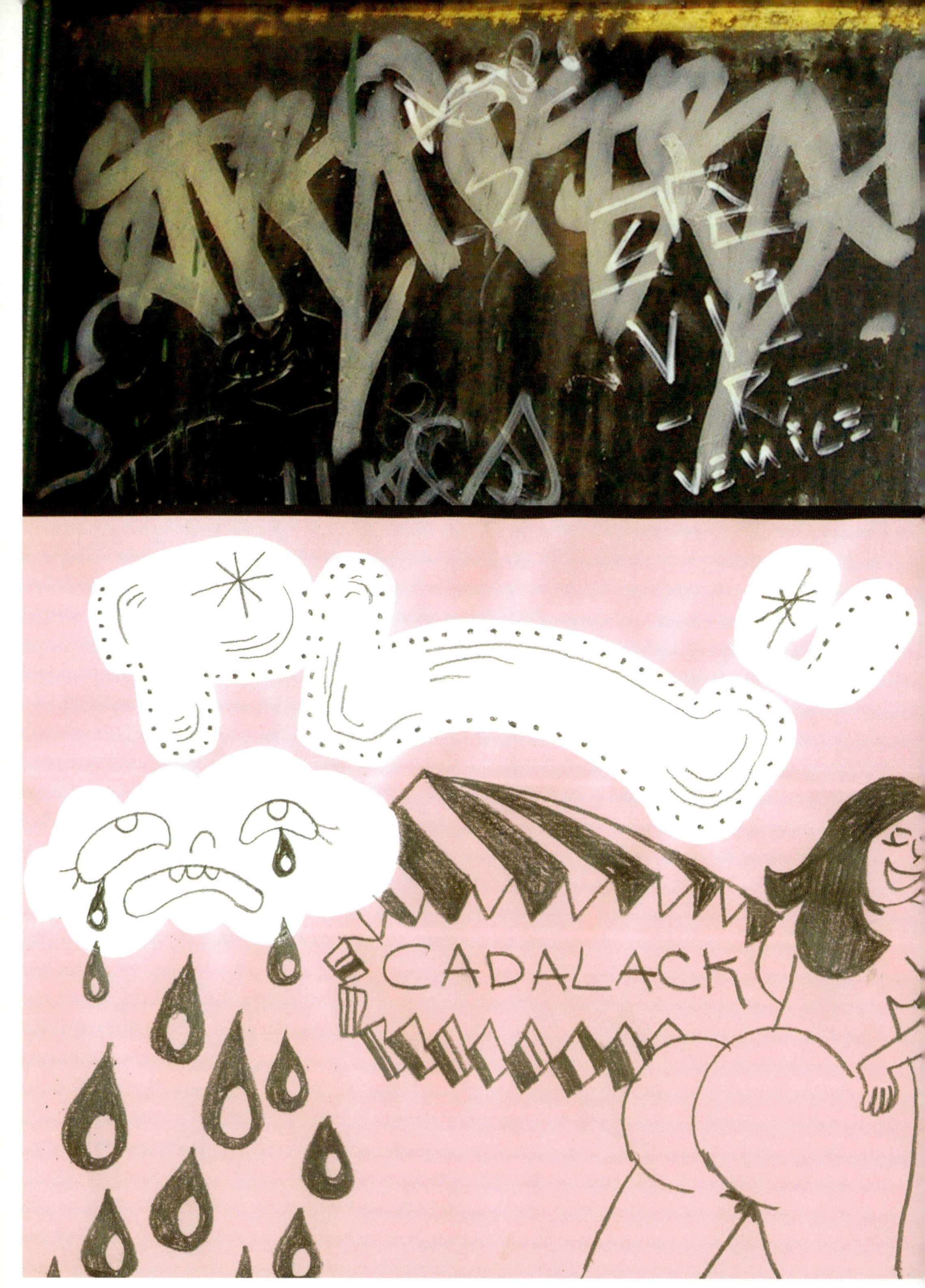
CADALACK

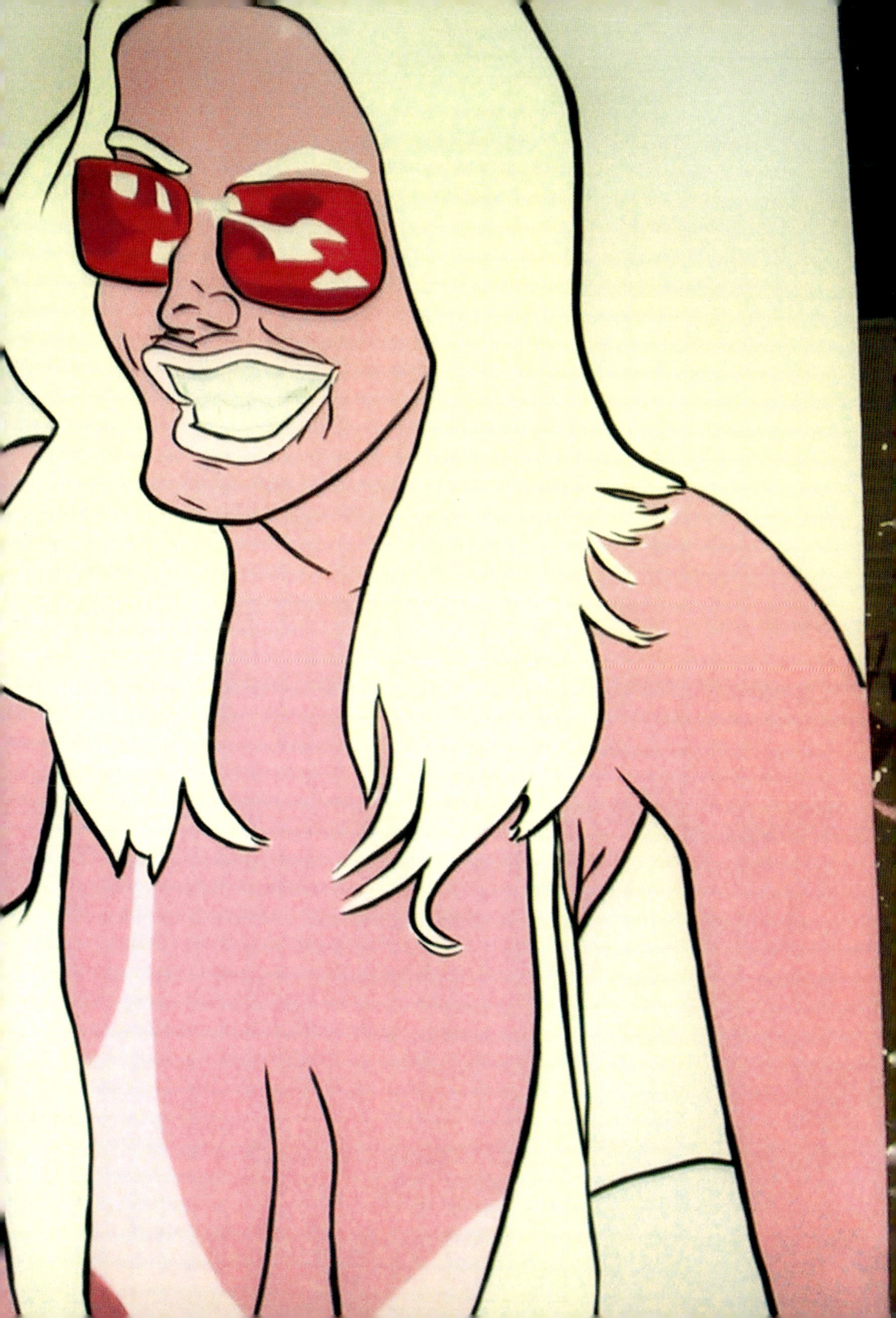

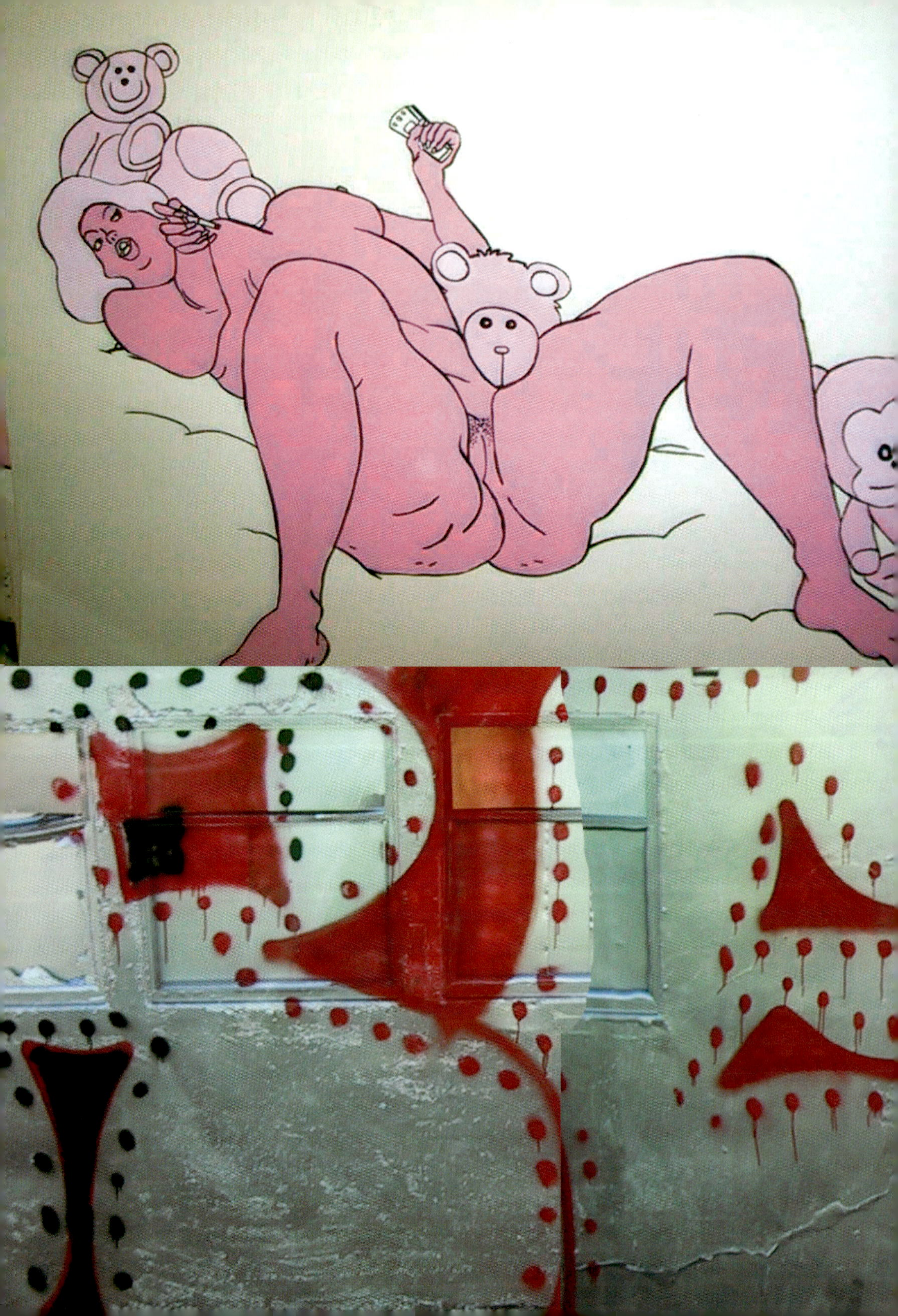

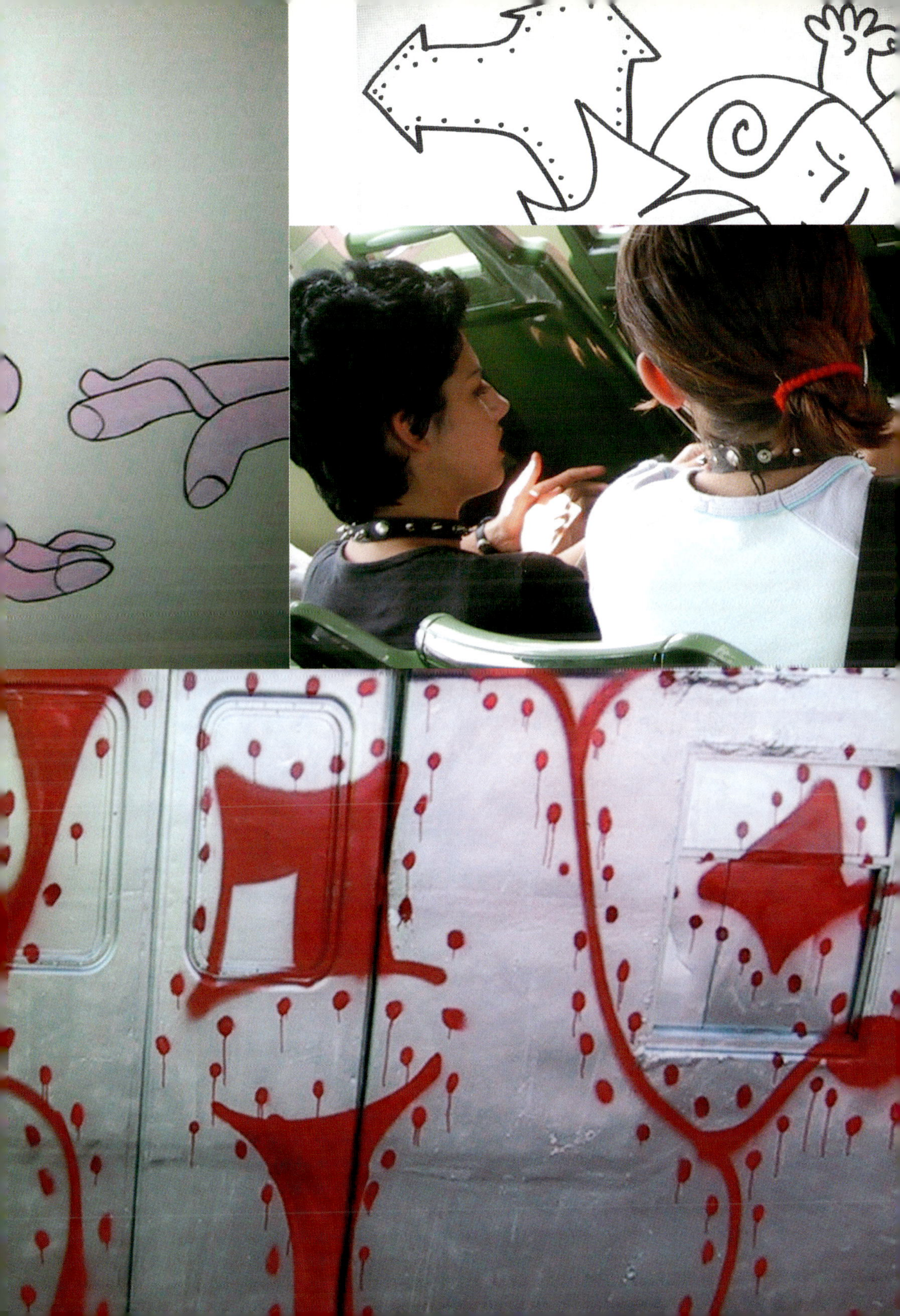

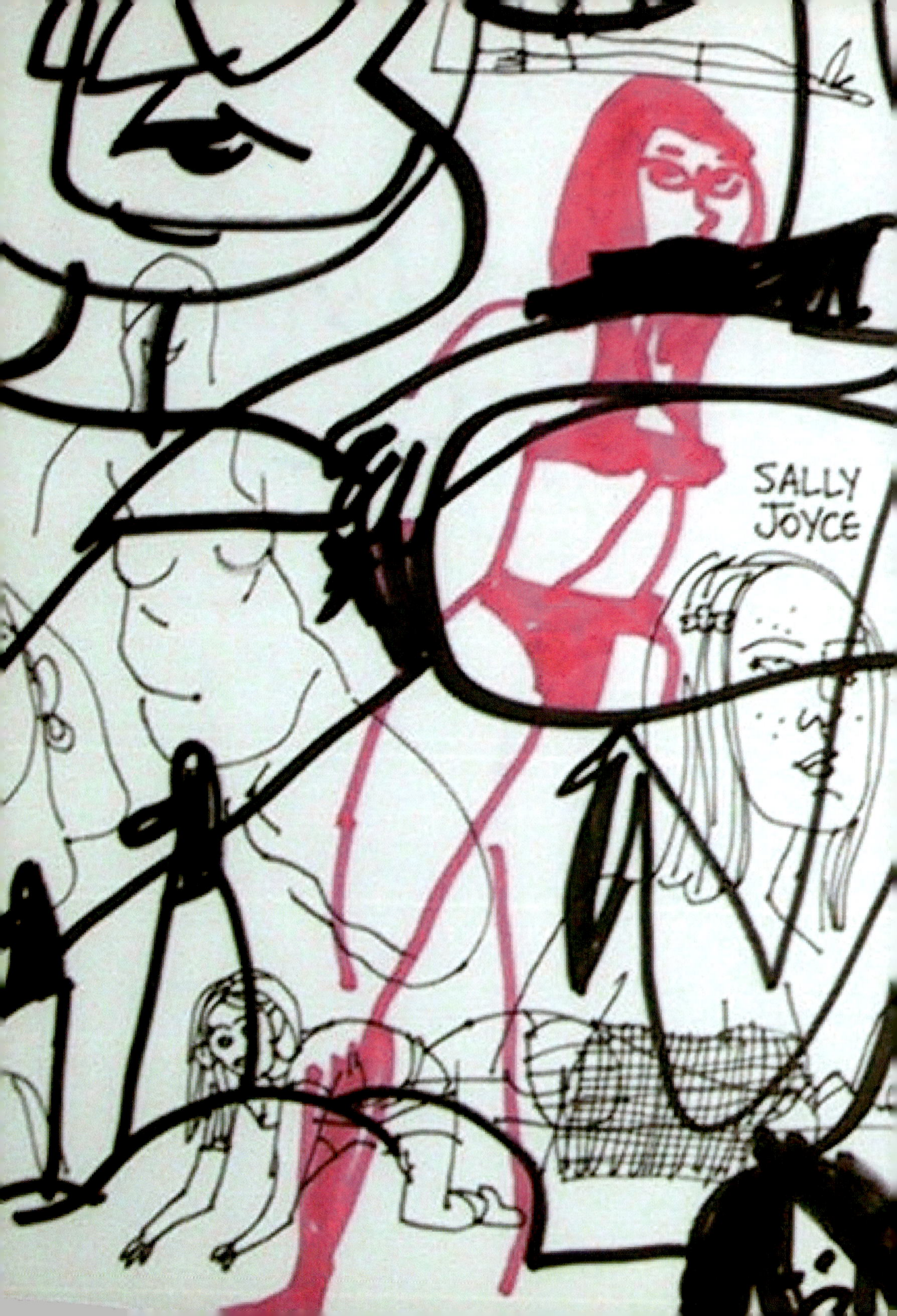
SALLY
JOYCE

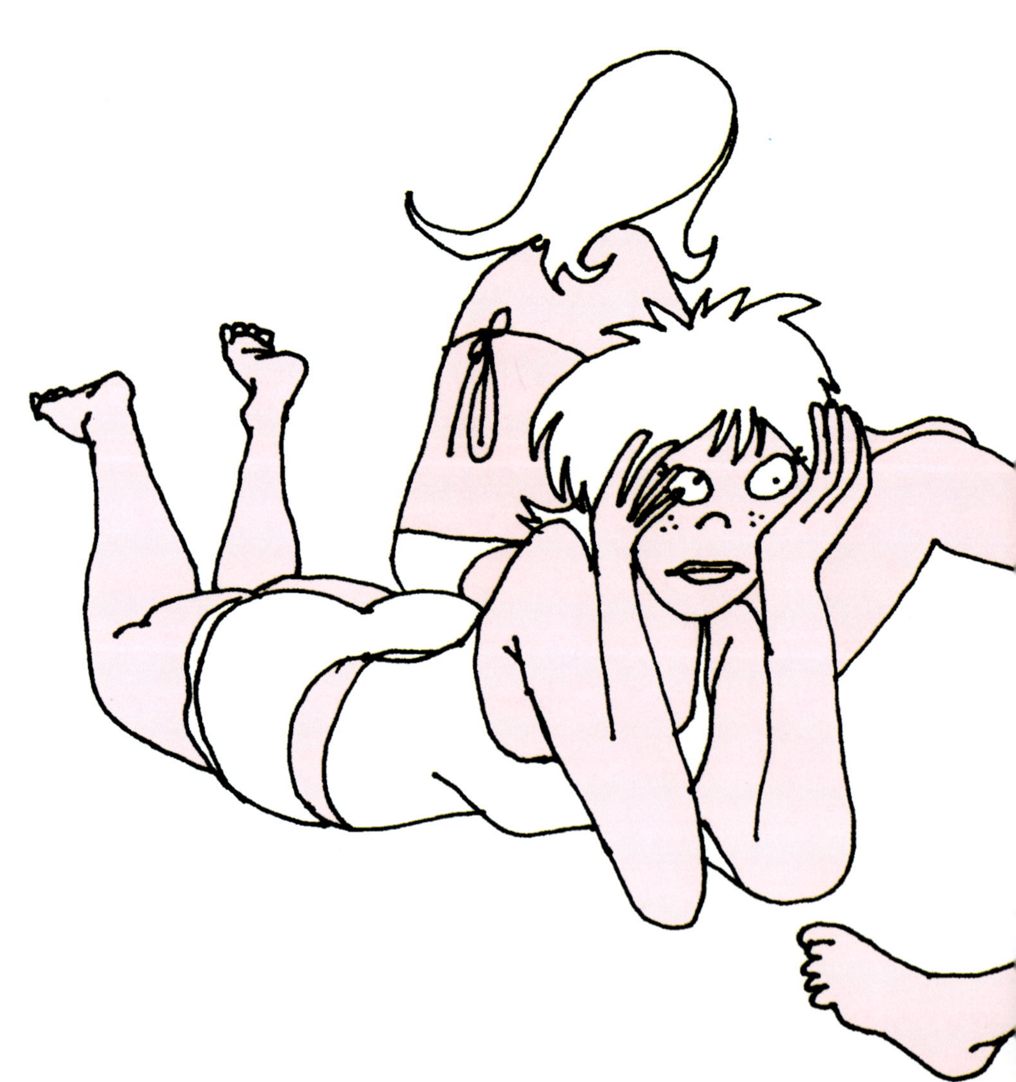

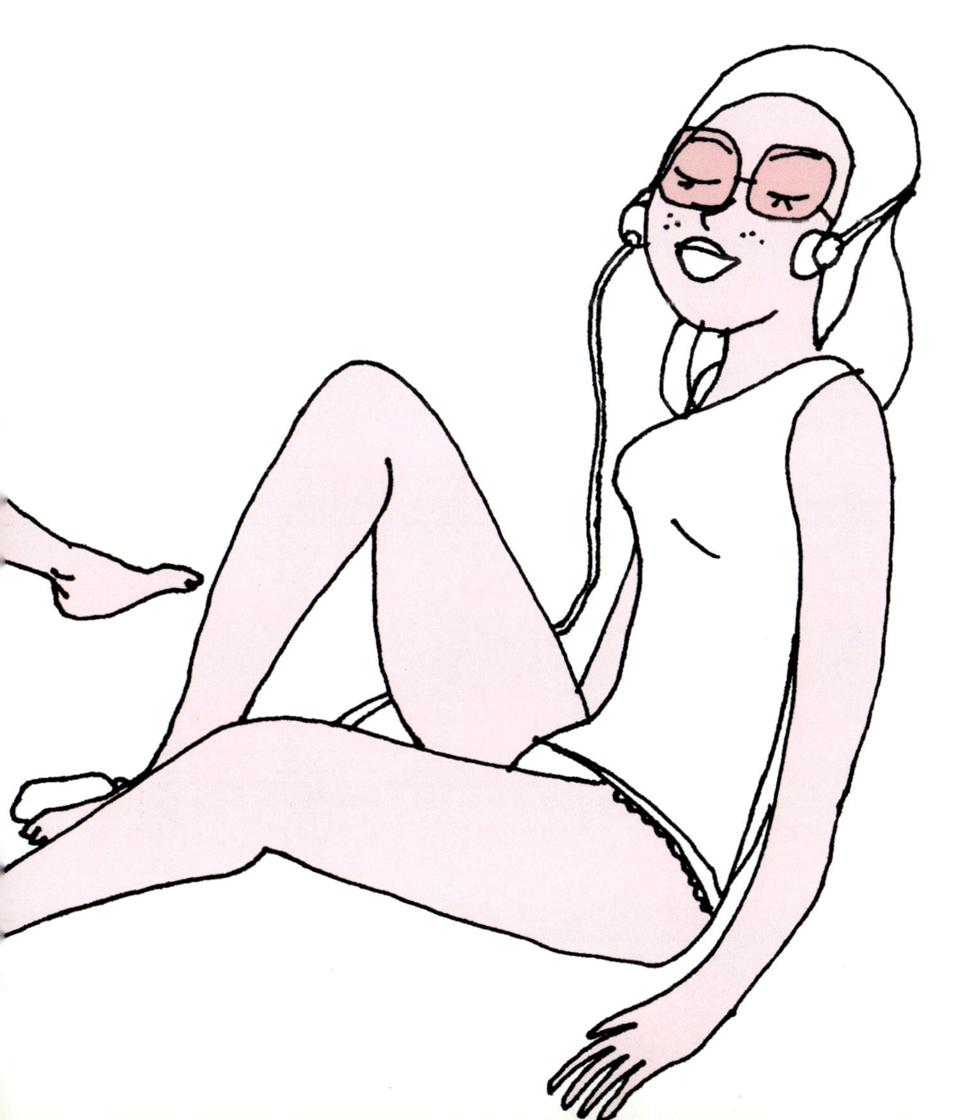

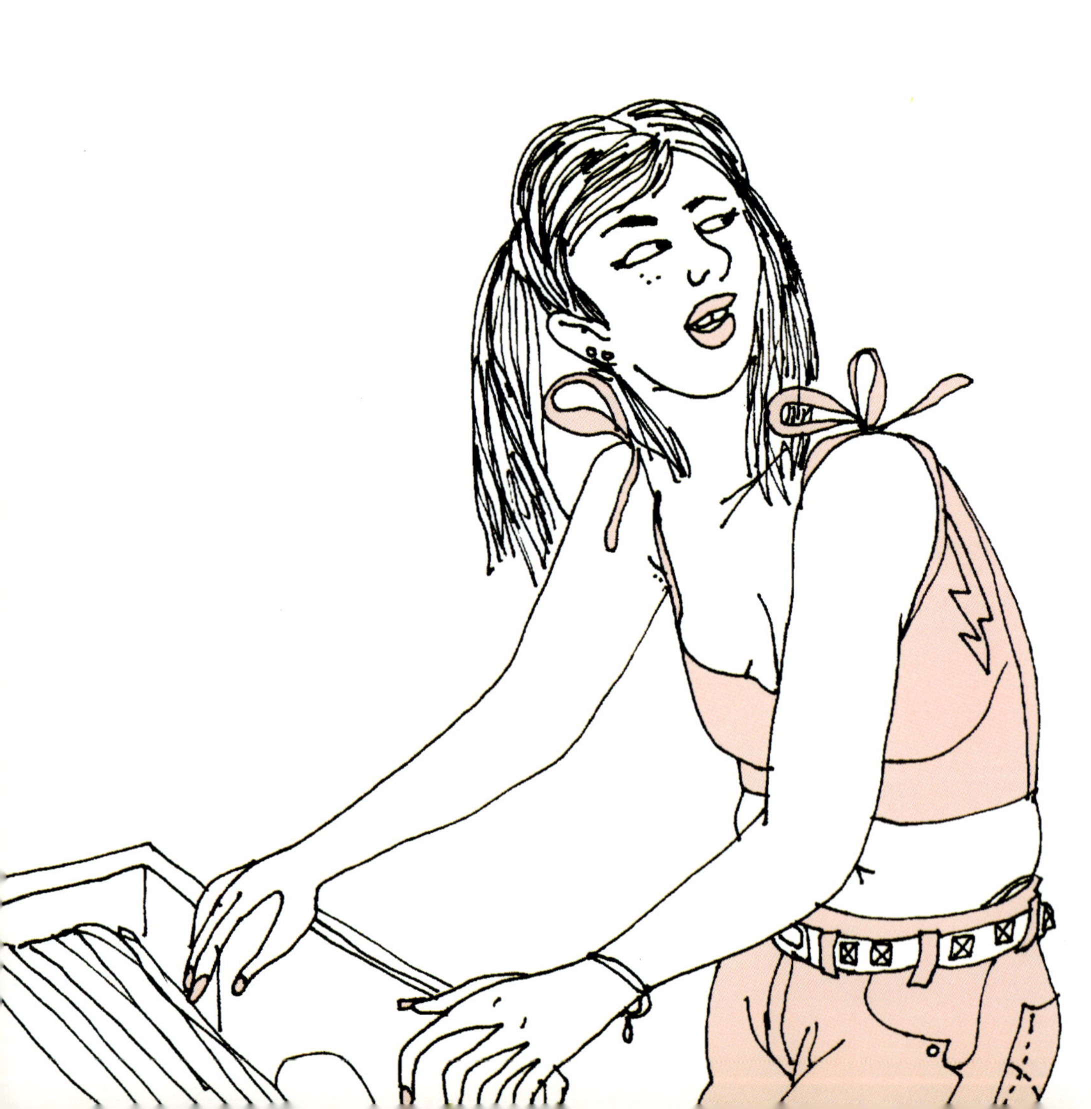

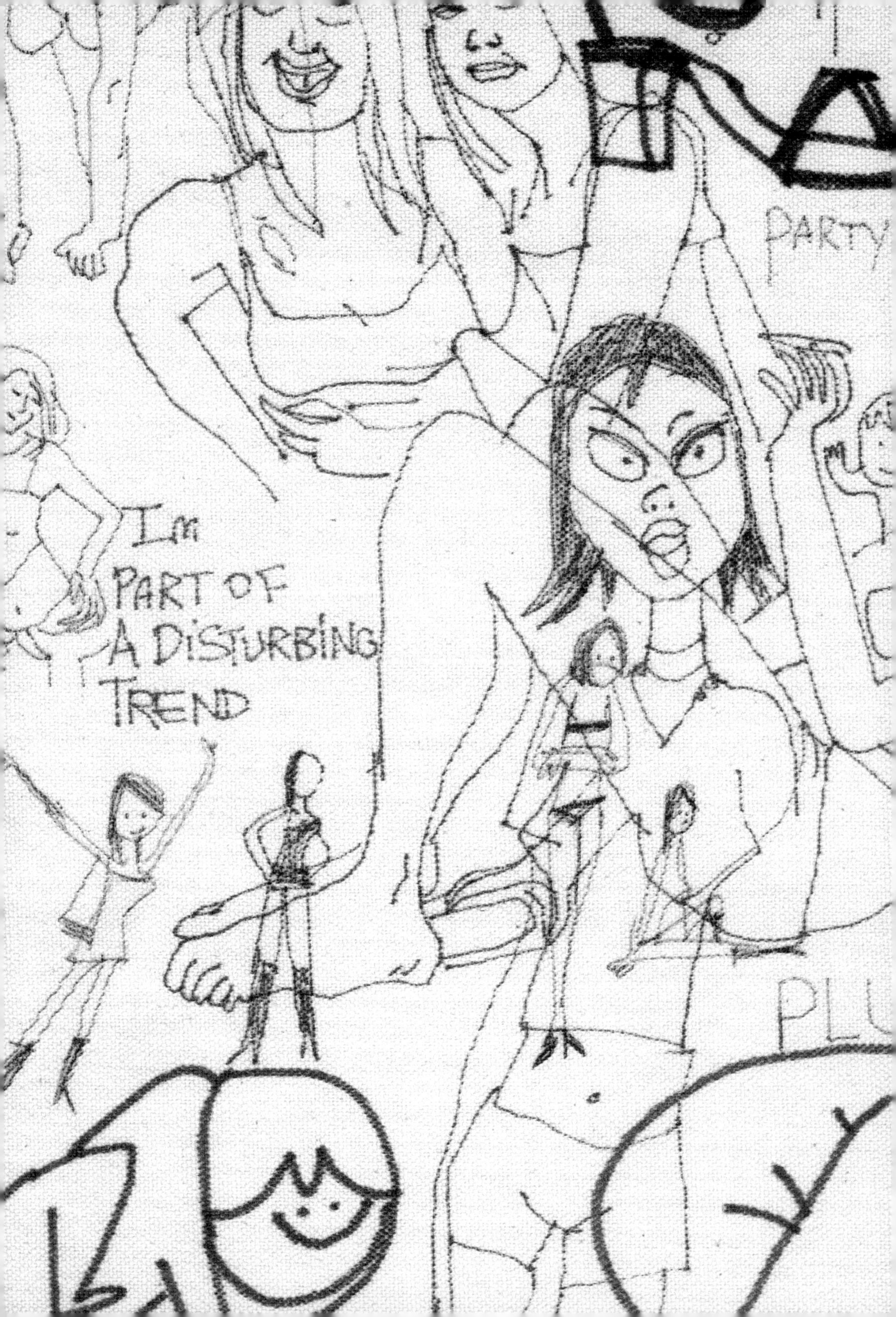
PARTY
I'm
PART OF
A DISTURBING
TREND
PLU

ITS
PTEEN JPEG

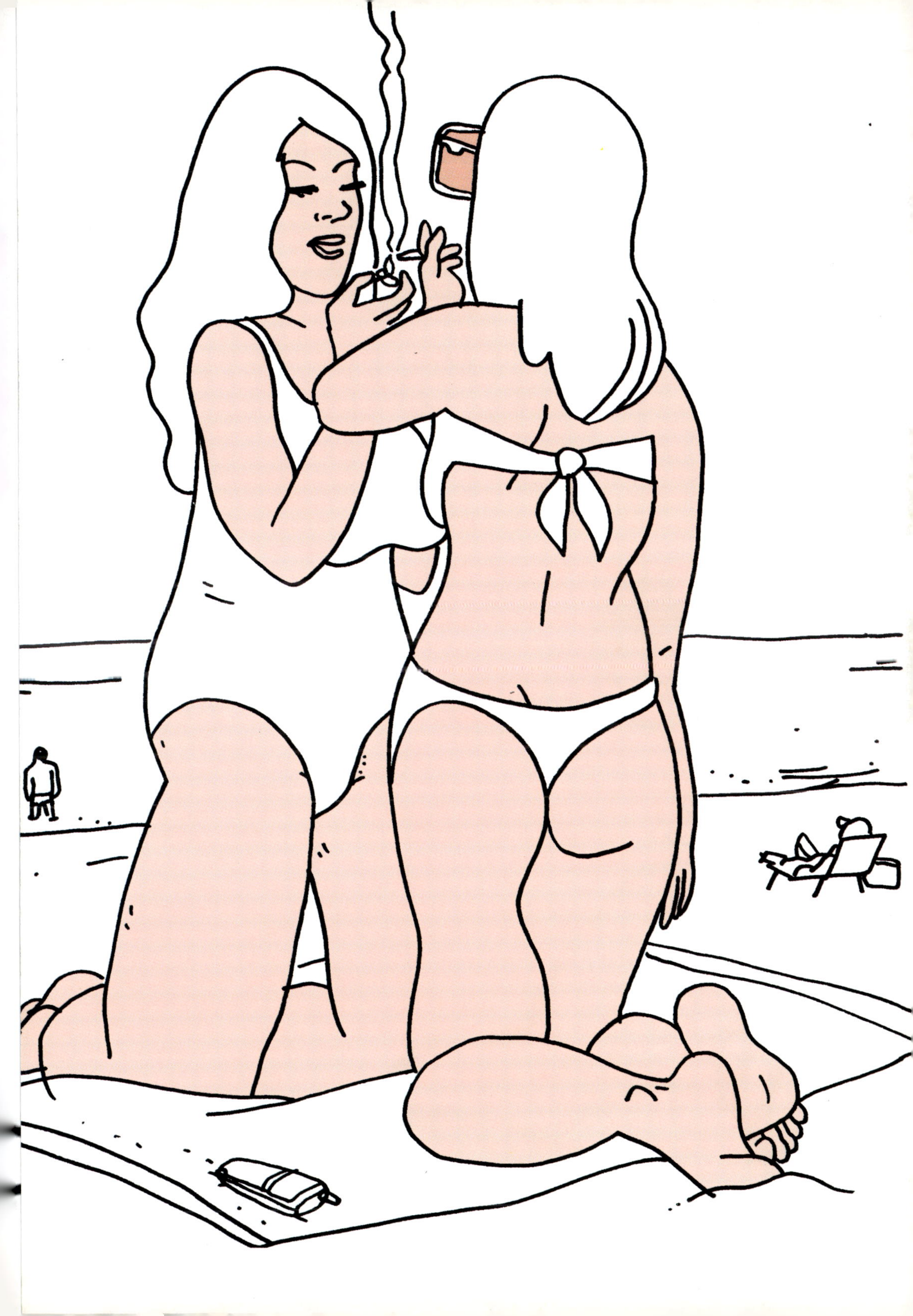

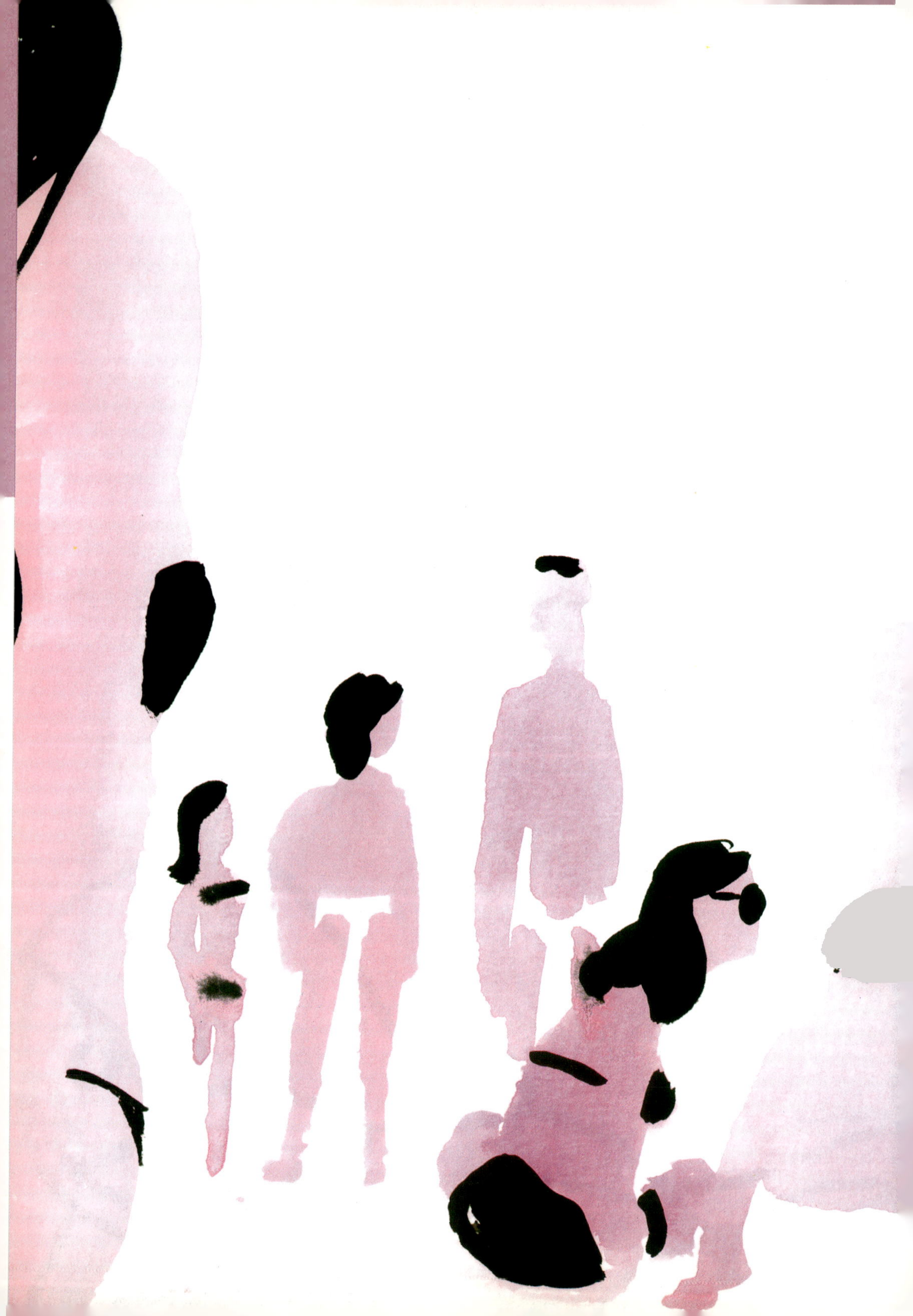

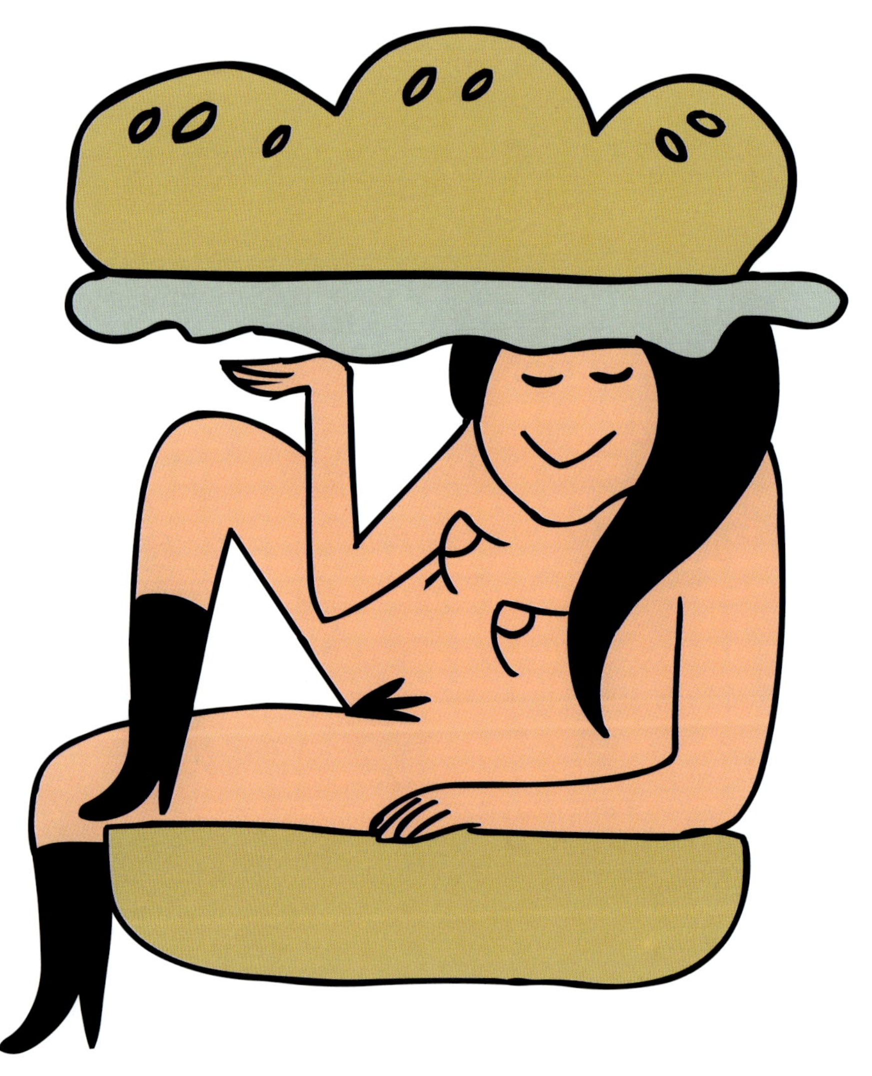

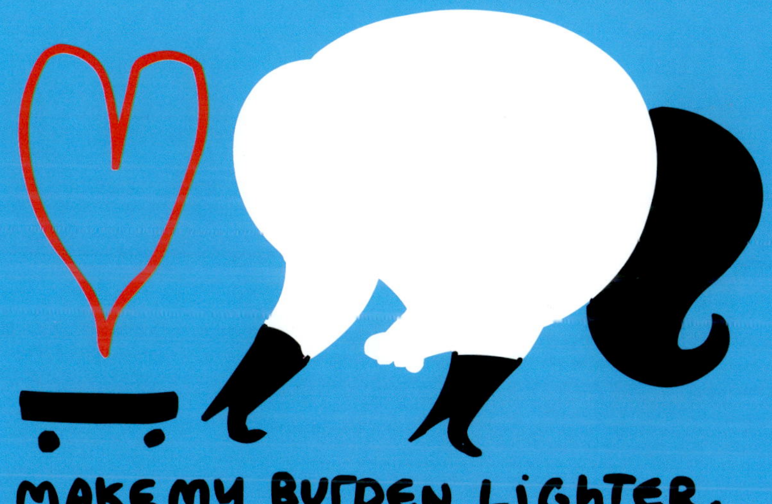
MAKE MY BURDEN LIGHTER.

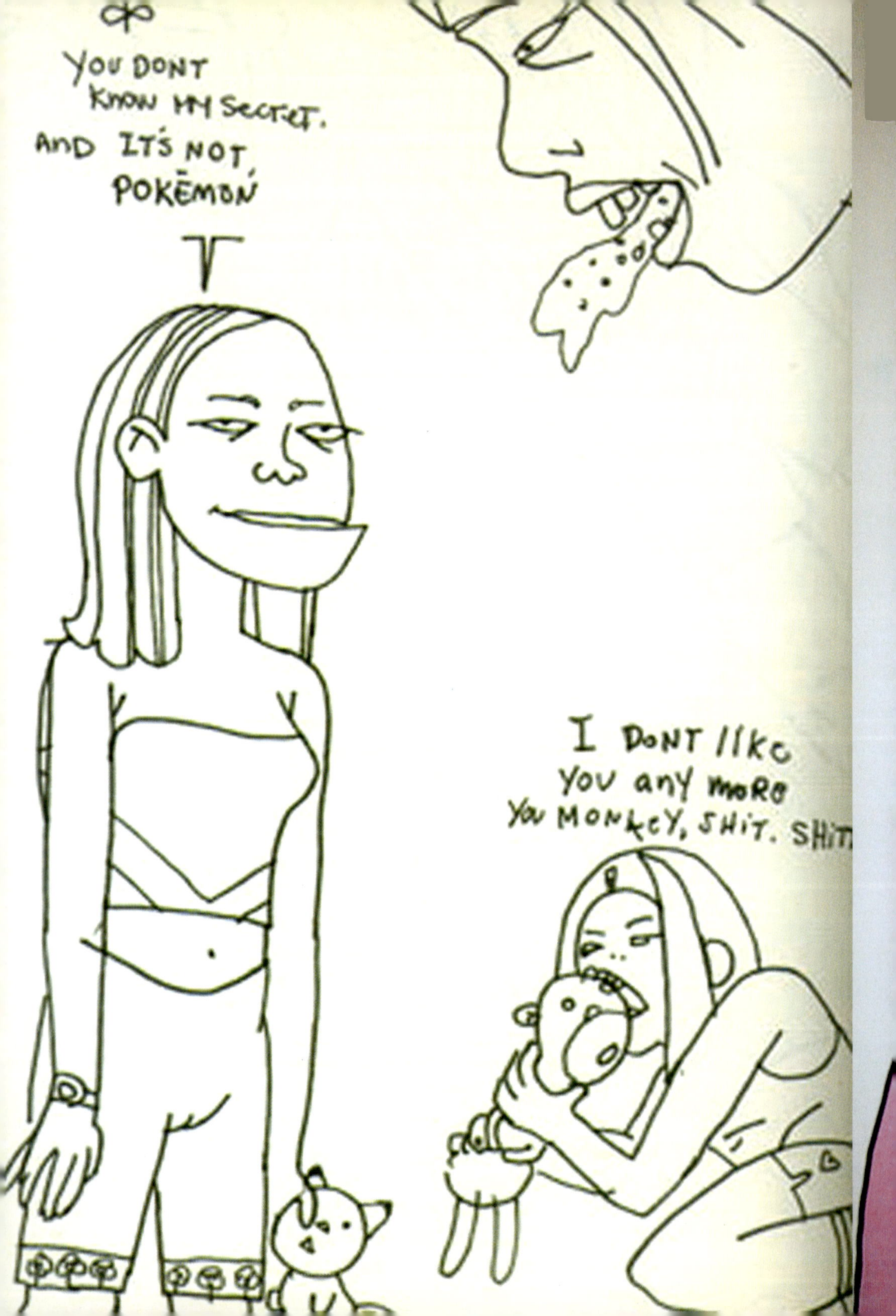
YOU DONT
KNOW MY SECRET.
AND IT'S NOT
POKĒMON'
I DONT like
YOU any more
You MONKEY, SHIT. SHIT

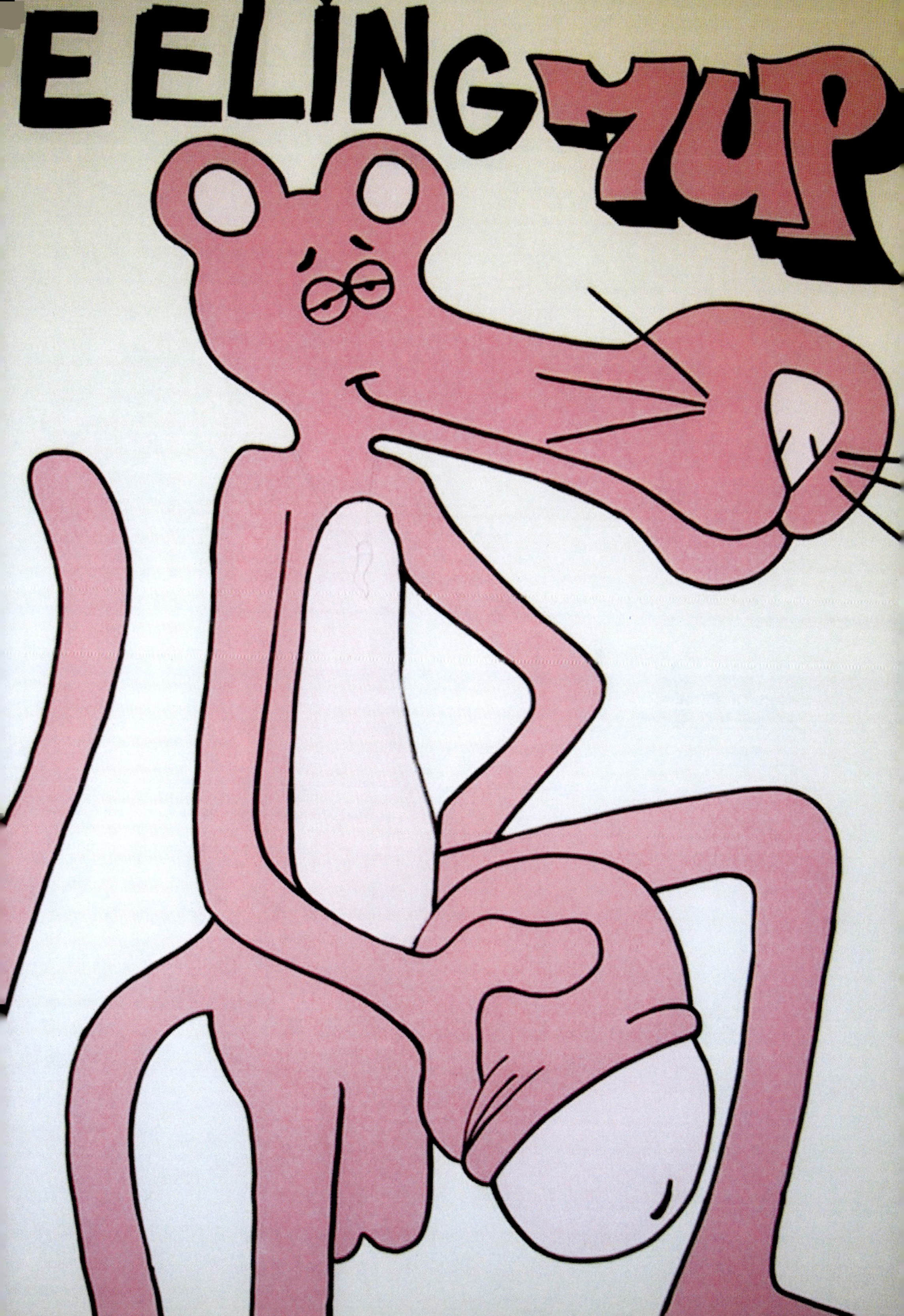
EELING
7UP

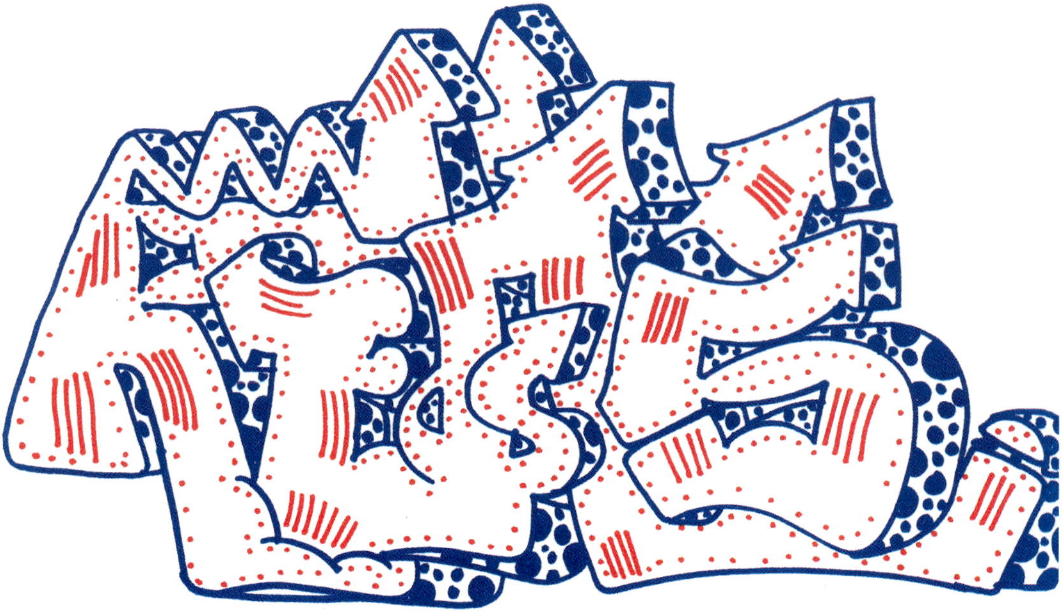

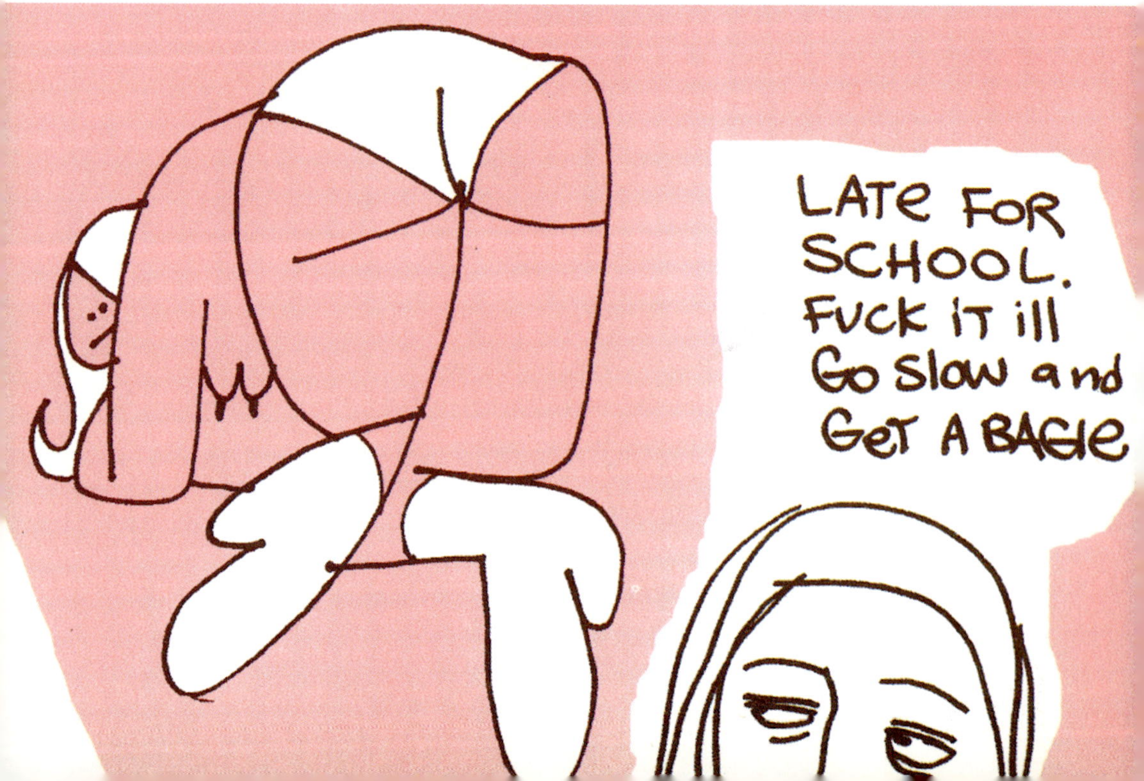

LATE FOR
SCHOOL.
FUCK IT ill
GO SLOW and
GET A BAGIE

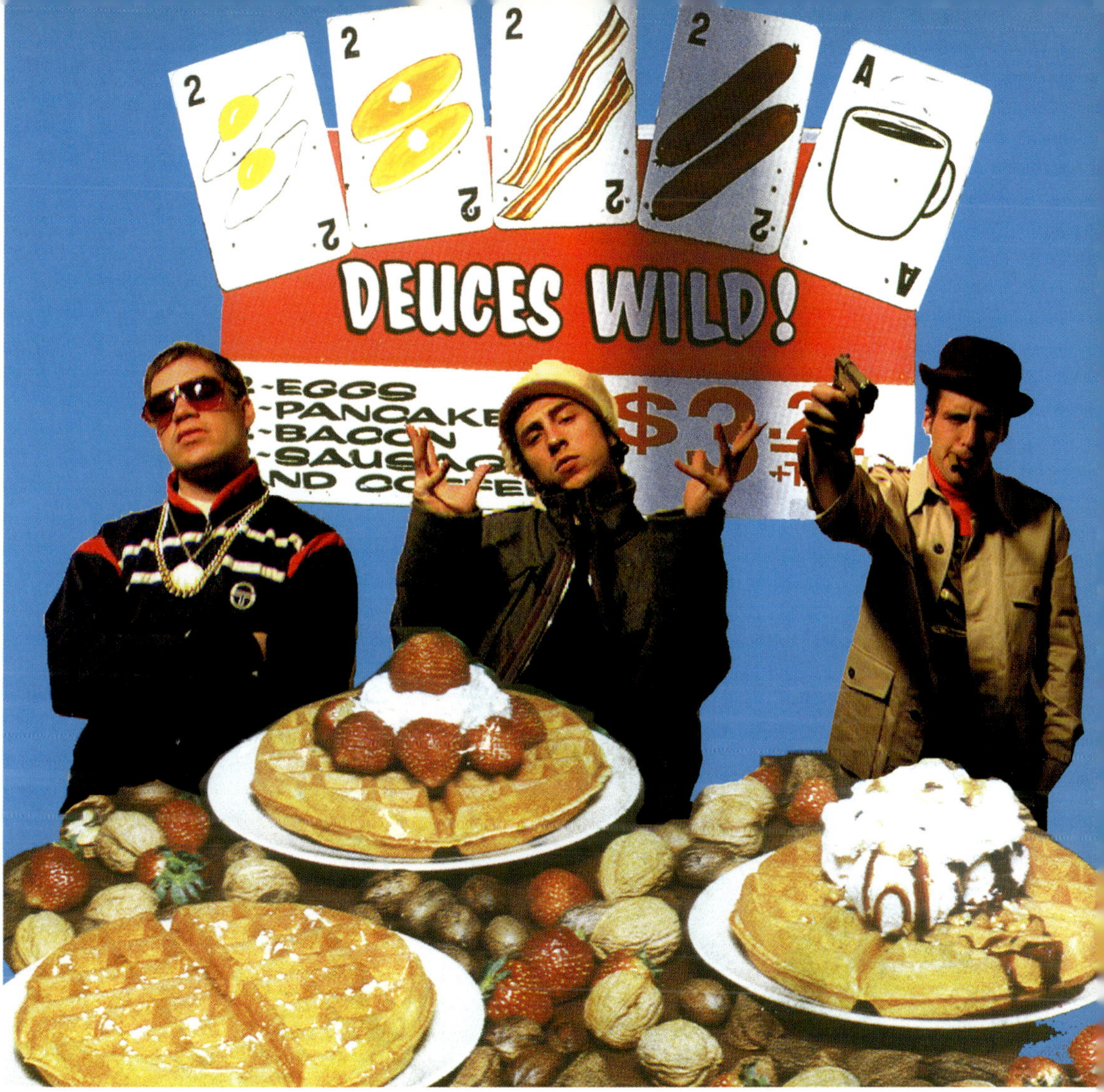

DEUCES WILD!

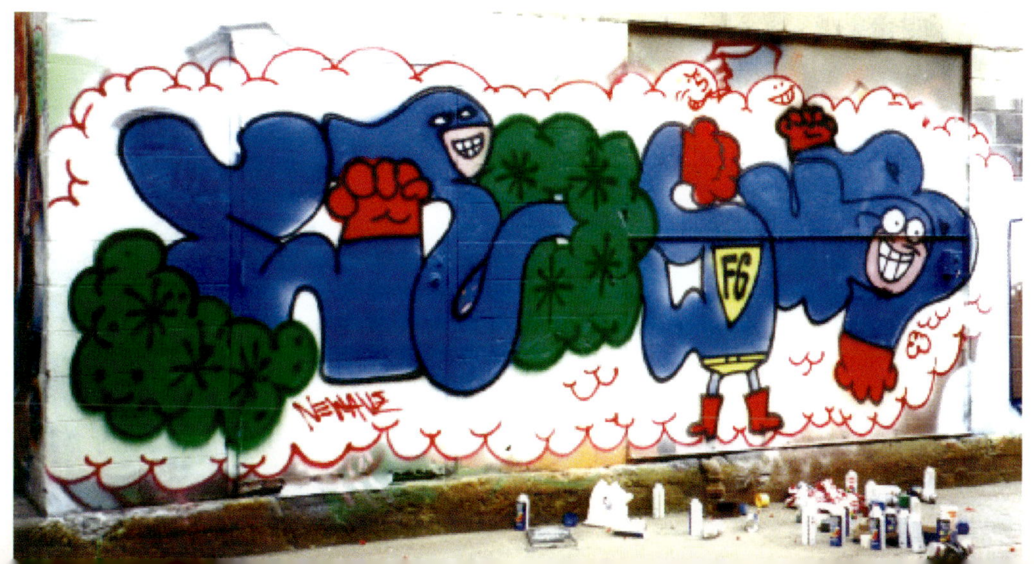

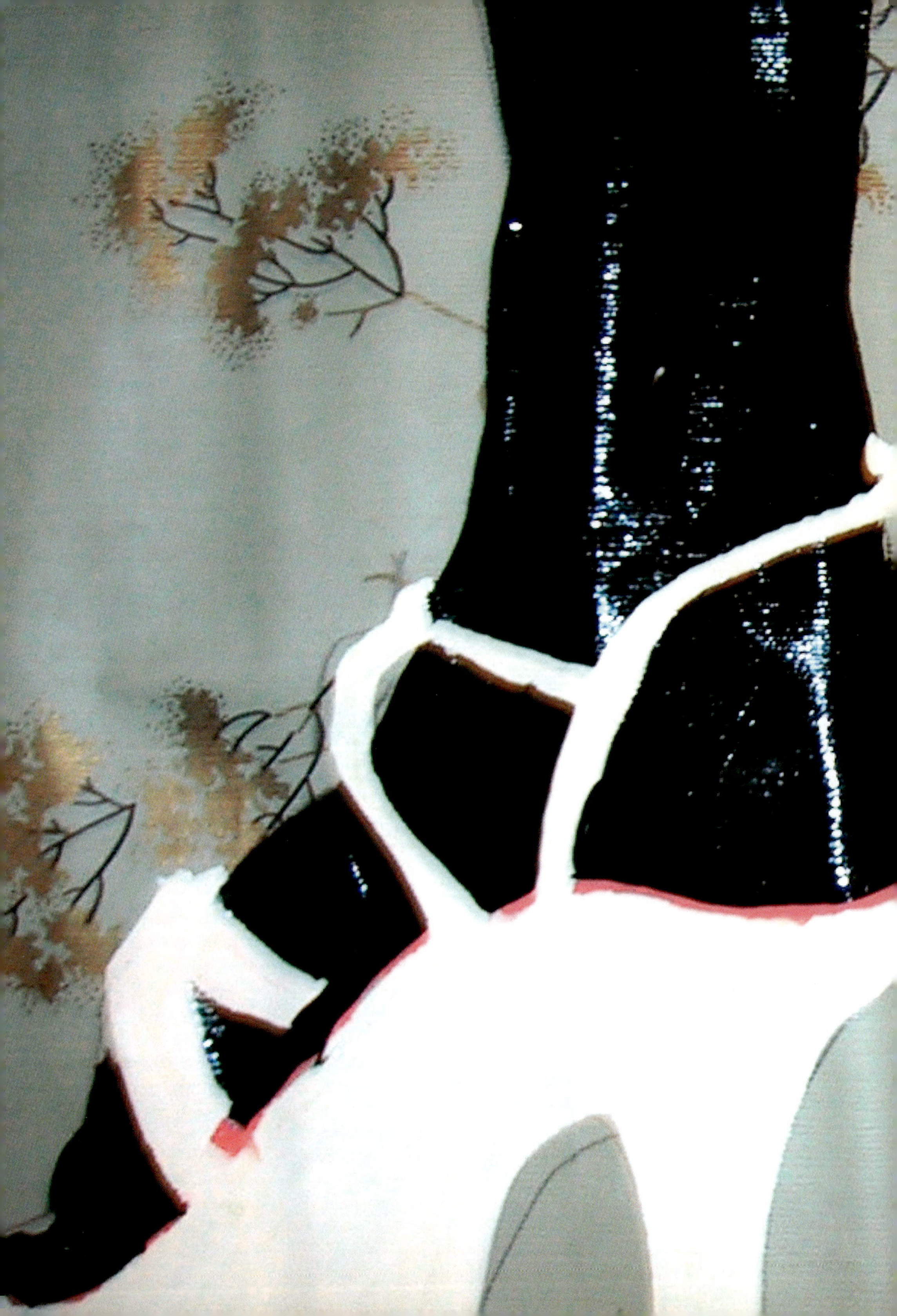

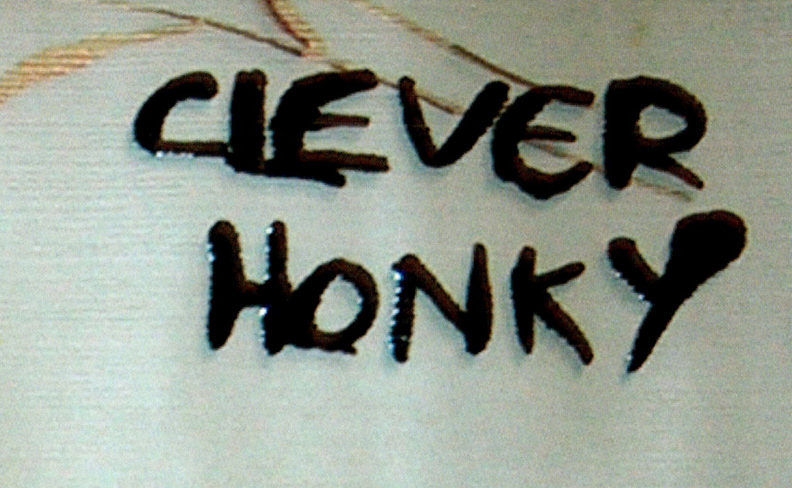
CLEVER
HONKY

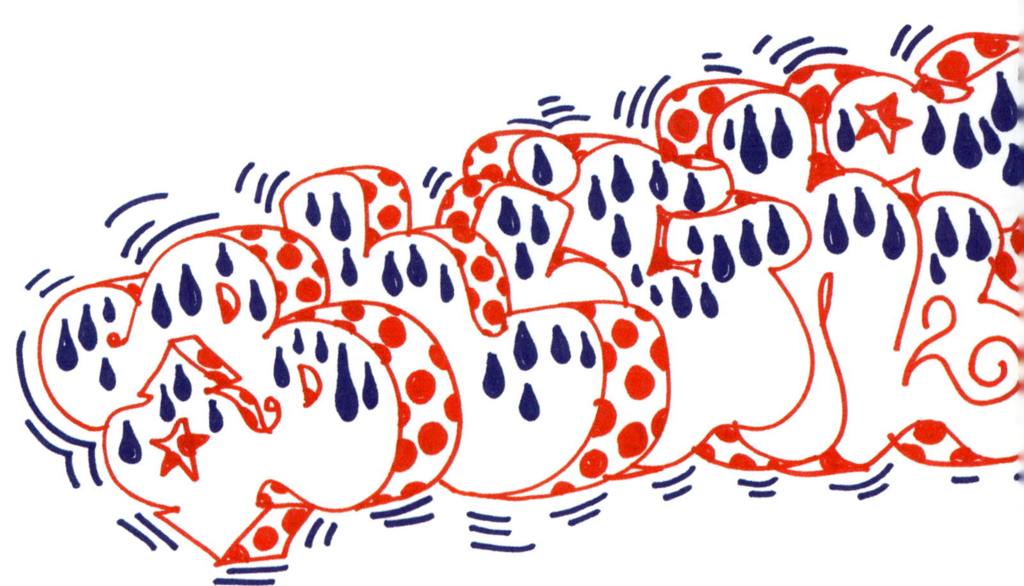